# MINNESOTA'S
# OLDEST MURDER
# MYSTERY

*The Case of Edward Phalen:*
*St. Paul's Unsaintly Pioneer*

*Gary Brueggemann*

BEAVER'S POND
PRESS

ISBN: 978-1-59298-535-7
Library of Congress Control Number: 2012916823

Cover oil painting *Chapel of St. Paul,* ca. 1845, by John Schmitt. Courtesy of the Minnesota Historical Society.
Book design by Ryan Scheife, Mayfly Design
Typeset in Bembo

Printed in the United States of America
First Printing: 2013

17   16   15   14   13          5   4   3   2   1

Beaver's Pond Press, Inc.
7104 Ohms Lane, Suite 101
Edina, MN 55439-2129
(952) 829-8818
www.BeaversPondPress.com

To order, visit www.BeaversPondBooks.com
or call (800) 901-3480. Reseller discounts available.

*Dedicated to my father, Walter J. Brueggemann (1919-1996)—
who grew up near the site of the Ben Gervais Cabin and passed on to me
his love of history and attachment to places.*

# CONTENTS

# INTRODUCTION

Anyone familiar with the City of St. Paul is familiar with the name Phalen. "Phalen" abounds in St. Paul's place-names: Lake Phalen, Phalen Creek, Phalen Park, Phalen Golf Course, Phalen Boulevard, Phalen Drive, Phalen Corridor, Phalen Elementary School, Phalen Recreation Center, Phalen Ice Arena, to name a few. Indeed, by any count, Phalen is among the most widely-used place-names in the city. Yet, how many people familiar with the name "Phalen" know much, if anything, about the person whom all those landmarks honor? Oddly enough, it may be fewer than the total number of public and commercial places that include "Phalen" in their name.

The man for whom so many places are named is ironically one of the most vilified and denigrated characters in early St. Paul history. Although clearly one of the founding pioneers of St. Paul—he was the first settler of both the downtown district and St. Paul's East Side, north of East Seventh Street—Edward Phelan (or Phalen or Felyn)* is not treated kindly by nineteenth century historians. In his early account of St. Paul, the city's first historian J. Fletcher Williams (1834-95) characterizes Phelan as "immoral, cruel, revengeful and unscrupulous." Williams writes that Phelan was "regarded by the other settlers as a bad [and] wicked man," whom most civil people "avoided as a dangerous person."[1] Williams' unflattering depiction was echoed by the first official historian of Minnesota, Rev. Edward D. Neill (1823-

---

* Originally spelled "Phelan," the name was eventually misspelled "Phalen," resulting in the current spelling of place-names throughout St. Paul. The text of this book uses the original spelling to refer to Edward Phelan.

93). Neill reported that "Phelan was considered…a bad…man," who was "boastful and unscrupulous in all his ways."[2]

Frank Bliss, author of *St. Paul, Past and Present* (1888), had only one good thing to say about Phelan: "He was…of fine appearance but most avaricious and revengeful in his disposition."[3] Alix Muller, the last local historian to publish in the nineteenth century (1899), also reported that Phelan "bore a rather unsavory reputation.[4]" W. B. Hennessy, the first local historian to publish in the twentieth century (1906), only added more negatives to Phelan's profile. Hennessy wrote that Phelan was "quarrelsome and vindictive" and "much given to the drinking of whiskey.[5]" But the ultimate indictment of Phelan's character came from Williams, Neill, and Bliss, who all flat out accused Phelan of committing the first murder in St. Paul.

Was the namesake of all those St. Paul landmarks really a murderer? Was he truly "immoral, cruel, revengeful and unscrupulous," not to mention "bad," "wicked" and "dangerous"? Who really was Edward Phelan?

Historians who study centuries past are at the mercy of the dead—those people who lived before us who took the time to record their time on earth. Unfortunately for St. Paul history, not enough people in Phelan's time took the time to record a fuller portrait of him. Indeed, good eyewitness accounts of the man from people who knew him are sadly lacking. None of the above descriptions of Phelan, in fact, came from writers who actually met him. The fact is, very little is known about Edward Phelan, and his guilt in a murder has never been proven. But the lack of firsthand descriptions of the pioneer with the "unsavory reputation" is not the only problem we face in the quest to uncover the real Edward Phelan and find the truth about the murder he allegedly committed.

Phelan lived in St. Paul from 1838 to 1850, a time and place where for a decade there were no newspapers to record his deeds, no census takers to record his vital statistics, and mostly no local government to record his business and real estate transactions. Phelan settled in St. Paul before there was a St. Paul. He claimed land there nine years before any part of the present city was surveyed and platted into precisely identified real estate. Phelan was a frontiersman who lived in the Upper Mississippi wilderness long before the territory of Minnesota was created by Congress and President Polk in 1849. Like most rough frontiersmen, or "backwoodsmen," Phelan was not an articulate man. Unlike the well-educated and eloquent gentlemen of his day, who typically took the care to preserve their thoughts in letters and diaries, Phelan left behind no diaries, no letters, and no memoirs, probably because he never bothered to pen them. He also left behind no known children and was never recorded as having been married. Consequently, uncovering Edward Phelan's life is a much more challenging undertaking than chronicling the life of an upper class gentleman from the same era, who often had descendants and left behind personal papers, documents, and even portraits and photographs of himself and his family. Adding to this challenge is the fact that virtually all of Phelan's local contemporaries—the St. Paul pioneers who knew Phelan and could reveal information about him—shared his lower class status and likewise left few if any written accounts or documents.

Nevertheless, despite the shortage of details about Phelan, enough records exist to piece together some semblance of his life and also cast better light on the murder charges against him. Much of what will be presented here about St. Paul's first murder case has never been published before, except for one compilation of old county documents published in 1999 by the Washington County Historical Society.[6] Indeed, what follows will not only be the first comprehensive coverage of the Phelan murder case but the first comprehensive coverage of Edward Phelan's life. Unlike modern "true crime" writers who can draw on police reports, extensive readable and reliable court transcripts, photographic evidence, detailed newspaper accounts, and personal interviews to cover the crimes they report, I could not draw from any of those sources for the crime I was investigating, simply because they either do not exist, or in the case of personal interviews, simply aren't possible. Fortunately, the sources I did uncover were still sufficient to solve most of the mystery of the first recorded murder case in St. Paul—the longest running murder mystery in Minnesota.

This book was a slow-growing project that began partly with research initiated in the 1970s, but developed mostly from an accidental discovery I made in 1994. For over thirty years I have been exploring both Minnesota and St. Paul history and sharing my findings with others through teaching, writing, and conducting historical tours. In 1978 I was privileged to create the first-ever college accredited course on the history of St. Paul for Inver Hills Community College. In developing that course, I strived to research every decade of my hometown's long and colorful past. But of all the interesting eras I studied, I found myself most drawn to the pioneer period. The founders of St. Paul fascinated me. They were not the sort of people one would normally associate with the founding of an important city. They were poor, uneducated, inarticulate, and unpretentious; none were born in the United States, and most could barely speak English. (French was the dominant language.) Yet, those humble backwoodsmen, farmers, and whiskey traders firmly planted a settlement that evolved into the great capital city of Minnesota. Edward Phelan, a former Fort Snelling soldier and native of Ireland, was one of those founding pioneers.

I first encountered Phelan in the early 1970s when I read J. Fletcher Williams' 1876 classic, *A History of the City of Saint Paul and of the County of Ramsey, Minnesota,* at the Minnesota Historical Society library on Cedar Street. Williams' colorful depiction of Phelan and his intriguing account of Phelan's alleged murder of his roommate, John Hays, in 1839 captured my interest. During the 1980s I spent more time investigating Phelan while researching and writing the *East St. Paul History Calendar(1985),* which included a special feature on Phelan and the creek and lake named after him. By the 1990s, however, I had moved on to a major Minnesota history project: writing full profiles of all sixty-two delegates of the historic Stillwater Convention, the 1848 assembly that launched the creation of the territory of Minnesota. Strangely enough, Phelan was one of those delegates, but appeared far down on the list of names I was researching. One of the first delegates I focused on was the president of the convention, Joseph R. Brown—one of the greatest, most colorful founding fathers of Minnesota. My research of Brown brought me back to the Minnesota Historical Society library, in its new location, where I found several boxes of Joseph R. Brown's papers and made the most exciting discovery of my life.

There was Brown's original *Justice of the Peace Casebook* for the years 1839-41, the period when he was the only legal civilian authority for St. Paul (or "Pig's Eye," as it was first known until late 1841). Astonishingly, inside that antiquated docket book was part of the long lost record of the Phelan murder case. J. Fletcher Williams had searched in vain for those records before he published his book in 1876. Henry Castle, author of the three-volume *History of St. Paul and Vicinity*, also failed to uncover them before he published his work in 1912. If the records were declared lost in 1876 and were still lost in 1912, who would expect that they would turn up in the late twentieth century preserved in the very historical society that J. Fletcher Williams had been the secretary of and librarian for twenty-six years? But turn up they did, right in Joseph R. Brown's *Casebook*.

My excitement soon gave way to frustration when I saw how illegible much of Brown's handwriting was. I spent hours trying to transpose Brown's faded writing, but I wasn't confident that my transcription was entirely accurate. As exhilarated as I was about my discovery, I wasn't sure what to do with it. I eventually decided to put the material on hold for a future article in *Ramsey County History* magazine. Thirteen busy years passed and when I finally found time to begin the Phelan article, in the summer of 2007, I discovered that Brown's *Casebook* had been put on microfilm, which made it even more difficult to read. After many hours at the microfilm reader, I eventually managed to transcribe most of the relevant records. What I deciphered was exciting material but to my great frustration there remained several parts of Brown's handwriting that I could not deci-

*A page from Justice of the Peace Joseph R. Brown's casebook. Photo courtesy of the Minnesota Historical Society.*

pher. Exasperated, I almost gave up the whole project, concerned that those undeciphered parts perhaps included some of the more critical sections of the document.

Fortunately and fatefully, I refused to quit. After I finished transcribing the legible parts of Brown's *Casebook* that covered the murder inquiry, I began searching my own extensive personal library for any material on the life and times of Edward Phelan. I then made another surprising and fortuitous discovery: a book I had purchased in 1999, but had not fully read, *Minnesota Beginnings: Records of St. Croix County, Wisconsin Territory, 1840-1849,* published by the Washington County Historical Society, included the complete transcription of Brown's 1839 *Casebook.*[7] I couldn't believe it. For eight years I had a book shelved in my own library that held a fully typed transcription of Brown's *Casebook!* I thought *Minnesota Beginnings* was merely a modern reprint of the rare 1941 publication of the Wisconsin Historical Records Survey, *Wisconsin Territorial Papers, St. Croix County, Oct. 5,*

*1840–April 2, 1849*, which I had often used in my research of Minnesota pioneers.[8] But the Washington County publication included three important additions: an expanded introduction that reviewed the legal history of the county, which originally included all of present Minnesota east of the Mississippi, over one hundred mini-biographies of early settlers, and most significantly of all, Joseph R. Brown's full 1839–1841 *Casebook*, with introductory comments. To both my surprise and delight, I discovered that two of the contributors to that impressive work were a talented couple I knew and respected, local historian Don Empson and editor Kathy Vadnais, who were former residents of my own West Seventh Street neighborhood. Another key contributor was the book's general editor and president of the Washington County Historical Society, Nancy Goodman, one of the best authorities on Joseph R. Brown. In 1996, two years after I discovered Brown's *Casebook*, Nancy and her husband Robert Goodman, published the first modern biography of Joseph R. Brown. The Goodmans' exhaustive research of Brown inevitably led them to their own discovery of his *Casebook*, and ultimately to its inclusion in *Minnesota Beginnings*. With the collective talents of Nancy Goodman, Don Empson, Kathy Vadnais, Brent Peterson, and other contributors of the Washington County Historical Society's publication, the transcription of Brown's *Casebook* was much better than my efforts in a handwritten notebook. In addition to transposing illegible words, their transcription impressively added proper punctuation and paragraphing to Brown's grammatically challenged writing. Understandably then, I have relied heavily on the Washington County Historical Society's clear and clean transcription of Brown's *Casebook*.

My article on the Phelan murder case evolved into a much larger project. It became clear after a few months of writing that the subject could not be confined to the limits of a magazine article. The story of Phelan and the murder he was accused of cannot be quickly and easily told. It is not a simple story of a murder, nor a simple biography of a man. Both the man and the murder case are complicated by the strengths and weaknesses of the surviving evidence and the glaring difficulty that the murder occurred over 170 years ago, in a place that no longer exists. Most of the primary evidence comes from Joseph R. Brown's *Casebook* records. That raw material has never been fully analyzed, let alone integrated with other evidence into a credible interpretation of the murder that Phelan allegedly committed. Only a book can do justice to this intriguing, complex subject, and I hope this one will come close to doing that. Readers will find that this is not a book where the author simply tells a story and the readers just sit back and enjoy the telling. This author wants the readers to be involved in the process of solving the murder mystery. I make the examination of the evidence transparent so every reader can see exactly how judgments are made and conclusions are drawn.

When I began this work I had no strong predisposition for or against Edward Phelan, nor any desire to be either his defender or his detractor. My only goal was to uncover the truth about him and the murder he may or may not have committed. I believe I have done that here; only the souls of the long dead characters in this historical drama could know for certain how close I have come to uncovering the truth.

# PROLOGUE

On a Friday in late September 1839, nineteen years before Minnesota became a state and two years before the village of St. Paul was founded, the battered body of a middle-aged Irishman was found by some Dakota Indian boys. The corpse had washed up along the shore of the Mississippi River, about seven miles downstream from Fort Snelling, near the ancient Indian landmark the white soldiers and settlers called Carver's Cave. It was the body of John Hays, a popular former soldier, who prior to his disappearance twenty-one days earlier, had been sharing a log shanty with his friend and business partner, Edward Phelan, a few miles upriver from the cave. Before the year was over Phelan would be arrested and charged with the murder of his friend. Was he guilty of the crime or was someone else the murderer?

# CHAPTER ONE

## Edward Phelan's Shadowy Past

Although much of Edward Phelan's life remains a mystery, the out-line of his biography can be traced. Thanks to his military records, we know that Phelan was born in Londonderry, Ireland in 1811, the same year that George III (the king of Great Britain and Ireland who lost the American Revolution) was declared insane and a year before the British and Americans began a new conflict: the War of 1812.[1] A port city in Northern Ireland on the River Foyle, Londonder-ry's history is well chronicled. Founded in the sixth century, Lon-donderry (also known as Derry) is an ancient city, scarred by over a thousand years of bloody battles and destructive foreign invaders. Vikings burned the medieval town and pillaged the land seven dif-ferent times. Later, in the early 1600s, English and Scottish Protestant soldiers and settlers conquered the city, burned Catholic churches and changed its name from Derry to Londonderry. They also built walls around the city "to protect them from Irish rebels." And those walls still stand as Derry's most distinguishable landmark. From the seventeenth century on, bitter and bloody struggles between Prot-estants and Catholics, English, Scottish and Irish indelibly marked the life of the city and county of Londonderry.[2] The long troubles of Northern Ireland are well documented, but the relevant point is that Edward Phelan was born and likely raised in that troubled land. If Phelan was in fact a rough character, it should come as no surprise: he came from a rough place.

We know nothing of Edward Phelan's parents, or even whether he came from a Catholic or Protestant family. The Phelan name is an old and very common Irish surname, originating from the Gaelic "O'Faolain." The name derives from the Gaelic word for "wolf" (faol); it dates back to at least the early eighteenth century and originated in southeast Ireland, in the region of Waterford and Kilkenny counties.[3] Given the Phelan name's ancestry, we might conclude that Edward Phelan did not come from one of the Scottish Presbyterian (Scotch Irish) families of Londonderry. If he was born Catholic, a faith the British tried hard to repress after their conquest of Derry, he left no traceable record of an affiliation with any Catholic church in America. His name does not appear in the 1841-50 records of the Catholic Chapel of St. Paul, the only church in St. Paul until 1848. However, the absence of his name does not prove that he was not Catholic. The Catholic Chapel of St. Paul was almost exclusively French, and Phelan could not speak French. He also could have been a lapsed Catholic, perhaps during his stay at Fort Snelling, where there were no priests available and the nearest Catholic services were over two hundred miles away.[4]

In addition to the mystery of his family, we do not know when, why or how Phelan left Ireland and immigrated to America.*[5] We do know that on June 8, 1835, ten years before the onset of Ireland's great potato famine, a twenty four -year-old "laborer" from Londonderry named "Edward Felyn"—who had "gray eyes, brown hair, fair complexion and was six feet two and one half inches high"—enlisted into the United States Army in New York City.[6] This is almost all we know of the physical features of Edward Phelan; there are no existing portraits or photographs of him. But historian J. Fletcher Williams notes one additional detail: he was a "muscular" man with "a splendid physique."[7] And one St. Paul pioneer who knew him added a few more characteristics: "Edward Phelan was one of those simple, plain, uneducated Irishmen."[8]

---

* An Internet search of early nineteenth century passenger lists of immigrants reveals several Edward Phelans but none that match the known biographical facts of the Edward Phelan who settled in St. Paul. An Internet search for any age-appropriate Edward Phelan in the genealogy records for Northern Ireland also turned up empty.

The uneducated Irishman with a splendid physique was assigned to Company E, Fifth Infantry and then eventually sent to Fort Snelling, the country's uppermost garrison on the Mississippi River and one of America's first lines of defense in the event of a British attack from Canada, Great Britain's last North American colony. Fort Snelling maintained a strength of about two hundred fifty soldiers, well supplied with cannon, muskets, and horses. Built in 1820 on a picturesque bluff at the meeting of the Mississippi and St. Peter's (now Minnesota) Rivers, the frontier fortress was a center for regional Indian affairs and the only mark of civilization in the land now known as Minnesota.* At that time Minnesota was the domain of two great rival tribes: The Dakota (Sioux), the first known inhabitants of Minnesota, occupied the wooded river valleys and prairies in the southern regions; the Ojibwe (Chippewa), who arrived later, occupied the boreal forests of the north.[9]

Phelan entered the army during the presidency of General Andrew Jackson—America's great hero from the last war against the British, the War of 1812—who also earned some of his fame fighting Indians. (Jackson's parents, coincidentally, were also immigrants from Northern Ireland, albeit they were Scotch Irish.) President Jackson's endorsement and enforcement of the controversial Indian Removal Act of 1830 coerced numerous Indian tribes east of the Mississippi to remove to the west. This would eventually lead to the United States government's purchase of Indian lands east of the Mississippi in present-day Minnesota. Significantly, that purchase, in 1837, opened up the future site of St. Paul for settlement and enabled Phelan to stake his claim there.

If the six foot two and one-half inch, "muscular" Irishman, whose last name meant wolf, joined the army for the excitement of combat, then he no doubt would have been disappointed at his assignment to Fort Snelling. Both the British and the Indians of the region

---

* The traditional term "Indian" rather than Native American is used throughout because it is the term used in excerpts and quoted material and was widely considered a neutral term prior to the 1970s.

(the Dakota and Ojibwe) were at peace with the United States; the duties of a Fort Snelling soldier were limited to the tedium of drilling, cleaning muskets and barracks, and doing a variety of farm work. In some respects, the soldiers at Fort Snelling were almost as much farm laborers as they were trained fighting men. Fort Snelling boasted one of the largest farms north of St. Louis, with pastures, large herds of grazing livestock, and cultivated fields exceeding three hundred acres. Phelan may have grown up farming in rural Londonderry, or may have learned to farm at Fort Snelling; whatever the case, when he later settled in present-day St. Paul, he made his living as a farmer.[10]

Phelan's three years in the army were seemingly uneventful, at least by the measure of his sparse military record. He started as a private and he ended as a private. He left no record of any meritorious conduct or of any reprimands for bad conduct. But was there something darker beneath the surface of this meager record? In the days when most men stood less than five feet eight inches tall, Private Phelan was an unusually big man. A height chart of the 232 soldiers at Fort Snelling for 1837-39 shows that Phelan was the tallest.[11] Moreover, Phelan was not just tall, he also had a "splendid physique" and was "muscular and active." Big, muscular men in the world of men typically commanded respect. One might surmise that a big strong man like Phelan would have emerged as a leader in the army. Even given the politics inherent in military promotions, one might expect that a man of Phelan's imposing stature would have earned at least one promotion. Why then did Phelan remain a private? Perhaps Phelan's intimidating size got him in trouble? He may have resented taking orders from smaller men and those smaller men in turn may have resented him for being bigger than they were? Or maybe his attitude, temperament, or character prevented his promotion? Maybe Phelan was too "active" (i.e., aggressive) and unruly to handle the restrictions of military discipline? The Rev. Edward Neill, a Philadelphia native who was St. Paul's first Protestant clergyman and the first secretary of the Minnesota Historical Society claimed that, "Phelan was considered by his superiors as a bad unscrupulous man."[12] Unfortunately, Neill never specified which "superiors" made that assertion. Did Neill interview some of Phelan's former officers when he began his historical research a few years after he arrived in St. Paul from Galena, Illinois, on April 23, 1849?[*13] Or did Neill merely collect anecdotes and rumors from the old locals who were available to him? There is no way of knowing, but to be fair to Phelan, there is at least a possibility that Neill's sources were secondhand.

We do not have to rely only on Neill's unsubstantiated claim to believe the validity of what he said about Phelan. J. Fletcher Williams, the dedicated librarian-secretary of the Minnesota Historical Society from 1867–93 who wrote the first and most detailed early history of St. Paul, would seem to be a credible authority on Edward Phelan. Arriving in St. Paul in 1855, three years after graduating from Ohio Wesleyan University and then working as a local newspaper editor prior to his employment at the Minnesota Historical Society, Williams was, in his own words, "very well acquainted with nearly all the early settlers," even before he began his ten years of research for his book. Most significantly, in preparing his work Williams claimed he "visited and secured the minute statements of every living pioneer of our city, whose address I could ascertain."[14]

Williams' book and other papers he left to the Minnesota Historical Society verify that he was not exaggerating about the extent of his research. Williams specifically stated that Phelan "by his own boasting had led a lawless and criminal life before entering the army, and was one whom most civil and well-disposed persons avoided as a dangerous person."[15] If Phelan openly admitted that he had a criminal past, then his low rank is not so puzzling and the circumstances surrounding his enlistment are partly revealed. Williams' use of the phrase "by his own boasting" implies that he heard these details firsthand from Phelan. But that would not have been possible; Williams

---

[*] The record reveals that Phelan had four commanding officers during his three years of service: Major John Bliss, Lt. Col. William Davenport, Capt. Martin Scott, and Maj. Joseph Plympton. With the exception of Scott, who died in 1847 during the Mexican-American War, all of Phelan's commanders were alive but no longer living in Minnesota when Neill began his research.

first came to St. Paul in 1855, five years after Phelan reportedly left for California, never to return again.[16] Williams' information must have come from those "minute statements" made by one or more of the pioneers he interviewed. Obviously, people who knew Phelan told Williams something about Phelan's boasts that he led a criminal life. Of course, it's possible that this unnamed source was merely one person, who either confusingly misstated Phelan's story or dishonestly distorted it. But the fact that Williams reportedly interviewed "every pioneer of the city" he could find makes it very likely that his information on Phelan came from more than one source. Indeed, there is a high probability that Williams' entire indictment of Phelan represented the consensus opinion of all the pioneers he interviewed. He said as much when he claimed that Phelan "was regarded by the other settlers as a bad, unscrupulous, wicked man." The truth may well be that Edward Phelan (the "wolf") was exactly who Williams' said he was: "an immoral, cruel, revengeful and unscrupulous" ruffian, who boasted that he "had led a lawless and criminal life."[17] If Phelan had a criminal past, how far back in his life did it reach? Did he engage in crime in Londonderry? Or on the streets of New York?

Phelan lived in New York City in 1835, a time when the city's Irish immigrant district, located in Lower Manhattan in the Sixth Ward, was notorious for being a brawling, sprawling, smelly slum, dominated by thugs and gangs. According to Herbert Asbury, author of the classic *The Gangs of New York* (1927), the district began when "freed Negro slaves and low class Irish, who swarmed into New York on the first great wave of immigration," established homes in the swampy part of Lower Manhattan. There, by the 1820s, such rough, lawless adjoining neighborhoods as the "Bowery," "Hell's Kitchen," and the "Five Points" made the district "the most dismal slum section in America," perhaps even "worse than the Seven Dials and White Chapel [the haunt of Jack the Ripper] districts of London."*[18] New

---

* Martin Scorsese's 2002 film *"Gangs of New York"* portrays the Five Points in the mid-nineteenth century and is based on Asbury's book.

York historian Gregory Cristiano described the Five Points slum as "a lurid geographical cancer, filled with dilapidated and unlivable tenement houses, of ill-repute and drunkenness and gambling. This was a place where all manner of crime flourished, the residents terrorized and squalor prevailed."[19]

Edward Phelan likely lived somewhere in the lawless Sixth Ward, perhaps in the "overwhelmingly Irish" neighborhood of the Five Points, before he enlisted in the army.[20] Was the big, muscular man from Londonderry a member of one of those gangs of New York? Or, had he lived that "lawless and criminal life" independently?

Placing Phelan in the context of the rough and tumble Sixth Ward prior to his enlistment raises intriguing questions about why he joined the army. Maybe he joined simply to escape the stench and hunger of the slums? Or maybe he enlisted to escape the gangs' vengeance? Perhaps his life was in jeopardy? Or, maybe he was coerced into the military by law officials in lieu of jail time for some crime he committed? Given that the notorious jail of the Five Points, the "Tombs," was not constructed until 1838, three years after Phelan's enlistment, it is probable that local criminals were sometimes cheaply punished by sentencing them to a forced enlistment in the army.[21] Frontier Fort Snelling was an ideal post to hold undisciplined, criminal soldiers because its remote location in the Upper Mississippi wilderness discouraged escape by desertion.[22] Coercion into the military by law enforcement officials in lieu of jail time for some crime Phelan committed would tie several of the known fragments of his life neatly together and might explain why he only served a minimum of three years and never received a promotion. It might also explain why Phelan would have bragged about his criminal past. Perhaps Phelan was the sort of guy who relished the notoriety of being a different kind of enlistee, one that was not a run-of-the-mill soldier, but a man who had lived an adventurous life as a gangster. Soldiers with criminal backgrounds were not rare, but maybe Phelan's escapades in New York were unusually colorful. All that might then explain why his superiors would single him out as a bad man, not so much because he behaved badly as a soldier (although he might have), but because they knew his background and were predisposed to see him as a criminal.

Whatever the circumstances of his enlistment, Phelan's likely residency in the crime-ridden slums of New York (not to mention maybe the slums of Londonderry) reinforces Williams' and Neill's unflattering depictions of him. Their descriptions of Phelan read like the characterizations of many actual men who came from the Five Points and Hell's Kitchen neighborhoods. One of the most feared and ferocious of the infamous Five Points gangs, the "Pug Uglies," would have fit Phelan's profile perfectly. According to Asbury, the Pug Uglies were "gigantic Irishmen, and included in their membership some of the toughest characters of the Five Points."[23]

# CHAPTER TWO

# Phelan Becomes the First Settler
# of St. Paul's Downtown District

Private Edward Phelan was discharged from the army at Fort Snelling on June 8, 1838, fifteen months after the Dakota and Ojibwe ceded their lands between the St. Croix and Mississippi Rivers to the United States under the Treaty of 1837, and five weeks before news of the Senate's ratification of the treaty reached the fort.[1] The land rush to the unsurveyed territory east of the Mississippi was already underway. A scattering of cabins dubbed Rumtown stood just across the river from Fort Snelling, in the area of what is now St. Paul's Hidden Falls Park.* This growing east bank settlement took its name from the fact that most of its residents were rum and whiskey traders. A few miles downriver, at the popular natural landmark called Fountain Cave, and just west of the present intersection of Randolph Avenue and Shepard Road, a notorious one-eyed, French-Canadian whiskey trader named "Pig's Eye" Parrant was finishing the construction of his shanty saloon. Just up the hill from Pig's Eye's place, at Buttermilk Falls and along Buttermilk Creek,** around the present corner of Duke Street and Palace Avenue, a family of French-speaking

---

* Rumtown was a sprawl of ten cabins stretching between the south and north ends of present-day Hidden Falls Park. Most of the cabins were saloons or in the vernacular of the day, "groggeries" or "whiskey shops."

**Buttermilk Falls was the cascade formed by the stream labeled "Buttermilk Creek" on James L. Thompson's "Map of Military Reservation Embracing Fort Snelling" (Oct. 1839), which meandered down the present James Street/Randolph Avenue hill on its run to the river. The falls was located near the present intersection of Palace Avenue and Duke Street. Palace Avenue was originally named Cascade Street. See note 24.

Swiss-Canadians named Perry (or Perret) were building their cabin and clearing some forest for their farm.[2] Clearly, the land grab was accelerating on the east side of the river and everyone at Fort Snelling was no doubt aware of it.

It was Phelan's good fortune to gain his release from the military at the beginning of the land rush. Exactly when he decided to take advantage of that timing and make a claim for himself on the east side of the river is not known. In spite of the great potential of the region, most discharged Fort Snelling soldiers left the area for more civilized surroundings. J. Fletcher Williams suggests that Phelan was influenced by a clever fellow Irishman and Fort Snelling soldier named John Hays and hints that another Irish soldier, William Evans, was also part of some discussion about the high value of the land across the river. Hays—a slender, five feet nine inch, blue-eyed, gray-haired native of Waterford, Ireland,* who claimed he was thirty-nine but looked much older—was, in the words of Williams, "a man of exactly the opposite characteristics of the ruffianly Phelan."* Williams elaborated:

> He was of middle age [in 1838]...his hair somewhat bleached with two or three terms in the Army. He was something of a martinet in discipline, precise and exact in his dress, bearing and actions, gained by his long military service. His form was spare but erect, and he had a dignified and respectable bearing that impressed everybody who met him favorably. Every one of the earliest settlers who knew John Hays speaks of him with unqualified praise, as an honest, courteous and clever old gentleman.[3]

In spite of these differences in character, manner, age, experiences, reputation, and rank (Hays was a sergeant), the odd couple of Phelan and Hays decided to team up and make land claims together. Sergeant Hays clearly initiated the idea; his military commitment extended

---

* Waterford is Ireland's oldest city, 190 miles south of Londonderry.

until April 25, 1839, almost a year after Phelan's discharge and probably too late for him to claim any of the better east bank parcels of property. Williams corroborates this, observing that Phelan did it "at the request of Hays."[4] The arrangement between the two Irish bachelors was simple. Phelan would select two choice tracts of land across the river. He would claim one for himself, the other he would claim and hold for Hays until the sergeant was free to join him. Williams clarifies that it was a *quid pro quo* arrangement. Hays "would furnish…some money" which Phelan "was to use in erecting a cabin, in which they would jointly occupy, when he came out of the Army."[5] Since Private Phelan had earned only about six dollars a month during his three years in the army, he was no doubt in desperate need of money to purchase the essential tools, supplies, and equipment to carve out a home in the wilderness. Thus, his partnership with the relatively wealthy veteran sergeant (who earned about fifteen dollars per month) may have been strictly an act of self-interest.[6]

Phelan successfully fulfilled his part of the deal by quickly staking claim to two select tracts of river land that would later become some of the most valuable real estate in St. Paul. Phelan's own land claim, according to Williams, was "a track of ground fronting the river, running back to the bluff, and bounded (approximately) by what is now Eagle and Third Street [Kellogg Blvd.] on the west, and St. Peter Street in the east."[7] In other words, his claim was the western end of what is now downtown St. Paul, an area marked by some of the city's most identifying landmarks – The St. Paul River Centre, Roy Wilkins Auditorium, Excel Energy Center, the Ordway Center for the Performing Arts, the Science Museum of Minnesota, the St. Paul Central Library, and Rice Park. But back in Phelan's day, the land was a wilderness of woods, swamp, meadow, and a cold spring (later called Rice Creek) winding down the limestone bluff. The tract Phelan claimed for Hays was "a claim adjoining his own on the east, fronting on the river, and running back to the bluff, extending probably from what is now St. Peter Street, down to somewhere near the present Minnesota Street."[8] In modern terms, the two claims that Phelan staked in June 1838 represent nothing less than the heart of St. Paul's downtown district.

Phelan's and Hays' Irish comrade, William Evans (1807-70), retired from the army around the same time as Phelan and also staked a claim in the summer of 1838. But his land was outside of today's downtown district, about one mile and a half further downriver from Phelan's claim, on the east edge of a mile-wide gorge, on the west end of present-day Dayton's Bluff. Evans, a bachelor farmer who had spent some years in pastoral Pennsylvania before joining the army, was, for a time, the only human inhabitant between Phelan and the Dakota Indian village called Kaposia (Little Crow's village), located about three miles down and across the river from Evans' cabin, at present-day South St. Paul. The village had a population of about three hundred people and twelve to fourteen large bark-covered lodges. They were one of seven bands of the Mdewakanton Dakota who had villages in the "Big Woods" of southeastern Minnesota, stretching from present-day Winona on the Mississippi River to present-day Shakopee, southwest of Minneapolis on the Minnesota River.[9]

Phelan's neighbor upriver at Fountain Cave, Pierre "Pig's Eye" Parrant, was notorious for selling whiskey to the local Dakota.* "An ugly looking," one-eyed, middle- aged, "bulky framed," French Canadian, who was "dark as an Indian," Pig's Eye was the first east bank settler to claim land downriver from Fort Snelling. Williams calls him "the founder of St. Paul."[10] On June 1, 1838, one week before Phelan was discharged from the army, Pig's Eye began building his crude shanty saloon about three miles downriver from Rumtown and nearly two miles upriver from Phelan's land. Though federal law had prohibited the trading of any "ardent spirits" in Indian country since 1832, Pig's Eye maintained that the law did not apply to his

---

* Fountain Cave was the landmark sandstone cavern near present-day Shepard Road and Randolph Avenue, remembered for its unending depth and the crystal stream cascading from its interior. It was located exactly where the present grain elevator now stands, one block west of Randolph and Shepard Road. The cave's entrance was destroyed in 1955 with the construction of both Shepard Road and the elevator. A historical marker highlighting the cave's history stands across Shepard Road from the elevator.

new establishment at the cave since it stood on the east side of the Mississippi— territory that was now no longer part of Indian country thanks to the 1837 treaty.[11] The Fountain Cave saloon quickly became a popular gathering place for men from Little Crow's Kaposia Village. And because his land was between Kaposia and Fountain Cave, Phelan would soon get used to the sight of the Kaposia customers traveling by (and across) his property to Pig's Eye's saloon.

According to Williams, Phelan decided to build his shanty "on the side of the bluff under Third Street, about where the Soap Factory now stands."[12] Translated into modern terms, that would mean the grounds of the River Centre Parking Ramp below Kellogg Boulevard, near Eagle and Exchange Streets. Williams described the first building erected on the site of today's downtown as "a log house – a mere hovel." That "hovel under the hill" was Phelan's home and, according to their agreement, Sergeant Hays' home when he came out of the army.[13] Williams says nothing about how long the two bachelors planned to share a cabin, but it was probably a temporary arrangement until Hays could build his own cabin.

According to Thomas McLean Newson (1827-1893), another former local newspaper editor who collected biographical sketches of St. Paul's early settlers, Phelan was assisted in the building of his cabin by a most interesting and important pioneer: James Thompson (1800-84).[14] Like Phelan, Thompson had lived a few years at Fort Snelling. But unlike Phelan, he never wore an army uniform. Thompson was a former slave, originally owned by President James Monroe's nephew, George Monroe. At Fort Snelling he was the property of first, John Culbertson, the fort's sutler* who brought him there from Virginia in 1827. Then Thompson was later purchased by Capt. Hanibal Day. Around 1836 Day took Thompson with him down to his new station at Fort Crawford, Prairie du Chien, Wisconsin, much to the sorrow of the "mulatto slave," who had to leave his Dakota wife behind. However, an abolitionist Methodist missionary there

---

* A sutler was a civilian appointed by the president to operate a general store inside a military post.

named Alfred Brunson (1793-1882) came to the rescue. Outraged that slaves were being kept that far north in supposedly free territory and also touched by the personal plight of Thompson, Brunson organized a fundraiser through the *Western Christian Advocate* newspaper and solicited enough funds by 1837 to pay Captain Day $1,500 for Thompson's freedom.[15] In gratitude for his liberation, Thompson freely served Brunson and other Methodist missionaries as both an Indian interpreter (he spoke the Dakota language) and as a carpenter, when they established a mission at Little Crow's Kaposia Village, across the river from present Pig's Eye Lake, in the spring of 1837. Ironically, when his work at the mission was completed around 1839, Thompson and his wife moved up to rowdy Rumtown, where he "ran a whiskey shop opposite Fort Snelling."[16] Newson, who interviewed Thompson when he was eighty-five years old, reported that the former slave claimed he had "aided in erecting and constructing the first house in St. Paul, which was owned by Phelan and Hays."[17]

Newson never reported the details of how Thompson came to aid Phelan in the building of his house. However, he did detail a colorful conflict between Phelan and Thompson that occurred sometime in 1839. One day in that year Thompson discovered that his pet pig was stolen and, suspecting Phelan of the crime, he trekked over to the big Irishman's shanty and found his pig there, fenced in a pen. Phelan was nowhere to be found, so Thompson simply "knocked off the boards" of the pen and then his well-trained pig "trotted home after him like a little dog, really glad once more to find his own master." When Phelan found out from another pioneer* what Thompson had done "he became terribly enraged" and stormed over to Thompson's place. (Newson never mentions where exactly Thompson lived.) Phelan aggressively demanded the return of "his pig." Newson literally recounts their dialogue:

---

* Newson said Phelan talked to Henry Jackson, St. Paul's first resident justice of the peace and the village's first American-born adult citizen. However, Jackson did not move to St. Paul until 1842, two years after Phelan left the present downtown area.

"It isn't your pig," said Thompson.

"It is my pig," said Phelan, "and if you don't give it up, I will lick you."

"You can't do it," said Thompson.

"Well, I will do it," replied the thief.

"Now see here," said Phelan, "I will meet you here tomorrow morning at 9 o'clock and if you lick me the pig is yours, and if I lick you the pig is mine."

"Agreed," said Thompson and the two departed.[18]

The "Battle for the Pig" did not look like a fair contest. The former slave was only five feet six inches and probably weighed no more than one hundred sixty pounds. Phelan, of course, stood over six feet two inches and was quite muscular. Despite his disadvantage in size, Thompson met Phelan at the time and place agreed upon. Newson's detailed narration of the fight almost reads like the words of a sportscaster:

> Phelan was a long-legged and long-armed man and so when the parties met he went for Thompson with his legs and feet, but Thompson dodged his many kicks, when all of a sudden he seized him by his nether extremity and immediately the brute and bully was upon the ground and Thompson pummeled him with his fists so thoroughly that he called for mercy. On gaining his feet he acknowledged that the pig belonged to his antagonist and invited "the boys" to his shanty, (Thompson among the rest) and treated them to five gallons of wine, and ever after that Thompson and Phelan were good friends.[19]

This is a classically American story: the big bad bully getting his comeuppance at the hands of the small righteous man. Yet it is also telling in what it reveals about Edward Phelan. Although it is only Thompson's version of the fight, as told to Newson, one can deduce a few plain facts about Phelan, assuming Newson's account is essentially true. One, he was a thief. Two, he was a liar. Three, he was a bully.

Four, he was a kicker more than he was a boxer, which in some places would have made him a "dirty fighter." Five, he wasn't as tough as he thought he was. And six, he wasn't a completely bad man: he confessed to his crime, he treated all the boys, including Thompson, to "five gallons of "wine," and made friends with the former slave who "pummeled him."

Whether the "Battle for the Pig" occurred before or after Hays moved in with Phelan was never noted. But on April 25, 1839, ten months after Phelan was discharged from Fort Snelling, John Hays retired from the army and moved into the "hovel under the hill" with Phelan.[20]

Later that summer, or the summer before, Phelan and Hays also partnered in the purchase of some cattle. Apparently Hays provided most of the money and Phelan provided most of the "bargaining" or price setting.[21] At least four of the cattle came from the herd of their neighbor Ben Gervais (1792-1875), a French Canadian farmer and one of the early founders of St. Paul.* In July 1838, a month after Phelan claimed his land, Gervais, his wife Genevieve (1804-1885), and their six children settled into the little glen just downriver from Fountain Cave, and about a mile and a half upriver from Phelan and Hays' shanty. Around the same time, Ben's younger brother Pierre Gervais (1803-1872), and his wife Sophie (1817-73) and infant daughter Elsie also settled downriver from the cave on land just a little east from his brother's claim.[22]

The population of the east bank was growing but was still far from resembling an established town. From the north edge of Rumtown (present-day Ford Dam) to William Evan's land five miles away (present-day Dayton's Bluff), there were just sixteen cabins scattered across the river bank in 1839. The residents of those frontier cabins—the only known dwellings then standing within the entire present city limits of St. Paul, with the exception of the nine or ten cab-

---

* Ben Gervais also donated a portion of the property for St. Paul's namesake chapel, founded the village of Little Canada, built the first commercial grist mill in Minnesota, and became, like Phelan, the namesake of a creek and a lake.

ins that some French Canadians built down around present Pig's Eye Lake in 1839—included only about thirty-three adults.[23] The vast majority of those settlers were, like the Gervaises, French-speaking immigrants from Canada. That included the French-speaking Abraham Perry family, who lived just up the hill from Ben Gervais at Buttermilk Falls. Originally from Switzerland, the Perrys immigrated to the Fort Snelling region after living at the Red River Colony in present- day Winnipeg, Canada.* The Perrys had the double distinction of being the first Fort Snelling area settlers to homestead downriver from Fountain Cave and the family that "at one time owned more cattle than all the rest of the inhabitants of what is now Minnesota," with the exception of Joseph Renville, at Lac Qui Parle.[24]

During the first week of June 1838, Abraham Perry (1776-1849), his wife Mary Ann (1790-1859), their adult son Charles (1816-1904), and their five daughters settled just east of Fountain Cave, with Fountain Creek as the boundary between their property and Parrant's.[25] Though Phelan and Hays did not speak French and had no known connection to Canada, there is no evidence that either of them had any problems with their neighbors. Years later one of the Gervais sons shared the following recollection about the first settlers of St. Paul with a local newspaper reporter:

> *The first settlers here all got on well together. They helped one another in every way and were always sociable and intimate. They were all plain people in moderate circumstances and everybody worked. Every family raised nearly all of its provisions, grains and vegetables*[26]

---

* Founded in 1811 by the Scottish Lord, the Fifth Earl of Selkirk, Thomas Douglas, under the sponsorship of the Hudson Bay Fur Company, the ill-fated Red River Colony was continuously plagued by blizzards, floods, droughts, locusts, and Indian attacks instigated and orchestrated by the rival Northwest Fur Company. Between 1821 and 1841, hundreds of colonists fled the colony in Red River oxcarts bound for Fort Snelling and beyond. The Gervaises and many of the Rumtown settlers were also immigrants from the Red River Colony.

# CHAPTER THREE

# A September to Remember:
# A Historic Birth and Mysterious Death

How well the two Irish housemates and business partners got along living in their little shanty is not clear; that would become a more relevant question in September 1839. For the pioneer settlers on the east side of the Mississippi downriver from Fort Snelling, that first week of September 1839 would be memorably marked by both a historic birth and an unforgettable death.

The birth was that of Basil Gervais, the seventh child of Benjamin and Genevieve Gervais, born on September 4, 1839, in their "little tamarack cabin" just below the bluff at the present-day intersection of Randolph Avenue and Shepard Road. For the rest of his life Basil Gervais would be known as "the first white child born in St. Paul." His mother Genevieve was undoubtedly assisted during his birth by the region's most experienced midwife, Mrs. Mary Ann Perry (1786-1859)—wife of Abraham Perry and mother of seven children—who conveniently lived just up the hill, less than a half-mile from their cabin.[1]

The unforgettable death was that of Sgt. John Hays, one of the most beloved settlers of the area and "respected by everybody." An "honest, courteous and clever old gentleman," Sergeant Hays' passing was not only the first recorded death in the place now named St. Paul, it was also the area's first recorded murder.[2] Unlike the birthday of Basil Gervais, the death of Sergeant Hays cannot be dated precisely, but the evidence suggests that Hays died only a day after the birth of the Gervais baby.

On Friday afternoon, September 6, 1839, Edward Phelan made a surprise visit to the cabin of Ben and Genevieve Gervais, but it is doubtful that he came to see the baby. In "the course of conversation," Phelan told Genevieve that his partner Hays "had crossed the Mississippi that day to go to Little Crow's village in search of a calf."[3] Although the recovering thirty-five-year-old mother was hard of hearing, Phelan spoke loudly enough that she heard the details of his story.

According to Mrs. Gervais, Phelan told her that early in the morning he and Hays were visited by an employee of fur trader Benjamin F. Baker, who was en route to the St. Croix River in a canoe. The man, "whose name [Genevieve did] not recollect," was told about the lost calf and Hays' intention to look for the Indians who had allegedly stolen it. The man

> offered [Hays] a seat in the canoe, which Hays declined, saying he would have a better chance of finding his calf, or the remains of it, by going down by land on the opposite bank of the Mississippi; by that means he might find the Indians in the act of feasting on the meat of the calf. When the man left the house, Hays accompanied him as far as the hill, after which he returned, breakfasted, dressed himself, and then Phelan went with him [Hays] across the river.[4]

Phelan would later add the detail that he "put Hays across the river in a canoe."[5] The conversation between Phelan and Mrs. Gervais took place while Ben Gervais was outside the cabin. Ben returned only in time to verify that some conversation had taken place between his wife and Phelan that "Friday."[6]

The significance of Phelan's conversation with Mrs. Gervais that day would become apparent when Hays' search for the lost calf turned into the mysterious disappearance of a lost man—and then even more significant when the case of a missing person turned into a case of murder. Phelan's comments about Hays to Mrs. Gervais on September 6 would become critical evidence since they were his first detailed explanation of why, when, and how his partner had left their farm. It would also lock Phelan into an account of the last time he saw Hays alive at a very early date, long before any murder investigation. To review, it was early Friday morning, September 6, after he had left him off on the other side of the river so that Hays could search for a lost calf on the same side of the Mississippi as Little Crow's village (Kaposia). According to Phelan, Sergeant Hays suspected that "the Indians" had stolen it.

During the official inquiry, Phelan also recalled that he visited the Gervais cabin again the next day, Saturday, September 7, to inform them of "Hays' disappearance." In other words, Hays never returned home from his trip to Kaposia. According to Phelan, the Gervaises "told him if [Hays] did not come [later] on Saturday, to notify them." Phelan further testified that he did just that, saying that "Sunday being a fine day went to Jervais [sic] and asked him to go with me and look for [Hays], being uneasy on his account. Jervais [sic] told me if [Hays] did not return to let him know, and he would aid in a search on Monday."[7]

In their later testimony of these events, neither Ben Gervais nor Genevieve Gervais made any mention of a visit by Phelan on Saturday, September 7, to inform them of Hays' disappearance. They both acknowledged that Phelan did return to their cabin on Sunday, September 8, and that was when they first learned of Sergeant Hays' disappearance. Genevieve Gervais added that Phelan told her "the probable cause of Hays' absence" was that "probably he had gone" to Hazen Mooer's place. (Hazen Mooer was a fur trader who lived fifteen miles downriver, on Grey Cloud Island, in present-day Cottage Grove.) Phelan said that Hays "had spoke of the possibility of his going there previous to his return." Mrs. Gervais informed Phelan that by a lucky coincidence, Joseph R. Brown, the Fort Snelling soldier-turned-fur trader, a resident of Grey Cloud Island and a justice of the peace, "was then at Mr. Perry's and could inform him whether

Hays had been there [at Mooer's] or not." (The Perry family lived less than half a mile from the Gervais cabin.) According to Mrs. Gervais, Phelan "replied that if his clothes were not so bad he would go but he did not like to go as he was."[8]

Once again, Ben Gervais was not part of the conversation between Phelan and his wife; all he could recall overhearing or understanding was "the observation that [the lost] calf had returned after the departure of Hays."[9] As we will see later, that was no insignificant recollection.

Genevieve Gervais' testimony was potentially incriminating against Edward Phelan. First, there was the discrepancy over which day Phelan first informed the Gervaises that Sergeant Hays was missing. Phelan claimed it was Saturday, the Gervaises testified that he didn't visit them until Sunday—the day he supposedly first realized that his partner was definitely missing. If Phelan was correct on that matter, then it provides some evidence that he had acted in a manner consistent with someone who was sincerely concerned about the welfare of his partner. On the other hand, if Genevieve and Ben Gervais' recollections were correct that it was not until Sunday when Phelan first told them about Sergeant Hays' disappearance then that would undermine the notion that he acted in a clearly concerned way. In other words, if Sunday was the correct day, Phelan should have realized that something was wrong when Sergeant Hays had not returned Friday night. If the Gervais testimony is correct, Phelan waited a full day and a half before notifying anyone that Hays was missing.

Genevieve Gervais' testimony about Phelan's reaction on Sunday to the news that Justice of the Peace Joseph R. Brown from Grey Cloud Island was nearby is even more incriminating against Phelan. Brown—the obvious official to notify of a missing person and moreover the neighbor of Hazen Mooer—was just a short walk away at the Perry cabin. Brown might well have known whether Sergeant Hays had been seen down at the very place where Phelan claimed Hays had "probably gone"—Hazen Mooer's place. Moreover, as an official of the law, Brown would know what should be done to try to find Hays. Yet, upon hearing this great fortuitous news that Justice Brown was virtually next door, what did Phelan do? He declined to see him merely because he wasn't wearing the right clothes.

Phelan's reaction here is certainly suspicious and not what one would expect from any concerned "uneasy" friend. It could, of course, be a sign of his consciousness of guilt. If Phelan had killed Hays, the last person he would want to talk to would be a law official who was from the place where Phelan claimed Hays was. Worse, Brown—the former Fort Snelling soldier—probably knew Hays and might have been able to detect flaws in anything Phelan said about him.

But there may be a less sinister explanation for Phelan's odd reaction. Since he was never known for his sensitivity or consideration of others, perhaps he did care more about how he looked to the Perrys than he did about gaining information about Hays. The Perry's had two mature daughters: twenty-four-year-old Sophia and thirteen-year-old Adele.[10] Maybe Phelan had a romantic interest in one of the Perry girls and he didn't want her to see him in his "bad" clothes. That should not have taken precedence over the urgency of gaining information about his missing roommate, but given all the negative depictions of Phelan, why would this man of supposed "low character" have his priorities properly in place?

Phelan, for his part, completely denied Mrs. Gervais' version of what he told her on Sunday, September 8. In an affidavit taken in November, he "denied the whole of her evidence, saying he had never told her anything of the kind, but that as she was hard of hearing, that she must have mistaken his words."[11]

In response to that affidavit, Genevieve Gervais replied, "I am confident this is the purport of his words. He knew I was hard of hearing, and spoke loud in consequence."[12]

In a contest over credibility, Edward Phelan, the ruffian with the "unsavory reputation," would have had a tough time competing against the hard-of-hearing, hard-working mother of seven, who was a devout Catholic and by all evidence, a woman of good moral character.[13]

On Monday, September 9, Edward Phelan finally began a search for Sergeant Hays, three days after he said he had transported him across the river. Accompanied only by Ben Gervais, Phelan searched the west side of the Mississippi, beginning at the place where Phelan said he had left Hays. Unfortunately, neither Phelan nor Gervais, nor any other witness of record, specified where exactly that place was.[14] We can only assume it was the closest landing place on the opposite shore of what the local pioneers called "Phelan's Landing," and what the later settlers would call the "Upper Landing," at the foot of Chestnut Street. Since present-day Harriet Island was then a true island, a crossing from Phelan's Landing would involve going downriver beyond the island's eastern (or lower) end, and cutting through the narrow passage between Raspberry (also known as Navy) and Harriet Islands. Thus, the most logical landing place for river crossings from Phelan's Landing would be the shoreline just west of the present Wabasha Bridge and just east of the Harriet Island main boat docks.

According to both Phelan and Gervais, the two men searched Sergeant Hays' supposed landing spot and found no traces of his footprints anywhere. Ben Gervais later offered an interesting interpretation of what he observed there:

> *At that place the beach was sand and gravel. Examined to see if any tracks were perceptible but could find no traces. Think a man with leather shoes would have left traces that would have been perceptible 2 or 3 days after he passed.*"[15]

How competent Ben Gervais was in the art of footprint analysis is not known. But he had previously spent three years working as a "trapper, guide and voyageur" for the Hudson Bay Fur Company, a career that included carrying canoes over a great many beaches and shorelines from Montreal to Winnipeg. He would have been very familiar with the sight of footprints on a beach and more experienced than most men in reading them.[16] We might then presume that the forty-seven-year-old former voyageur and trapper was making a sound judgment when he reasoned that "a man with leather shoes would have left traces that would have been perceptible two or three days after he passed." An obvious question arises: If Phelan left Hays off at that spot on the beach just three days earlier, why weren't there any traces of his footprints? Maybe rain washed them away? Although Phelan stated that the day before, Sunday, was "a fine day," another source noted that locally September 8 was "a rainy Sunday."[17] Had a Sunday shower erased Hay's footprints? Maybe, but perhaps Gervais factored recent rain into his calculation that footprints "would have been perceptible two or three days after [Hays] passed."

Phelan and Gervais (presumably in a canoe) continued searching the west shore as far down as Kaposia (Little Crow's village) and the Methodist mission house there, just north of what is now the corner of Concord Street and Butler Avenue in South St. Paul, where about three hundred Mdewakanton Dakota and the family of a white missionary resided. There at the mission house, in the words of Gervais, "Phelan inquired for Hays; they said he had not been there."[18]

The two men traveled back upriver, again searching the river bottoms for any sign of Hays. This time they found some tracks near the beach where Hays had supposedly walked. But both men agreed that the tracks went the wrong way: west toward the St. Peter's River instead of east toward Kaposia. Phelan made the following observation:

"The track was not that of Hays, as it was too old and the track was made by a round-toed shoe, while the boots Hays wore were square-toed."[19] Aside from those "old" round-toed, westward tracks, neither Gervais nor Phelan reported seeing any sign of Hays' trek along the beach during their ten-mile round-trip search of the west side of the river.[20] Phelan's mention of "old" tracks also implies the interesting suggestion that footprints can remain for longer than three days, even after a "rainy Sunday."

Two days later, on Wednesday, September 11, Phelan went to Fort Snelling to see one of Sergeant Hays' old comrades, Bartholomew Baldwin, a soldier who was married to a Dakota mixed-blood and who was one of the army's Indian interpreters.[21] Whether the visit was primarily to inform Baldwin of Sergeant Hays' disappearance or to enlist his help to search for him is unclear. In any case, Baldwin later testified that he first heard of Hays' disappearance on Tuesday and then joined Phelan in a search for him on Wednesday morning.

Baldwin and Phelan's search was essentially a repeat of the earlier search Phelan made with Gervais. Although Baldwin's testimony included much interesting information, his account of this Wednesday search was disappointingly brief. He only mentioned seeing some tracks on the beach where Phelan and Gervais had recently walked.[22] Phelan, however, provided much more detail about his search with Baldwin. He testified that Baldwin served as an interpreter when they went to the Kaposia village and that he "engaged…the Indians but could get no intelligence of any kind." Phelan further stated that he "enquired personally" about Sergeant Hays to the family of the Methodist lay missionary, John Holton, "but they had heard or seen nothing of him."[23]

After conducting two different searches, with two different men, on two different days, Phelan concluded that "the Indians must have killed [Hays]" and so he "made no further search" for his partner.[24] What led Phelan to that conclusion? No body had been found, and nowhere on Sergeant Hays' supposed route to Kaposia did Phelan, Gervais, or Baldwin see any signs of blood, or any Indian footprints, or anything indicating some kind of violent struggle. Moreover, Ben Gervais testified that he heard Phelan tell his wife on September 8 that "his calf had returned after the departure of Sergeant Hays."[25] If that were true, then presumably it had not been stolen by Indians ,and Hays would not have caught Indians in possession of it triggering a confrontation. Given that logic, what motive did any Indian have for killing Sergeant Hays?

During the later inquiry Phelan was apparently asked that critical question. (The inquiry recorded only answers, no questions.) He responded indirectly at first, saying that "he did not understand the Indian language" but that "Hays spoke a few words of it."[26] He also said that he had "no reason to suspect any particular Indian," but added that he did "not know one Indian from another."[27] However, Phelan then reported a past problem that Sergeant Hays had with one "particular Indian." (Unfortunately, that part of his handwritten affidavit is marked by a number of illegible words and very poor grammar. Fortunately, most of what was written can still be understandably translated.)

> *One young Indian came to the house about two months ago [August] and was taking aim with his gun at things in the house. Judged from what I saw that [Hays] told him to stop. I then left the house, and the two [were] together, and went up the hill back of the house; was not gone more than twenty minutes when I heard the report of a gun—saw the Indian outside the door, and asked Hays what was the matter, who said the Indian had been taking aim at a looking glass in the house, and that he had taken the gun from him and fired it outside the door, remarking that he had told the Indian if he came back he would club him. Followed the Indian up the hill, and saw him load his gun and he threatened to tell Waultietanka [Wakinyantonka, Chief Big Thunder\*] about it. [Hays] spoke of this affair afterwards, and said he expected to have some trouble with the Indians. [This] Indian was a very young man, about eighteen years of age. Never heard that [Hays] had difficulty with the Indians about the matter. No difficulty could have occurred without my getting a knowledge of it. Am not aware that [Hays] had any difficulty with any white man.*[28]

Phelan's story about the young, trigger-happy Dakota harassing Sergeant Hays has a ring of plausibility. It was not uncommon for Indians to harass the settlers of the Fort Snelling region. On October 18, 1838, the Perrys had complained to Major Lawrence Taliaferro, Fort Snelling's Indian agent (the federal official assigned to all Indian

---

\* Big Thunder was the chief of the Kaposia village who was also known by the non-Indians as Little Crow. He was the son of the first known Little Crow and the father of the most famous Little Crow, who led the Dakota during the great uprising of 1862.

matters in the region), that a band of Dakota "shot and killed three of their cattle and wounded a fourth."[29] A few years earlier, Mendota fur-trader-farmer Jean Baptiste Faribault filed a claim with Taliaferro for the reimbursement of fifty-nine hogs, four horses, and two bulls that various Dakota had stolen during a three-year span.[30] According to a story W. B. Hennessy reported in his little known book, *A History of the St. Paul Fire Department* (1909), Pig's Eye Parrant's Fountain Cave business was once violently plundered by some local Dakota:

> One day a steamer came tooting up the river and drawing at nightfall up to the bank in the neighborhood of Fountain Cave, near the Parrant establishment, dropped off three barrels of whiskey. The fact was noted by an Indian who had no liquor in him and no means, in the form of legal tender, of getting any in him. He observed that Parrant and a trusted friend rolled the barrels up the incline to a "lean-to" structure of logs which covered the entrance to a cave and formed protection for the Parrant cache. The Indian sent for assistance and that night there were doings on the banks of the Mississippi. The Indians looted the cache, knocked in the head of a barrel, and before Parrant knew what had happened, he was obliged to flee for his life. The Indians indulged in a wild orgy…and set fire to the "lean-to" and destroyed with it the two barrels of whiskey they had not bothered to take out. The money loss was not great…but it destroyed [his] entire stock in trade.[31]

Most dramatic of all, a few years after the incident with the Perry family, Adele Perry—now married to Vetal Guerin and living near what is now the corner of Kellogg Boulevard and Wabasha Street (on Hays' former claim) —experienced a terrifying ordeal, when "nine or ten Indians made an attack on the house, and tried to kill [her husband]." Williams covered this frightening encounter in vivid detail:

> They broke in the window and attempted to crawl in. Mrs. Guerin concealed herself under the bed, expecting to be murdered. Guerin

*seized an axe, and was about to brain the first pagan whose head appeared through the window. This would have been a very unfortunate affair for Guerin, had it happened, but luckily, before any bloodshed occurred, a friendly chief, named 'Hawks Bill', came up, and remonstrated them to leave. While they were parleying, Mr. and Mrs. Guerin, with the child slipped out of the door, and fled to Mr. Gervais house [their new home near present Kellogg Blvd. and Robert Street]. The Indians then went away, after shooting Guerin's dog with arrows.*[32]

Williams also reported another frightening encounter Guerin had with some "drunken Indians."

*At another time Guerin was leaning on the gate post of his garden when some drunken Indians coming up Bench street hill fired at him. A ball struck the post making a narrow escape for Guerin. Again, as he opened the door one morning, an iron-headed arrow whizzed past his head and stuck the door jamb.*[33]

Years later, Vetal Guerin summarized all the problems he had had with the local Dakota in early St. Paul. "Sioux Indians killed my cow and pig. I was much afraid at times. They killed several oxen and hogs. Several times tried to kill me."[34]

But the well-documented incidents between local Dakota and settlers is not the only reason that Phelan's story about Sergeant Hays' conflict with the young Indian rings true. Phelan's credibility is enhanced by his surprising conclusion that he "never heard that [Hays] had difficulty with the Indians about the matter." And he adds that "no difficulty could have occurred without my getting knowledge of it." Those concluding remarks are surprising because they undermine the most obvious reason a guilty Phelan would have had for telling the story: to divert attention away from himself and steer the investigation to another suspect. If Phelan wanted to blame his crime on an Indian, then one might expect him to do that directly and emphatically when given the chance. But Phelan did not do that. He was neither direct nor emphatic and indeed, seemed almost careful not to overplay the importance of Sergeant Hays' incident with the Indian.

Was Phelan being clever and coy? Or was he simply telling the truth?

The testimony of Bartholomew Baldwin somewhat confirms Phelan's Indian story. Baldwin recalled that during the day of their search "Phelan told me nearly the same story about the quarrel between [Hays] and the young Indian about two months ago, except that Phelan stated that [Hays] had, after firing of the gun, taken the flint from the lock, and Phelan did not say to me that he saw the Indian load the gun."[35]

Baldwin's revelation— that Phelan told him "nearly the same story" weeks before the investigation began in late September— makes Phelan's story a little more convincing. However, it still leaves the possibility that he invented the Indian incident, but simply did it back in early September. The two discrepancies that Baldwin noted were about seemingly minor details. Still, that could be a small sign that the story was fabricated. On the other hand, it could just be a common instance of two men having different memories of a conversation.

After Phelan and Baldwin's futile search for Sergeant Hays on September 11, there is no record that any subsequent searches were conducted by anyone. Four days after Phelan and Baldwin's trip to Kaposia on Sunday, September 15, Fort Snelling's Indian agent Lawrence Taliaferro penned an interesting entry in his journal:

*A man by name Hays, an Irishman lost. Supposed killed – even reported to have been murdered by the Chief Wa-kin-yan-ton-ka [Big Thunder]. No belief rests with me. I incline to the opinion that his neighbor, Phelan, knows something. Hays lived with him and had money.*[36]

Taliaferro's brief comments are loaded and intriguing. Where did the report that Hays was "reported to have been murdered by the

Chief Wa-kin-yan-ton-ka" originate, before a body was even found? Logically, it must have originated with Phelan. Phelan had told Fort Snelling soldier Bartholomew Baldwin about the alleged incident between Hays and a young unruly Dakota, including the remark that the young Dakota "threatened to tell" Chief Big Thunder about Hays' rough treatment of him. Baldwin probably told his fellow soldiers at the fort what Phelan had told him about an angry Indian threatening Hays with the wrath of Chief Big Thunder. Phelan may also have realized that anything he told Baldwin would get back to the soldiers at Fort Snelling.

If Phelan schemed to plant a plausible explanation of how and why Sergeant Hays could have been killed by Indians, then some of Taliaferro's comments suggest that the scheme was working, at least on September 15. Taliaferro's choice of the words "reported" and "murdered" in his journal entry imply that people at the fort were assuming by September 15 that Sergeant Hays had been murdered, and that the first murder suspect was Chief Big Thunder no less.

Superficially Chief Big Thunder was an easy suspect. According to Dakota missionary and historian Samuel Pond, "his features were repulsive, his manner ungainly and awkward and his disposition [was] unamiable" and he "had an ungovernable temper."[37]

When Big Thunder's father, the popular Cetanwakanmani (the first chief that Americans called Little Crow) died in 1834, the talk around Fort Snelling was that his son would be a very poor successor to the great chief.[38] Perhaps it was Big Thunder's known negative image that explains why people at the fort were quick to circulate a rumor that he murdered Hays. If Edward Phelan was the real murderer of Hays and had fabricated the incident about Hays' confrontation with an Indian, then it would have been a clever embellishment to implicate Big Thunder, knowing that people were already predisposed against him.

Major Taliaferro's journal entry also includes the notable statement that he had "no belief" that Big Thunder was involved with Sergeant Hays' "reported" murder. As the fort's Indian agent since its establishment in 1819, he was well acquainted with all the Kaposia chiefs including Big Thunder, with whom he had worked in developing an agricultural program at his village, and also in negotiating the Treaty of 1837.[39] Taliaferro had devoted twenty years of his life to working with the Dakota and probably knew Big Thunder better than any other non-Indian did; it's a significant point that he didn't believe Big Thunder murdered Sergeant Hays.

Major Taliaferro's concluding comment that he was inclined "to the opinion that Phelan knew something" because "Hays lived with him and had money" is even more intriguing. The veteran army officer and long-standing Indian agent, whose duties at Fort Snelling brought him into contact with more civilian, military, and native people than any other person in present Minnesota, not only quickly rejected the report that Hays had been murdered by Big Thunder, but he instantly offered his alternative suspect: Edward Phelan. Taliaferro offers two simple reasons: first, Phelan lived with Hays, and second, "Hays had money." Interestingly, Taliaferro was the first person on record to introduce the money motive into this crime. But how did he know that Sergeant Hays had money? Did he know the popular sergeant and learn it from him? That would have been most unlikely because of the impersonal way the major referred to the sergeant in his journal. Instead of calling Hays by name, he merely referred to him as "an Irishman."

More likely, he had heard about Sergeant Hays' money from someone at the fort who knew Hays, or had some knowledge of his wealth. Perhaps that someone was Indian interpreter Bartholomew Baldwin, who the Indian agent did know and probably saw quite frequently. But the best source of information on Hays' finances at Fort Snelling was the officer who actually held two hundred dollars of Hays' savings for safekeeping, Lt. Daniel H. McPhail. Lieutenant McPhail had likely been Sergeant Hays' immediate superior and eventually a friend; he would later be a key witness in the investigation of Hays' death.[40]

But what did Major Taliaferro know about Phelan? Given the gap between their ranks it would seem highly unlikely that the major knew Private Phelan personally. (Majors don't fraternize with privates.) However, given Phelan's height and bad reputation, it's possible that Taliaferro knew of Phelan from the officers who had dealt with him and that he had inside information about the former private's character and past behavior.

The fact that a man like Major Taliaferro—the veteran army officer and Indian agent, who was the legal authority over the region's fur traders and missionaries and was notably known for his impeccable honesty—was quick to suspect Phelan is telling. Although Taliaferro's suspicion may be early evidence of a rush to judgment against Phelan, the man with the bad reputation, it may also be yet more circumstantial evidence of Phelan's guilt.

# CHAPTER FOUR

# A Gruesome Discovery

On Friday, September 27, 1839 grim news about John Hays hit Fort Snelling. A Dakota named "Wabsheeda" (also known as Dancer) called at the office of Major Taliaferro "to say that his sons had found the body of Mr. Hays, lost some time ago, in the river near Carver's Cave."[1] The fate of Sergeant Hays was now finally known, twenty-one days after he had disappeared. After hearing Wabsheeda's story, Taliaferro sent him "at once" over to the fort's commander, Major Joseph Plympton, with the following letter:

*Agency House, Saint Peters, Sept. 27, 1839*
*Major: I have sent the bearer, a good Indian, to go with the gentle-*
*men who are in quest of the identity of Mr. Hays' body, now in the*
*water near Carver's old cave. The Indian will conduct them to the*
*spot being so directed by his chief [Big Thunder], if requested so to do.*
*Very respectfully, your obedient servant,*
*Law. Taliaferro, Indian Agent*[2]

It is not clear who Taliaferro meant in his reference to "the gentlemen who are in quest of the identity of Mr. Hays' body." Presumably they were some of Hays' friends at the fort. There is no chance, however, that any of those "gentlemen" were Edward Phelan.

According to Phelan's later testimony, he first heard of the discovery "at sundown on the evening of the 29th," two days after the news reached Fort Snelling. A settler downriver named John Campbell, who presumably lived somewhere below present Mounds Park, near the historic natural landmark called Carver's Cave, located in present Dayton's Bluff, apparently visited Phelan and told him that "he and the Indians had found it near his place."* Phelan "considered it too late" that day to go down and view the body, but decided he would go "the first thing in the morning."[3] The next day, Monday, September 30 at "about sunrise," Phelan went downriver and saw the body Campbell had told him about. It was "so disfigured" that the only way he could identify it as Sergeant Hays was by his "long nose," Hays' distinguishing feature.[4] Phelan's reaction to seeing the gruesome, disfigured, and decaying remains of his partner was unfortunately never recorded. Phelan's comments about the clothes Sergeant Hays was wearing were recorded on a page of his affidavit that is now too blurred and illegible to transpose. The following is the best that can be deciphered:

> *Deceased did change his clothes having on his [?] a blue coat and oxford grey pantaloons. Deceased was missing [?] didn't like to appear [?].*[5]

Although Phelan's original testimony about what he saw and did when he saw Hays' body lacks detail, he elaborated during a later cross-examination. "When he was found his head and shoulders were out of the water. [I] hauled him partly on the beach and covered the corpse over with grass and sand."[6]

Interestingly, this was the state of the body when Fort Snelling's official medical examiner found it: on the beach and covered with grass and sand. If Phelan's dating of events was correct, then it's puzzling that Fort Snelling's commander Maj. Joseph Plympton waited three days after receiving Taliaferro's September 27 message before

---

* Who John Campbell was and when he settled near Carver's Cave is another mystery. Williams, the great chronicler of St. Paul's early settlers, never mentioned him as one of the town's pre-1840 pioneers. Carver's Cave was named for Jonathan Carver, the English explorer who found the ancient cave "with Indian hieroglyphics" in 1766 and later publicized it in a popular book. The Dakota called the cave "Waukon Teebee—the house of the spirits." See endnote 3.

he sent the appropriate military personnel down to retrieve and examine the body. The critical fact is that Phelan was able to handle the body himself before any military investigators could examine it. Did Phelan tamper with any evidence on the murder victim? Of course he did – he later admitted that he moved the body and covered it with grass and sand. Why did he do that? He never explained.

In any case, the same morning that Phelan reportedly moved and covered Sgt. Hays' body (Monday, September 30), Major Plympton assigned Hays' friend Lt. Daniel L. McPhail to lead a "dispatchment of men from the garrison...to the place where the deceased was reported to have been found for the purpose of ascertaining...how he came to his death."[7]

The "dispatchment of men" included Bartholomew Baldwin and two notable figures: Fort Snelling's famed sutler, Franklin Steele (1813-80), who later became the founder of the town that evolved into the City of Minneapolis, and Fort Snelling physician Dr. John Emerson (1803-43) who was best remembered as the owner of Dred Scott (1799-1858), one of the most famous slaves in American history. Scott would later sue for his freedom on the grounds that his slavery at Fort Snelling was illegal because the fort was within "free territory," where slavery was prohibited by federal law. The infamous Dred Scott Case would reach the Supreme Court in 1857, and the court's controversial landmark decision against Scott and the whole concept of "free territory" would help trigger the Civil War.[8]

Dred Scott's owner, Dr. Emerson, was the most critical member of McPhail's party because he would serve as the official medical examiner. Yet, the fact that the group included at least two friends of Sergeant Hays—McPhail and Baldwin—and most likely a third (why else would storekeeper Franklin Steele come along?) ensured that this "dispatchment of men" would not be dispassionate about their mission.

As the army's flat-bottomed Mackinaw boat rowed downriver, McPhail reportedly saw Phelan coming upriver, again, presumably in a canoe. McPhail testified that Phelan was "on his way to the garrison for the purpose of making known that the deceased had been found, he having been down and seen the deceased in the morning early, and covered as he was found."[9] McPhail's ineloquent account of his encounter with Phelan is vague and confusing. Aside from the above statement, he only related that he "met Phelan a little below his house, took him down with me. Saw him previously, however, above, he being on his way to the garrison."[10] Apparently Phelan, "on his way to the garrison," met the McPhail group, learned of its mission, quickly returned home to beach his canoe, then jumped on board the Mackinaw boat moments later to help guide them to the body.

When McPhail, Emerson, Baldwin, Steele, Phelan, and other unnamed men on board the Mackinaw reached the body of Hays, Dr. Emerson took charge of the unpleasant work they had to do. McPhail's later testimony provided the best details about Emerson's examination:

> *Found the deceased laying upon his back, feet in the water, and covered with grass and sand. The Dr. caused him to be uncovered and washed for the purpose of making an examination, which was done, and resulted in the discovery of the deceased having come to his death by blows inflicted upon the face with some heavy weapon, breaking both jaw bones, upper and lower, also the temple bone, together with the cheek and other bones belonging to the face....After the examination I caused the deceased to be buried. The deceased was found perfectly naked.*[11]

McPhail's statement that the "deceased was found perfectly naked" would seem to contradict Phelan's jumbled comment that Hays had on "a blue coat and oxford grey pantaloons." However, given that Phelan was present with McPhail, Baldwin, Steele, and others at Dr. Emerson's examination of the body, it does not make sense that Phelan would later contradict the doctor and all those credible witnesses by stating that the body had clothes on it when he first saw it. Doing so would only draw more attention toward him and raise the obvious question: What happened to those clothes that Phelan saw on Sergeant Hays, just a short time before McPhail's party found him naked? More likely Phelan's jumbled comments were referring to the clothes Sergeant Hays was wearing on the day he disappeared. (Another witness will be presented later who swore that Phelan told him on September 6 that "Hays had put on his best clothes" when he trekked to Kaposia.)[12] In any case, there were in fact no clothes on the remains of Sergeant Hays. Dr. Emerson's own testimony of his examination was much more concise, but his references to "James Hays" instead of John Hays are evidence that either the doctor was not one of Hays' personal friends, or John Hays was also known as "James Hays."

> *On hearing that the body of James Hays was found, I proceeded in the company with several others to examine the aforesaid body, and found that it was mutilated in a shocking manner—the bones of the face were broken into several pieces, as if done with some mighty weapon. I have no hesitation in declaring it as my belief that the death of James Hays was caused by the aforesaid injuries.*[13]

Dr. Emerson's statement is surprisingly brief and vague. Unlike a modern-day coroner's report, which would provide a detailed description of the state of the body and lengthy analysis on the cause of death, Dr. Emerson devoted only two sentences to the matter. But such was the extent of medical inquiry on the American frontier in 1839.

Hays' burial is also revealing of life on the frontier. Instead of bringing the body back for interment in the fort's cemetery, McPhail's dispatchment simply buried Hays right there near Carver's Cave. We can only assume that the bones of Sergeant Hays lie there still, probably underneath either present-day Warner Road or the railroad tracks below Dayton's Bluff. (Carver's Cave, the ancient natural landmark where the body was "near," still remains inside Dayton's Bluff, though its entrance is no longer accessible.)

After Dr. Emerson's conclusion that Sergeant Hays' death was the result of blows from "some mighty weapon," there could be no question that he was a victim of foul play. Indeed, based on McPhail and Emerson's description of his wounds, we can conclude that Sergeant Hays was not just murdered, he was over-killed.

# CHAPTER FIVE

# Phelan's Arrest and the Hearing
# on All Saints Day

Since Hays was a civilian at the time of his death, the investigation of his murder was technically not a military matter. The closest civilian authority was Minnesota's first justice of the peace, Henry Sibley (1811-94)—the regional head of the American Fur Company and virtually "law west of the Mississippi" (and north of the Zumbro River)—who lived in an impressive stone house that still stands today in Minnesota's oldest town, Mendota. Sibley took charge of the murder investigation immediately and quickly identified a prime suspect: Edward Phelan. There was no chance that Sibley would be intimidated by the size and strength of the big Irishman: Sibley himself was six feet two inches and a strong, athletic frontiersman who was reportedly the best bare-knuckles boxer on the Upper Mississippi and "the finest shot in the country." Even Edward Phelan probably would have acknowledged that the "law west of the Mississippi" was also the toughest guy west of the Mississippi. But Sibley wasn't just tough, he was an educated gentleman. His father, Solomon Sibley, was a preeminent judge in Detroit and a former justice of the Michigan Supreme Court, and Sibley himself had been a respected justice of the peace since 1831.[1] Thomas Newson praised the man destined to become Minnesota's first congressman and first state governor as "a really good man—an honest man—a moral man—an able man— an upright man—a worthy man."[2]

41

## Phelan's Arrest and Testimony

According to J. Fletcher Williams, "Phelan was at once arrested by warrant issued by Henry H. Sibley, as Justice of the Peace, and…was examined before that officer."[3] Williams gave the warrant's date as September 28, but the only surviving official document connected to the case notes that Phelan gave his testimony "before H. H. Sibley, Esq., a few days after the body had been found," and according to Taliaferro's journal entries, Indians had reported finding the body on September 27, and Phelan and the military detachment found and examined the body on September 30.[4] In other words, the warrant may actually have been dated in early October. Phelan's testimony before Sibley was preserved in an affidavit that Williams was never able to find. Interestingly, the document ended up in the hands of Joseph R. Brown, who copied it into a casebook that he eventually filed with a large volume of papers that he donated to the Minnesota Historical Society. Some of Phelan's testimony from that affidavit has already been presented, but the rest of it is equally crucial evidence for assessing his guilt or innocence in the murder of Sgt. John Hays. According to the affidavit:

> *Hays disappeared about the 6th or 7th of Sept., day of the week Friday. He had lost a calf, which he supposed the Indians had taken, and he hoped by visiting Little Crow's Indian Village to find the meat of it. About 9 or 10 o'clock of the above named day I put Hays across the river in a canoe, and he requested me to look out for him towards evening, which request I complied with, but he did not make his appearance.*[5]

Phelan then gave his account of when and how he looked for Hays and much later found his body, as we have seen, and his testimony in response to Sibley's cross-examination follows:

*Do not know where he was in the habit of keeping his money and papers. Know nothing about his private affairs. Was upon very friendly affair with deceased, but he was not communicative with regard to his pecuniary affairs. He was not in the habit of speaking to me about his money matters. Only once he spoke and said he had two hundred dollars in the hands of Lt. McPhail, that when deceased had heard of surveyors coming to survey the "Land Grant" as was supposed. I observed to deceased that it might be necessary for us to sell off our stock of cattle, when he replied that he had more than money enough to purchase a quarter section of land [160 acres], which was about the quantity we intended to claim. This was a short time after General [John] Wood had arrived at Fort Snelling. Deceased did not mention his having any other money besides the two hundred dollars in the hands of Lt. McPhail. Had no reason to suppose he had any other money. He was not in the habit of counting his money before me. The last time deceased came to the fort, gave him fifty cents of money, as he said he wished to pay his ferriage across the Mississippi. Am not aware of any person being as intimate with deceased as myself or that know more of his money affairs.*[6]

Phelan's testimony cries for clarification. He said he and his roommate had "a very friendly affair" and he believed no one was "as intimate with the deceased" as himself, but he claimed he knew nothing about "his private affairs." He said he gave Hays "fifty cents of money" to pay his ferriage across the river, yet the evidence suggests that Sergeant Hays was the partner who "had money" (Taliaferro's words) and young Private Phelan was the partner who lacked money. Why would Phelan have to lend fifty cents (over two days' pay) to the relatively rich sergeant for his ferriage fee?

Unfortunately, Sibley's interviews with other witnesses who could either verify or deny Phelan's statements, especially those about Hays' money matters, have been lost. In fact, the only document preserved from Sibley's investigation is a copy of Phelan's original affidavit. Williams, who interviewed Sibley, reported that "General Sibley thinks he preserved a copy of the evidence taken—but has been unable so far to find it in his mass of papers."[7]

Sibley's further cross-examination gave Phelan a final chance to clarify his testimony:

> *Never sent to Pine Bend to see if deceased had been there. When deceased crossed the river he had no weapons, neither did he express any fear of the Indians. It was not the intention of the deceased to take the remains of the calf had he found it at the Indian village; he merely wished to satisfy himself whether he [the Indian] had it or not.*[8]

Phelan's clarification of his testimony adds some interesting detail to his story but may also cast more suspicion on him. First, Phelan admitted that when Sergeant Hays was missing he never tried to find out if he had gone to Pine Bend, a place just across the river from Grey Cloud Island (and Hazen Mooer's trading house), where the small Dakota village of Medicine Bottle was located. Mrs. Gervais had testified that Phelan told her on September 8 that Hays "had probably gone to Mr. Mooer's."[9] Second, Phelan claimed that on the day Hays supposedly crossed the river and headed to Kaposia in search of the missing calf, he was alone and unarmed, yet not fearful of the Indians. These details—that Sergeant Hays was unarmed and not fearful of the Indians—do not fit well with Phelan's earlier testimony about a violent confrontation Hays had with a young Dakota over a gun just a month before, an "affair" over which Hays "said he expected to have some trouble with the Indians."[10] Third, according to Phelan, the reason that Hays was traveling to Kaposia was not to regain the calf or its remains but merely to find out if the Indians had taken it. Taken together, the last two points do not make a very credible story: Sergeant Hays, (who only "spoke a few words" of Dakota), walking alone and unarmed, makes a roughly five-mile trek to the Dakota village to ascertain whether Indians stole his calf—not to regain the animal but only to prove that the Indians took it. This is not a very convincing story. An argument could be made that perhaps Hays thought he needed proof of the theft in order to convince the Indian agent, Major Taliaferro, to compensate him for the stolen calf. (The Indian agent had authority to compensate settlers for any livestock stolen by Indians.) But if that was Hays' reason for trekking to Kaposia, it was a rather foolish one. It would have been easier and safer for Hays to report the theft to Taliaferro and request an investigation of the matter. After all, that was the Indian agent's job. Indeed, Taliaferro wouldn't likely have approved of someone like Sergeant Hays, who could not speak Dakota, launching his own investigation of a potential Indian crime. Another smarter and safer alternative might have been for Sergeant Hays to invite his Indian interpreter friend, Bartholomew Baldwin, to join him in the search. Taliaferro might have approved of that idea. If Phelan's story about Sergeant Hays was true, then Hays appears to have been a rather reckless and foolish man. However, this characterization of Sergeant Hays is not consistent with what we know about him.

Exactly what evidence Sibley gathered in his murder investigation is not known, but Williams confidently asserted that "Hon. H. H. Sibley, who carefully sifted the evidence on the examination of Phelan, says it was such as to leave no doubt of his guilt."[11]

## The Case Transfers to Joseph R. Brown

No matter how strongly Sibley felt about Phelan's guilt, sometime in October 1839 he turned the case over to another justice of the peace. The issue was jurisdiction. Sibley's authority was limited to the west side of the Mississippi, the area designated since 1838 as Iowa Territory. Sibley's license was issued by Clayton County, Iowa Territory and places on the west side of the river, like Fort Snelling, Mendota, Red Wing, and Wabasha, were subject to the laws of Iowa Territory. But Hays' body was found on the east side of the Mississippi, and all evidence seemed to point to his being murdered there; therefore the investigation, prosecution, and expenses of the case fell under the jurisdiction of the area east of the Mississippi, designated as Wisconsin Territory since 1836. Eight months before Phelan's arrest, the closest Wisconsin lawman to Phelan's Landing would have been over two hundred fifty miles downriver at Prairie du Chien. However, on February 15, 1839, Joseph R. Brown of Grey Cloud Island became a justice of the peace of Crawford County. As Wisconsin Territory's westernmost county, Crawford County included all of present-day Minnesota east of the Mississippi, but Prairie du Chien was its county seat.[12] Hence the need to remove the case to Joseph R. Brown and the county and territory he represented.

Like Sibley, Justice Brown was not one to be intimidated by the likes of Phelan. A "good sized man" of "iron will and muscular frame," Joseph Renshaw Brown (1805-70) was a rugged, fearless frontiersman who had lived an adventurous life in the "Indian country" for twenty years.[13] Born in southern Pennsylvania and raised mostly in northern Maryland, Brown was the grandson of a Scottish immigrant and the son of Samuel Brown, a poor Methodist minister "of high principles, good education and keen intellect." Joseph R. Brown ran away from a printer's apprenticeship at age fourteen or fifteen and joined the army as a drummer boy and fife player. The army immediately sent him west to join the Fifth Infantry's mission of constructing the first American fort in present-day Minnesota. He could later boast that he was one of the soldiers who built Fort Snelling. After retiring from the military in 1828 at the rank of sergeant, Brown became a fur trader. He was initially employed by the American Fur Company but later operated as an independent trader and worked ambitiously in over a dozen posts stretching from Lake Traverse to Lake Pepin and beyond.[14] Minnesota's second justice of the peace— and the first one assigned to the settlement that became St. Paul— may or may not have known the murder suspect personally. Sergeant Brown had retired from the military about seven years before Private Phelan even arrived at Fort Snelling. By the time Phelan was serving at the fort, Brown was clerking in a fur post over two hundred miles away at Lake Traverse. However, during 1838 and 1839, when Phelan was farming his claim in present-day St. Paul, the two men would have had several chances to meet because Brown was then making a number of trips between his Grey Cloud Island post and his new "extensive whiskey shop," just across the Mississippi from Fort Snelling.[15] In fact, documents show that on at least two occasions during this time, Brown was at the home of Phelan's neighbor, Abraham Perry, albeit the second occasion was a community meeting held six weeks after Phelan's arrest. But the first occasion was the visit Brown made to the Perry home on Sunday, September 8, 1839—the same day Phelan visited the Ben Gervais family (the Perry's closest neighbors) to inform them of Hays' disappearance.

Other evidence reveals some interesting reasons that Brown was at the Perry cabin that day. September 8 was the exact same day that "15 or 20 Indians" deliberately tore down the roof of Brown's whiskey shop across from Fort Snelling.[16] A Dakota named Red Hail claimed that the vandals were put up to it by Taliaferro, who strongly disapproved of liquor trading and was frustrated by the rise of the Rumtown saloons. Though Taliaferro adamantly denied the charge, Brown and his partners who ran the "whiskey shop" were convinced that the Indian agent was behind the attack on their business.[17] Given Taliaferro's honest reputation, it is possible that one of Brown's competitors at Rumtown or Mendota deviously instigated the vandalism. In any case, it is quite likely that Brown's visit to the Perrys that Sunday was connected to his investigation of the destruction of his saloon.

There were two good reasons that his investigation would have brought him to the Perry home. First, eleven months earlier the Perrys had been victims of a Dakota attack on their cattle. Brown probably would have been interested in hearing the Perry's explanation of the incident. Second and more importantly, one of the temporary residents of the Perry household was Abraham and Mary Perry's son-in-law James Clewett, a partner of Brown's in the vandalized whiskey shop. Obviously, Brown needed to talk to Clewett, who was one of the regular operators of the saloon, and a logical place to look for him was at the Perry home.

There is no evidence that Brown ever had any direct dealings with Phelan prior to Phelan's arrest in late September 1839. And there is nothing in the record of Brown's life to indicate that he would have been predisposed to judge Phelan unfairly. If anything, that record could be construed to show that Brown might have been more predisposed to favor Phelan's defense, that Hays was killed by Indians. In addition to the incident of the "15 or 20 Indians" who vandalized his whiskey shop, and earlier attacks on his livestock by marauding Dakota, Brown himself had been shot in the shoulder by an angry Dakota at Lake Traverse, and even worse, one of his employees trading further west was murdered by a Dakota horse thief.[18] Whatever predisposition he had, if any, one of Brown's friends specifically praised him for being a "close observer of men...and a man of honorable principles."[19] If that was an accurate characterization of Brown, then those traits would serve him well in handling the first civilian murder case in the region that became Minnesota.

Exactly when and how Sibley transferred the case to Brown is not known. Sibley and Brown were old fur trading friends, so it was probably an amicable and informal arrangement. Interestingly, Brown and Sibley would later collaborate in creating a new territory called Minnesota out of parts of the former Iowa and Wisconsin Territories. The name, a Dakota word that means "water like the sky," was Brown's idea. Of all the founding fathers of Minnesota, Joseph Renshaw Brown and Henry Hastings Sibley were clearly the greatest.* Yet, their preserved collective work on the Hays case is not very impressive by modern standards. It would of course be absurdly unfair to criticize the frontier justices for not producing clear, clean, perfectly verbatim transcripts when they had no stenographers and the typewriter had not yet been invented. If their transcriptions were often illegible, poorly punctuated, and grammatically flawed, it is worth bearing in mind that they had to write everything by hand; in Brown's case it was a tremendous amount of writing. Also,

---

* See Rhoda Gilman, *Henry Hastings Sibley* (Minnesota Historical Society, 2004) and Nancy & Robert Goodman, *Joseph R. Brown* (Lone Oak Press, 1996).

one can imagine the difficulty they had to secure witnesses in the days before railroads and even true wagon roads reached the region, when the fastest way to go from Fort Snelling to Phelan's Landing was about an hour-long canoe ride. Steamboat travel during the 1830s was very irregular, with only an average of twenty-five steamboats reaching Fort Snelling each year.[20] Moreover, justices of the peace were not full-time positions. Both Sibley and Brown also had burdensome responsibilities as fur traders, not to mention unavoidable workloads in their domestic affairs. (Brown, for instance, also did some farming.) Yet despite all these obstacles, a frontier justice of the peace was expected to serve as a combination policeman-prosecutor-court reporter-judge when a criminal case came in. In any case, the record of the murder investigation they left behind is what it is: a poorly written, incomplete, somewhat confusing collection of depositions, with not one question to the witnesses recorded and only the briefest concluding summation of the evidence.

There is a strong probability, however, that the original record was more extensive and impressive. Eventually the case ended up in the court at Prairie du Chien, the county seat, and this court lost all records of its proceedings, likely including documents originating from Sibley and Brown. Joseph R. Brown deserves credit for saving the only legal documents preserved from this historic case.

### The Testimony in Brown's Casebook

It is Brown's "*Justice of the Peace Casebook for St. Croix County*"—the county he helped create in 1840, which included all of present-day Minnesota east of the Mississippi and roughly north of Lake Pepin—that records those testimonies that have been quoted thus far, as well as several more. Brown's casebook is essentially a crude collection of depositions, with a few added responses to cross-examination questions, though none of those questions were recorded. The book opens with the following formal notation:

*On the 31st day of October, 1839 I issued a warrant for the arrest of
Edward Phalen, suspected of having murdered James Hays, who was
his partner on a farm in Crawford County, near the "Cave" on the
Mississippi. H. C. Mencke was appointed special constable to act in
the case. The warrant was duly served and the prisoner having been
brought before me was put upon examination at 11 o'clock Nov. 1,
1839 when the following testimony was adduced.*[21]

Brown never noted where he conducted his "examination" of
the "prisoner" but it probably was at his whiskey shop, across from
Fort Snelling.

The first deposition Brown recorded was Dr. Emerson's testimony (describing the severe injuries to Hays' head). Phelan's testimony follows and Brown introduced it with these words:

*The prisoner said he had no further explanation to give of the dis-
appearance of Hays than that contained in his affidavit before H. H.
Sibley, Esq. a few days after the body was found viz.*[22]

Phelan's main testimony was not what he told Brown on November 1 but the testimony he gave before Sibley in September or early
October. Apparently Brown simply copied the affidavit into his casebook. Presumably the original document was later sent to Prairie du
Chien and eventually became part of the lost records of that courthouse. Phelan's testimony before Sibley has already been covered, but
Brown conducted his own cross-examination which will be best
saved for later.

The deposition of Bartholomew Baldwin, the fourth witness in
Brown's casebook behind Emerson, Phelan, and McPhail, follows and
provides important testimony and one part of it helps Phelan's defense.

*Never saw anything about Phelan's building to lead me to suppose he
had killed deceased, nor never heard anything which would lead me
to suppose so. Have often been at the house of the deceased. He never*

*spoke about his money matters, but on one occasion when I took him across the river he had a mind to buy an Indian girl. I told him he had better buy a cow, and he remarked that he had money enough to buy a cow and the girl too, and he said he thought he could buy the latter for fifty dollars and fifty more would be enough to buy the cow.*[23]

Baldwin was with Phelan during their search for Sergeant Hays on September 11, five days after Phelan claimed his partner disappeared. So Baldwin's statement about never seeing anything incriminating "about Phelan's building" is not as helpful to Phelan's defense as it might first appear. Finding no evidence of a murder at Phelan's cabin five days after Hays' disappearance would hardly disprove that Phelan murdered Hays. The possibility obviously remains that Phelan could have murdered Hays at or near his cabin and then simply cleaned up the evidence of the crime. Or, he could have murdered him farther away from his home. Baldwin's remarks about Hays' finances confirm Phelan's claim that Hays didn't talk about his "money matters." They also indirectly support Phelan's statement that McPhail held two hundred dollars for Hays.

### Buying an Indian Wife: A Possible Scenario

Baldwin's anecdote that Hays was willing to spend fifty dollars "to buy an Indian girl" could be imaginatively interpreted to show another possible motive Phelan might have had to kill his partner. Consider the following scenario:

Bachelor Hays desperately wanted a female companion for either his wife or mistress. But in the Upper Mississippi frontier of 1839 the chances of finding an available white woman willing to have him were about as good as his chances of finding gold on his land. The only white women available on the local frontier were a few daughters of soldiers, missionaries, and backwoods settlers, but the competition for those women would have been too great for a gray-haired, long-nosed man like Sergeant Hays. Realistically, the only way that Sergeant Hays could have found a woman would have been to do what the fur traders did: marry an "Indian girl." However, by virtue of their business, the fur traders were very close to the Indians and knew how to properly arrange marriages with the daughters or sisters of the Indian men who were their partners in trade. Sergeant Hays was not a fur trader and did not have a close relationship with the local Dakota. If he wanted an Indian wife he would have to find someone who had a relationship with the Dakota, spoke their language, and knew how to arrange a marriage to a Dakota girl. For Sergeant Hays that perfect someone was his friend Bartholomew Baldwin, who was both an Indian interpreter and married to a Dakota mixed-blood. Thus, it's possible that when Sergeant Hays told Baldwin that he wanted to "buy an Indian girl," he was doing so specifically because he needed Baldwin's help. To "buy an Indian girl," as bad as that sounds, did not literally mean buying a girl like a Southern planter might buy a slave. Rather, Dakota fathers and brothers followed a custom similar to the European custom of dowries, except they did not traditionally receive money. According to missionary Samuel Pond, who knew the marriage customs of the Dakota quite well, "almost any kind of property might be given in exchange for a wife, such as horses, guns, cloth, kettles, etc.," but the offering of the goods must follow a certain formality.[24] Baldwin would have known these customs since he was married to a Dakota woman.

Returning to the scenario: Sergeant Hays would eventually tell his bachelor housemate Phelan about his idea to spend fifty dollars for an Indian wife and then inform him that if he did, he would want to move out of the shanty and build a home of his own. Hypothetically, Phelan might have wanted an Indian girl too, but he had no money and he did "not understand the Indian language" and might have gotten jealous and resentful of Sergeant Hays. He might have brooded over the prospect that his rich partner was going to get a girl, and he was going to be left alone. He might also have felt perturbed that Sergeant Hays was going to splurge fifty dollars on a girl when there were more practical things they needed to buy, especially things that Phelan could share in like food, liquor, and farm equipment. And so, hypothetically, it was from those feelings of jealousy and resentment that Phelan's desire to murder Hays developed.

The critical point of this scenario is that the murder motive may not have been directly the desire for Sargeant Hays' money but rather jealousy and resentment of Hays' ability to buy an Indian girl. In other words, Phelan's motive here was not just about "coveting thy neighbor's goods," it was also about "coveting thy neighbor's wife" (or potential wife).

## Baldwin's Further Testimony

The rest of Baldwin's testimony provides relevant, intriguing details about what he saw on the day Hays was buried.

> *On the east bank of the Mississippi some distance above where the body was found, as passing through the bottom after attending the burial of the deceased, I observed a trail, the bushes and herbage being much beaten down. Also saw grey hairs sticking to the herbage, think they may have been wolf hairs—there being many tracks of wolves along the trail. Do not think they were hairs from head of deceased, as his hair had been cut a short time before his disappearance, whereas the hairs seen by me were long. Have no reasonable cause to suspect any particular person of having murdered deceased. Have never heard any threat made against him by either white man or Indian. Had not seen deceased for four or five days previous to his disappearance. Was well acquainted with him. He wore very grey hair in color somewhat resembling the hair of a wolf.*
>
> *As we were coming down the boat (being one of the crew on that day) to bury the body, an Indian on board told me that his son had seen the corpse of deceased some distance above where we found it. The place pointed out by the Indian was near where I found the grey hairs, and my search was in consequence of the information I received from the Indian.*[25]

Baldwin's full testimony is both interesting and perplexing. On the one hand, some of his statements would seem to vindicate Phelan. The following are the most compelling:

> *Never saw anything about Phelan's building to lead me to suppose he had killed deceased nor never heard anything which would lead me to suppose so....Have no reasonable cause to suspect any particular person of having murdered deceased. Have never heard any threat made against him by either white man or Indian.*[26]

These statements are strong assertions in defense of Phelan, mainly because the man who made them was a uniquely qualified witness. Baldwin was "well acquainted" with Sergeant Hays and likewise well acquainted with Phelan. He had also been at their house "often." In other words, he was a good friend of Sergeant Hays and maybe even a good friend of Phelan's. Outside of ex-soldier and neighbor William Evans, he probably knew both men better than any other witness, or any other person who recorded their opinion about the victim and the suspect. Given Baldwin's unique perspective, his opinion about Phelan's guilt or innocence merits particular consideration. And his opinion was clear: he had "no reasonable cause to suspect" that Phelan murdered his friend. That doesn't prove Phelan was innocent—history is filled with the cases of proven murderers, whose friends mistakenly believed that they were innocent—but it is a powerful testament for his defense.

On the other hand, some of Baldwin's testimony about finding "grey hairs" and "beaten down" brush "some distance above where the body was found," after an Indian had told him that his son had earlier seen the body in that very area, is potentially devastating. Although Baldwin didn't specify where that disturbed brush was, "some distance above where the body was found" would have been very close to—if not on—Phelan's property. Phelan's land was only about one and a half miles up from the Carver's Cave vicinity "where the body was found." If what the Indian told Baldwin was true, then somehow

Hays' body was moved from the place it originally washed ashore. Did Phelan, who definitely had access to the body before it was officially examined, move it off his land and down toward Carver's Cave?

Conveniently enough, the cave was a celebrated Indian landmark, known by the Dakota as "Wakon-Teebee—dwelling house of the Spirit."[27] If Phelan was Hays' killer, then it would have been sensible for him to move Hays' body further away from his land and closer to a site directly associated with the Dakota. That way when the officials found the body their suspicions might be more directed to the Dakota than to him. Of course, it is possible that the river could have naturally carried Sergeant Hays' body down toward the cave. But what about the "beaten down brush" that Baldwin observed at the site where the Indians first saw the body? Was that trampled brush some sign of struggle at the scene of the murder?

Clearly Baldwin tried to temper that potentially incriminating evidence by stressing his belief that the gray hairs on the trampled brush came not from Sergeant Hays' body being dragged through the "herbage," but rather from wolves that left "many tracks" along the trail. Baldwin explained that the gray hairs he saw there were too long to be Sergeant Hays' because he knew that Hays had recently gotten a haircut. Were those gray hairs on that trampled brush near Phelan's Landing from roaming grey wolves, or were they from the battered head of Sergeant Hays, whose hair was as grey as a wolf?

Another witness would present a much different perspective about the trail with trampled down brush. What's more, that man and still another witness would reveal some powerful new information about the case's most critical dates: September 5 and 6, 1839, the night before and the morning of Sergeant Hay's supposed errand across the river. Most significantly, they would provide credible eyewitness accounts of where Phelan was and what he was doing on September 5 and 6, details that Phelan failed to mention in his original affidavit. Collectively their testimonies would be devastating to Phelan's defense.

## Two Critical Witnesses

The witnesses were two obscure lumbermen from the St. Croix River: Stephen Scott, presumably a former Fort Snelling soldier who "knew Hays very well," and John Foy, Scott's companion, who had just recently moved from Indiana and was "not acquainted" with either Sergeant Hays or Phelan.[28] Both men testified that on their way to Mendota "on Thursday night, the 5th of September…[they] slept at the house of Wm. Evans." Evans lived about one and a half miles downriver from Phelan's shanty, on Dayton's Bluff, somewhere around the corner of present-day Conway Street and Mounds Boulevard. Both men distinctly recalled that "about nine o'clock at night" someone unexpectedly came to Evans' cabin. It was Edward Phelan. In the words of Foy:

> *Phelan came into Evans house that night about nine o'clock; he had a large canoe paddle in his hand, was bareheaded and his clothes muddy. He said he had fallen from a log in crossing a creek, while looking for a calf, which he had lost, and had lost his hat. Phelan slept that night at Evans' house.[29]*

Scott gave virtually the same account, only he didn't mention Phelan's muddy clothes and used different wording, saying Phelan got "bewildered in the dark" in explaining how he lost his hat "in crossing a creek." Neither man added anything more about the events of that evening.[30]

Their accounts of the next morning, September 6, were even more interesting and collectively provide some of the most incriminating evidence against Phelan. Their testimonies are strikingly similar and consistent on most points. According to Scott:

> *We left there in the morning after having breakfasted; when we left the house the prisoner was still there. We embarked at probably 8 o'clock in the morning, but seeing a canoe coming from the other*

*side of the river, we stopped on a sand bar about 30 rods [165 yards] above where our canoe lay, and waited until the canoe referred to came up. Messrs. [Henry C.] Mencke, [James] Clewett, and a Frenchman was in the canoe. We got some liquor from them and then proceeded on our way. It could not be over half an hour from the time we left Evans' until we reached [or left?] the sand bar.*[31]

Foy estimated that they "waited near Evans' Landing about ten minutes" for that canoe to arrive and then "we remained long enough to get a bottle of liquor, say about ten minutes."[32]

Although Scott's testimony is worded "until we *reached* the sand bar," it is possible that he meant to say, "until we *left* the sand bar." There is, of course, a big time difference between the words "reached" and "left." If he did mean "reached," then the time they "reached the sand bar" would not include the additional twenty minutes that Foy said they spent waiting for those canoeists and, after they arrived, obtaining a bottle of liquor from them.

After leaving the men in the other canoe, Scott and Foy paddled upriver. Scott said: "We did not stop anywhere between the sand bar and Phalen's Landing." Foy said: "Do not think we were more than half an hour from Evans' house to the landing place of the deceased." Scott estimated it differently: "We were not more than half an hour coming from the bar to Phalen's Landing."[33] But by Foy's estimate, they spent twenty minutes at the sand bar.

Although their travel time will prove to be important, what they saw on the wide, bending river will be more significant. In the plain, powerful words of Foy:

*While we were about one and a half miles from Phalen's Landing, we saw a log canoe ascending the Mississippi. Above the landing some distance the canoe went out from shore, near half way between that and the Island, turned and came down the Mississippi to the landing place, where he went ashore, when we were about 30 rods [165 yards] below. Am positive the prisoner got out of the canoe. Am*

*positive no canoe crossed the Mississippi from the time we left Evans'
Landing until we got to Phalen's. Am positive Phalen did not cross
the Mississippi when I saw him in the canoe, and as the canoe was
in sight all the time, am positive that it was him that was ascending
the river.*[34]

Scott told virtually the same story:

*Previous to landing we saw a canoe coming down the river; it landed
at Phalen's Landing while we were forty or fifty yards there from.
Am well acquainted with Phelan and am sure he got out of the canoe.
Do not think it possible that canoe could have crossed the river. We
first saw the canoe some distance above Phalen's Landing; had it
come from the opposite shore when we first saw it, it must have come
around the head of the large island, which would have required an
half an hour to do, and we certainly would have seen it.*[35]

The two critical points of Scott's and Foy's stories thus far are:

1. Phelan stumbled into William Evans' cabin at about nine
o'clock Thursday night with no hat, muddy clothes (although only
Foy added that detail), and carrying a canoe paddle. He reportedly
said he was looking for a lost calf and dropped his hat while crossing a creek.* The question is: If he had walked to Evans' house (a fact
deduced not only from Scott's and Foy's accounts, but also from the
testimonies of William Evans and Phelan himself), why was he carrying a canoe paddle? Dr. Emerson's intriguing response to Joseph
R. Brown's cross-examination was intentionally not presented earlier
with the rest of his testimony in order to save it for this very occasion.

---

* That creek may have been the very stream that was later named for him. "Phalen's Creek"
used to flow into the Mississippi River just below present Dayton's Bluff.

*Believe the wounds inflicted on the deceased could have been so inflicted by a canoe paddle, and the wounds bore the appearance which induced me to believe that such an instrument might have been used.*[36]

If Phelan had beaten Sergeant Hays' face bloody with a canoe paddle that night (Dr. Emerson had also stated that "all the bones of the face were broken in several pieces"), then he would have needed to wash the splattered blood off his clothes. That would explain why his clothes were muddy and presumably wet when he entered Evans' cabin. In other words, Phelan could have simply fabricated his story of accidentally falling into the creek to hide the real reason his clothes were muddy: that he had intentionally waded into the muddy creek or maybe the river to wash away incriminating blood splatters from his body and clothes. Perhaps the blood on his clothes would not wash off with plain water so he covered the blood stains with mud. Given that Sergeant Hays' body was found in the river, and if Phelan did kill Hays, he certainly would have gotten wet and muddy when he dumped the body in the river.

2. Scott and Foy left Evans' house at around eight o'clock in the morning (Scott's estimate) on Friday, while Phelan was still inside. The men then canoed only about "30 rods" (or 165 yards if Foy correctly defined a rod as 5½ yards) upriver, when they reached a sand bar. The sand bar was probably near the mouth of what was later called Phalen's Creek, which widened where Trout Brook joined it just before it flowed into the Mississippi River. At the sand bar the men noticed another canoe crossing the river so they stopped and waited for the canoe to reach them. About ten minutes later the canoe, with three men inside, reached the sand bar. Scott knew two of the men and somehow managed to get a bottle of liquor from them. After spending just enough time to acquire the liquor, "say about 10 minutes," the men proceeded upriver, where about a mile and a half from Phelan's Landing they saw a "log canoe" (which was slower than a bark canoe) going upriver along the shore, "above the landing some distance." Then the canoe abruptly headed toward the middle of the

river, turned around and returned downstream to the landing and reached it when Scott and Foy were still "40 or 50 yards" downriver. Both men positively identified the lone canoeist as Edward Phelan. Scott and Foy reached Phelan's Landing no more than a half an hour after they left the sand bar. Or, according to Foy, about thirty minutes after leaving William Evans' house. Thus, the estimated time that they saw Phelan in the canoe was between eight thirty and nine o'clock, if we assume Scott's starting time of eight o'clock. Foy never gave a starting time but he would later testify that they arrived at Phelan's Landing "about 8 o'clock in the morning." In his original testimony, Phelan said that he took Sergeant Hays across the river at "about 9 or 10 o'clock" Friday morning; he never said anything about returning home after spending the night at Evans' cabin, a rather significant detail to omit. Scott and Foy both agreed that Phelan was still in Evans' house when they left it Friday morning around eight o'clock. (Scott's time). A key question: How long did Phelan remain there?

## Corroborating Testimony: William Evans

William Evans' testimony confirms most of Scott's and Foy's stories, and adds a few details to it, including what happened after the two men left his house.

> *I recollect that Phalen slept at my house when Scott and another man slept there, but do not recollect the day of the month or week. Phalen came about dark to the house, said he had lost his way while looking for a calf, and that he wished to remain all night, as he could not find his way home in the dark. He had a paddle in his hand when he arrived. Do not recollect observing mud on his clothes. He left in the morning after brekfast, about the time Scott and the other man left, probably a few minutes after. Said he would look for his calf on his way home, and if did not find it, Hays would go to Little Crow's Village in search of it.*[37]

An immediate question: How did Phelan know that Sergeant

Hays would go to Little Crow's village to search for the calf? Sitting inside Evans' house, over a mile away from where Sergeant Hays was (hypothetically), how did Phelan know what Hays would do?

Before considering Evans' estimate of how long Phelan stayed at his house on the morning of Friday, September 6, one other part of his testimony needs to be examined: his testimony that he did not recall observing mud on Phelan's clothes. This may be a small opening for Phelan's defense. If Phelan's clothes were not muddy or wet, or visibly bloody on the night he came to Evans' house, then that would be strong exculpatory evidence that he had not assaulted and murdered Sergeant Hays that evening. But Evans' failure to recall the state of Phelan's clothes is not necessarily a contradiction of Foy's very specific recollections of "the night of Thursday, the 5th of September." (It is noteworthy that Evans also could "not recollect the day of the month, or the week" of the night in question.) Foy specifically testified that Phelan arrived at Evans' house that night "bareheaded and his clothes muddy." He even detailed Phelan's account of how he had lost his hat: "He said he had fallen from a log in crossing a creek." Although Scott did not specifically mention Phelan's muddy clothes, his testimony is not inconsistent with the critical points of Foy's statement. Scott also recalled Phelan telling them how he had lost his hat: "[He] got bewildered in the dark, that in crossing a creek he had lost his hat." Scott's testimony does not contradict Foy's additional details of Phelan falling "off a log" and getting "his clothes muddy." In other words, both Foy and Scott's recollections of that night specifically mention some problem Phelan told them he had "crossing a creek." Given that fact, it would be reasonable to deduce that a man who loses his hat while crossing a creek in the "dark" wilds would surely get a little wet and muddy in the process. Thus, even though Scott did not mention it and Evans did not recall it, Foy's recollection of Phelan's muddy clothes is perfectly plausible.

But a more critical question is this: What prompted Edward Phelan to tell Foy and Scott about an incident he had crossing a creek? Was he just making conversation or did his sudden appearance at Evans' cabin—wet, muddy and "hatless"—necessitate some explanation?

On the important matter of Phelan's actions on Friday morning, September 6, Evans' recollections are very valuable. Thanks to Evans' testimony, we know that Phelan left Evans' house "a few minutes after" Scott and Foy left and that presumably he was going to return home the same way he came: on foot. How long would it take Phelan to walk the mile and a half from Evans' house to his own cabin? Phelan himself gave the answer. During Brown's cross-examination of him, Phelan said "a man may walk from Evans' to my house in about a half an hour."[38] Therefore, if Phelan left Evans' house "a few minutes" after eight o'clock (Scott's time), we can assume that he arrived at his landing sometime around eight thirty. Interestingly enough, eight thirty was about the same time that Scott and Foy saw him alone in a log canoe "ascending the Mississippi...some distance" above his landing and then turning around and returning to his landing.

## Phelan's Problem

Here is Phelan's problem: In his own testimony he claimed that he "put Hays across the river" on Friday morning "about 9 or 10 o'clock."[39] But how could he have been able to do that given the time frame the testimony has logically established? In other words, is it reasonable to believe that Phelan had enough time to: leave Evans' house around eight o'clock, hike thirty minutes to his shanty, get Sergeant Hays (who might not be instantly ready to go—more about that later), walk down to the landing (three blocks below), get in his log canoe, paddle upstream beyond the upper end of present Harriet Island (about four blocks), cross the river there (which was not as quick a place to cross as downriver at the lower end of the island), deposit Hays on the west shore, cross the river again around the upper end or head of the island (Scott estimated that crossing at that point would take about half an hour), and then return down to his landing, hop out of his canoe, and start up the hill to his cabin, before Scott and Foy arrived there between eight thirty and nine o'clock?

Scott and Foy both testified that Hays was already gone when they visited Phelan's cabin shortly after they arrived at his landing. Scott swore that Phelan told him then and there that "he had just put Hays across the river—he had gone to Little Crow's Village to look for a calf." In other words, Scott and Foy supposedly witnessed Phelan transporting Hays across the river while on their way to his landing. Despite what he claimed, it would seem that Phelan not only didn't have enough time to paddle Sergeant Hays across the river but his estimate of "9 or 10 o'clock" was too late to be plausible. During Brown's cross-examination, Phelan tried to deal with that time problem by changing the time of his Friday river crossing. At this point he testified that "he put deceased across the river around 7 o'clock," two or three hours earlier than he originally estimated.[40] However, that doesn't help him. Credible witnesses contradict that time—according to Scott's clock time, Phelan would have still been in Evans' cabin at seven o'clock—and the whole issue of time is relative. Whether it was seven or eight or nine o'clock doesn't change the fact that Phelan left Evans' house Friday morning on foot "after" Scott and Foy had left in a canoe and those men saw him alone in his log canoe less than an hour after they left Evans' house. They both adamantly maintained that they not only didn't see him cross the river but that it would have been impossible for him to do so during the time they saw him. Foy testified that Phelan's "canoe was in sight all the time" and they first saw him when they were "about one and a half miles from Phalen's Landing."

So far it seems that Phelan cannot escape from the time frame logically deduced from the accounts of other witnesses. His only hope of defense is the possibility that someone can show that Scott's and Foy's time estimates are not accurate, and that both their vision and memory of events are unreliable. Otherwise, his story of transporting Sergeant Hays across the river on Friday morning is simply not plausible. If that story can be proven to be false then Phelan's whole defense falls apart; if Phelan did not take Hays across the river that morning, why did he say that he did? The answer is obvious: to cover up his murder of Hays. Thus, the glaring critical issue is the credibility and reliability of witnesses Stephen Scott and John Foy.

## Two More Witnesses: Clewett and Mencke

Unfortunately for Phelan, Scott's and Foy's accounts of events are supported by two additional witnesses: James Reuben Clewett (or Clewit) and Henry C. Mencke (or Menck), two of the men in the canoe that encountered Scott and Foy at the sand bar on Friday morning, September 6, 1839. Although Clewett's and Mencke's time estimates differ a little from Scott's and Foy's, the differences are not enough to undermine the collective credibility of all four witnesses.

James R. Clewett, a veteran fur trader (born in England in 1810 and conspicuous because of his English accent), was an interesting witness. He was one of Joseph R. Brown's partners in the vandalized whiskey shop* and also the husband of Rose Perry; their marriage on April 9, 1839 was later heralded as the "first white marriage in St. Paul."[41] His testimony provides interesting details about what he saw that Friday morning, as well as another perspective of the key events related by Scott and Foy.

> *I was ascending the Mississippi in a canoe, in company of H. C. Mencke and [Pierre] Jervais [Ben Gervais' younger brother, sic], on a Friday morning about 8 o'clock to the best of my recollection. We landed on a sand bar, near Evans' Landing, where we found Stephen Scott and John Foy whom we saw ten or fifteen minutes before we landed. Remained on the sand bar fifteen or twenty minutes, and left it about the time the other canoe left. Scott and Foy having a bark canoe, and nothing in it, went much faster than we did in our canoe,*

---

* In our modern-day judicial system, a judge would recuse himself from a case if a personal or business associate appeared in the case. But these were different times and the old Wisconsin Territory was a very different place. Minnesota in 1839 was a small world where it was virtually impossible for any justice of the peace not to have had some previous contact or knowledge of a witness.

*being loaded. Suppose they must have gained one-third the distance between the sand bar and Phalen's Landing, which took us about three-quarters of an hour. When we reached Phalen's Landing, we saw the bark canoe drawn upon shore. From half a mile above the bar, until we got to Phalen's, we could have seen a canoe had it crossed near that point. Think it not possible any crossed while we were traveling that distance. Saw a log canoe at Phelan's Landing. I think it would require ten minutes for a man in a canoe to cross the Mississippi at Phelan's Landing.*[42]

On closer examination, Clewett's references to time are not that different from the estimates of Scott and Foy. First, he agreed with Scott's Friday morning starting time of about eight o'clock, although he references their starting point as the sand bar near Evans' Landing, not Evans' house. Foy never gave a starting time, but working backwards from the later times he did give, a reasonable guess for his starting time would be roughly around seven-thirty. Second, Clewett estimated that it had taken his canoe "ten or fifteen minutes" to reach the sand bar from the point on the river where they first saw Scott and Foy. Foy said it was ten minutes, not much difference there. Third, Clewett said they remained at the sand bar about "fifteen or twenty minutes," whereas Foy said it was only about ten minutes.

Scott was not specific but said "it could not be over a half an hour from the time we left Evans' house until we reached the sand bar." Scott did not say how long they were at the sand bar, but again, he might have meant that the entire time spent between leaving Evans' house and leaving the sand bar was "no more than" thirty minutes. If that is what he meant, then his summary estimate of thirty minutes maximum would be very close to Clewett's total estimate of twenty-five to thirty-five minutes. However, if that is not what Scott meant, then his summary estimate is very difficult to calculate. In any case, Clewett's estimate of the time spent at the sand bar does not directly contradict what Scott did or did not say about it. Fourth and most significantly, Clewett also estimated that because of Scott and Foy's fast, lightly loaded "bark canoe," they made the trip from the sand bar to Phelan's Landing about one-third faster than Clewett and his companions did. Since Clewett estimated that his heavily loaded canoe took three-quarters of an hour (forty-five minutes) to reach Phelan's Landing, then we can logically deduce that a canoe going one-third faster would make the same trip in thirty minutes, the same amount of time Foy said it took to go from Evans' house to Phelan's Landing, and the maximum amount of time that Scott said it took them to go from the sand bar to Phelan's Landing.

Clewett's canoe mate, Henry C. Mencke, is another interesting witness. "A foreigner" (perhaps he was German or Swiss), Mencke was a local whiskey trader, also closely associated with Brown; along with Clewett, he was one of the proprietors of Brown's whiskey shop.

Although Major Taliaferro disliked Mencke, he was the one Brown appointed as special constable to arrest Phelan.* "Constable" Mencke confirmed Clewett's account on most points, but none of the discrepancies helped Phelan.[43]

*I suppose it was about seven o'clock in the morning on Friday, the sixth of September last as I was ascending the Mississippi in a canoe with J. Clewet and Pierre Jervais [the younger brother of Ben Gervais,sic]. I landed on a sand bar, a short distance from Evans's Landing. Scott and Foy arrived at the sand bar about the same time we did. Saw them on shore at Evans' Landing within twenty minutes previous to our landing on the sand bar. Did not remain on the bar to exceed fifteen minutes. Scott and Foy left the bar, say five minutes before us. Suppose it took us about three-fourths of an hour from the bar to Phalen's Landing. From the difference in the speed of the two canoes, suppose Scott and Foy traveled that distance in nearly half the time. From about three-fourths of a mile above the bar we could have*

---

* When Indians burned down Brown, Clewett, and Mencke's saloon in 1839, Mencke accused Taliaferro of encouraging the Indians to do it. Menck then somehow got a deputy marshal's badge from Clayton County, Iowa and tried to arrest the Major for arson. Taliaferro was spared from being taken to jail by the commander of Fort Snelling. See endnote 43.

*seen a canoe cross from Phalen's at all times, saw none crossing either way. Suppose a person in a canoe might cross and recross the Mississippi opposite Phalen's Landing in twenty minutes.*[44]

If Clewett's testimony added maybe ten minutes to the window of time Phelan had to plausibly transport Hays across the river before Scott and Foy arrived at his landing, Mencke's testimony quickly took that away and maybe even subtracted more minutes from that already small window. Although Mencke's Friday morning starting time of "seven o'clock" was the same as Phelan's revised estimate, that earlier time does not help Phelan for the same reasons given previously. More importantly, Mencke's estimates on the critical matter of how long Scott and Foy stayed at the sand bar, and how long they took to reach Phelan's Landing from the sand bar, were either roughly similar to other witnesses' estimates, or even lower than most. For instance, he said that the time he and his crew spent at the sand bar "did not exceed 15 minutes." That is not inconsistent with Foy's estimate of ten minutes, and reasonably close to Clewett's estimate of fifteen to twenty minutes. But he also said that "Scott and Foy left the sand bar say five minutes before us." Thus, Menck was inferring that Scott and Foy's stay at the sand bar was actually closer to ten minutes, the same as Foy's estimate. Even worse for Phelan, his estimate of how long it took Scott and Foy to reach Phelan's Landing from the sand bar was considerably less than both Clewett and Scott's estimates. Mencke calculated that "Scott and Foy traveled that distance in nearly half the time" they did. (In other words, "nearly half" of forty-five minutes.)

Mencke also calculated that it would take a person in a canoe about twenty minutes to "cross and recross the Mississippi opposite Phalen's Landing." However, Mencke obviously did not realize that Scott and Foy, in their speedy canoe, first observed Phelan canoeing upriver from his landing, near the head of present Harriet Island. Thus, Phelan would not have been able to cross the river at the point Mencke considered ("opposite Phelan's Landing"), which was the shortest, most logical crossing point from his landing. Last but not least, Mencke strongly agreed with the three other witnesses in canoes that morning, that nowhere on their voyage to Phelan's Landing did they observe any canoe crossing the river. Clearly, Clewett's and Mencke's testimonies do not undermine the credibility of Scott and Foy. The credibility of Scott and Foy is most critical, not only for what they have testified thus far but for the testimony to come, which is even more devastating to Phelan's defense than the first part of their testimonies.

## Scott and Foy: The Story Continues

After witnessing Phelan from a distance paddling up and down the river in a log canoe, before he docked at his landing and "immediately" headed up the hill to his home, Scott and Foy arrived at Phelan's Landing. In the words of Foy, "we landed alongside Phelan's canoe about 8 o'clock in the morning."[45] Scott and Clewett would have disputed that time, but the significant point is that they arrived at the landing between thirty and sixty minutes after Scott and Foy last saw Phelan up close in Evans' house. What happened next is best told by Stephen Scott.

*After landing Foy started immediately up the bluff toward Phalen's house. I remained a few moments, and when I started I took a trail that led apparently through the bottom where the road passes in the winter, which is shorter than the summer road. I followed the trail some ten rods [75 yards], when I came to where the road abruptly terminated, and the herbage had been trampled down very much for some distance round, and there I saw a considerable body of blood, around which there was drops of blood on the herbage. The blood appeared fresh—do not think it had laid over a day at the farthest. From this place there was no trail but the one to the river. Do not recollect to have seen any tracks in the trail in the vicinity of the blood. It appeared as though some heavy body had been laying, and I was under the impression at the time that one of the cattle had been wounded by the Indians, and had lost the blood I saw. I do not recollect to have seen any signs of cattle in the vicinity. The bottom was wet at the time, and did not look like a place cattle would frequent— cannot say there was any appearance of anything having been dragged along the trail, although the herbage was much beaten down around the river by the trail, and then took the road up the bluff to Phalen's house, where I found him and of whom I inquired for Hays. He told me he had just put Hays across the river—he had gone to Little Crow's Village to look for a calf—and that Hays had put on his best clothes. I enquired [sic] if any of their cattle had been hurt, at the same time telling him of what I had seen at the bottom. He answered it must have been some of Jervais' cattle, as none of theirs had been wounded. Phalen showed me where he was building a root house, he said something about not agreeing with the manner in which Hays threw out the earth, but do not recollect he had any dispute with Hays on that or any other subject. Knew Hays very well—did not see him about the premises. Suppose it was nine o'clock when we left Phalen's house.*[46]

Earlier it was Scott who said they had left Evans' house at about eight o'clock. Thus, by now stating that they left Phelan's house at "nine o'clock"—after obviously spending several minutes there—he was saying in effect that they arrived at Phelan's Landing *less than an hour* after they left Evans' house. That revision is much closer to Foy's estimate of thirty minutes.

John Foy's account is not as shocking and elaborate because he did not use the same trail to Phelan's cabin that Scott did, but it is not inconsistent with Scott's story.

*Went directly from the landing to the house, found Phalen there. Left Scott at the landing. Was not acquainted with deceased. Had seen no other person about the premises but Phalen and Scott, who came sometime after me. Went with Scott and Phalen to where a root house was building. While there prisoner stated that he and his comrade (Hays) had some dispute as to where the clay thrown up in digging should be put. Phalen wishing to throw it down the hill, while Hays insisted on throwing it up the hill. Remained about fifteen minutes at the house. When we returned to the landing we saw a canoe with some Indians in it near the landing.*[47]

Scott's discovery of "a considerable body of blood," which "appeared fresh" and "drops of blood" on the surrounding "herbage," some "10 rods" (or seventy-five yards) from Phelan's Landing, is powerful, incriminating evidence against Edward Phelan by itself. But added to that are the incriminating comments that Phelan apparently made when both Scott and Foy conversed with him up at his cabin. First, he told them, in Scott's words—and presumably in the presence of Foy—that "he had just put Hays across the river—he had gone to Little Crow's Village to look for a calf—and that Hays put on his best clothes." Yet, when Scott told him he had seen blood on the trail and that "it appeared as though some heavy body had been laying" there and he "was under the impression at the time that one of the cattle had been wounded by the Indians and has lost the blood [he] saw," Phelan apparently appeared uninterested. "He answered it must have been some of Jervais' cattle, as none of theirs had been wounded."

Consider: Here is a man who claimed he had just taken his partner across the river to look for a lost calf downriver at the Indian village. Yet when someone told him that just below his cabin there were glaring signs that an animal might have been butchered there, he immediately concluded, without even going to look at the bloody site, that it "must have been some of Jervais' cattle, as none of theirs had been wounded." Anyone would argue that Phelan's response here was odd. Two obvious questions arise: Why would Phelan say that none of his cattle were wounded when he had just told Scott and Foy, and even Evans the night before, that he and Sergeant Hays were missing a calf? How could he be so sure that the "big body of blood" that Scott saw on the river bottom trail was not the blood from the missing calf?

The answers would seem to be as obvious as the questions: allegedly, Phelan knew that the blood wasn't from a calf not only because the calf wasn't really missing, but also because he was the only person who knew the true source of the blood: the battered head of his partner, Sergeant Hays, whom he had killed.

## Phelan's Neighbors, the Gervaises, Provide More Information

But luckily for Phelan, at least part of his response to Scott—the possibility that his neighbor's cattle could be the source of the blood—could be partly supported by that very neighbor and his son. Ben Gervais and his fourteen-year-old son Alphonse Gervais (1825-1904) testified before Justice Brown and both confirmed that their "cattle frequently ran in the bottom below Phelan's house." Ben Gervais explained that there was "a road from [his] house going that way that the cattle made." Alphonse added that their cattle went there to feed on the "bottom grass."[48]

> *They were in the habit of going there, before the frost struck the grass in the prairie. Have driven my father's cattle from there several times during the summer.*[49]

However, both father and son testified that they never saw or heard of any blood down at the river bottom. Ben Gervais elaborated:

> *Know of no cattle having been wounded during the Summer or Fall. Think if any of my neighbor's cattle had been wounded I would have heard of it. Never heard of any blood being found in the bottom, cannot conceive how it could get there. Never observed that my cattle bled from the sores in their feet—do not believe that any quantity of blood could have issued from them.*[50]

Alphonse concurred with his father:

> *Passed through the bottom frequently never saw blood there. My father had cattle diseased in the feet, but never saw blood to issue*

*from them. Know of no cattle having been killed or wounded by the Indians during the summer. Have been in the bottom since the disappearance of Hays and found cattle there. Have been in the habit of seeing Phalen and Hays frequently. Never saw any sign of dispute or ill-feeling between them. Do not know of them ever having quarreled.*[51]

Ben Gervais echoed his son's last remarks:

*Never heard of any misunderstanding between Phalen and his partner. Think I would have perceived it, had such been the case; they always appeared to be on good terms with each other.*[52]

If Stephen Scott's sworn testimony about seeing that fresh pool of blood at the river bottom on September 6 was true, then Ben and Alphonse Gervais gave convincing testimony that the blood did not come from their cattle, or probably anyone else's cattle. Nevertheless, Ben and Alphonse Gervais did give some help to Phelan's defense. Young Alphonse in particular might be one of the best defense witnesses Phelan has. His last remarks in support of Phelan's good relationship with Hays are compelling. Ironically, years later when Alphonse was an adult, he told J. Fletcher Williams a very different story about Phelan. According to Williams:

*Alphonse Gervais stated that he saw blood on Phelan's clothes, and that, when Phelan's cabin was searched, bloody clothes were found beneath the floor. He stated, moreover, that he found the place, near the cabin, where the act was committed, being led thither by a very sagacious dog he owned, who smelled the blood, and plainly, traced the route by which the body was dragged to the river from thence.*[53]

What Alphonse Gervais reportedly told Williams decades after he testified as a fourteen-year-old boy is, if true, the most incriminating evidence against Phelan yet uncovered. The obvious question is: why didn't Alphonse Gervais tell that story to Joseph R. Brown back on November 1, 1839? There is no way of knowing for certain now, but all things considered, it is unlikely that he deliberately lied to Williams, telling him some sensational fabrication about what he saw years before at his old neighbor's place. We know that Williams interviewed several other witnesses and participants in the murder case, including Alphonse's own parents and Henry Sibley, who was widely respected and the case's original investigator. Surely one or more of those knowledgeable and mostly honorable pioneers would have exposed any false story they heard about the case when Williams consulted with them. What's more, the evidence is strong that Williams, the former newspaper editor and long-time dedicated secretary of the Minnesota Historical Society, was very conscientious in quoting his sources correctly and attaining overall accuracy in his reports.[54]

Still another factor to consider in determining the credibility of Alphonse Gervais was the reputation that the Ben Gervais family had for being good, honest, humble, God-fearing, family farmers. The evidence is overwhelming that the Gervaises were devout Catholics. Ben Gervais donated some of the land for St. Paul's first church, the historic Catholic Chapel of St. Paul, and he also helped found the second Catholic church in Ramsey County, St. John the Baptist in Little Canada. In fact, the first mass in Little Canada was held in the Ben Gervais cabin.[55] A family legend has it that in order to get baby Basil Gervais baptized by a priest, Genevieve and one of her older sons took the infant in a canoe and paddled over 250 miles to St. Gabriel's Catholic Church in Prairie du Chien. The records of that parish verify Basil's baptism there.[56] But the most telling hint of the Gervais family's character comes from the words of Ben and Genevieve's locally famous son (and Alphonse's brother), Basil Gervais. In a newspaper interview on May 6, 1894, Basil referred to his notoriety as the "first white child born in St. Paul," and revealed much about his values and character:

*As for being the first white child born in St. Paul, I suppose I ought to be proud of it; but after all was it not an accidental circumstance? How can one help it where he was born?*

*To live a good life is better than all such things. I can tell you what gives me more pride than anything else. I have never been a rich man and never expect to be. I am only rich in my children. I have not been able to give them wealth or a very good education, or many advantages; but I have always tried to teach them to be good men and women and do right as best they could, and never do any disgraceful or mean thing and to trust in the good God to take care of them. And they please me by their conduct oh, very much. I have quite a brood of them to be sure, but one never came that was not welcome; and the dear little fellows, though I have had to hustle pretty hard to care for them, they are worth all the trouble and they help me what they can and we get along all right and I am satisfied. I hope they may grow up to be much better off and much better every way than their father, but if they cannot be well off and good at the same time, then let them be good and poor. And me—why sir, honestly I tell you the truth, I would much rather people would say of me, "there goes Basil Gervais, and he is a good man," than they should say nothing else but "there goes Basil Gervais, and he was the first white child born in St. Paul."*[57]

Unfortunately, Alphonse's beliefs and values were never printed in the newspaper, but those articulated by his brother Basil Gervais— "to be good men and women and do right…and never do anything disgraceful or mean…and to trust in the good God"—likely reflected the core values of the entire Gervais family. It's hard to imagine that Alphonse Gervais would make up an elaborate story about Phelan and then, even worse, repeat it to a historian who he knew would preserve it for posterity.

If the graphic story that the adult Alphonse Gervais told Williams was not fabricated, then why didn't young Alphonse tell Justice Brown that story? Perhaps he had told it earlier in testimony before

Justice Henry Sibley, and that deposition, quite plausibly, was part of the documents that were lost at Prairie du Chien. But it is surprising that Alphonse's testimony before Justice Brown was so very short and focused mainly on the issue of whether injured cattle were the source of the blood in the river bottom. Indeed, from its appearance in Brown's casebook—its brevity, narrow scope and the order of its placement—Alphonse's deposition has all the characteristics of a narrow rebuttal testimony. If that is what it is, then it's possible that Brown had Alphonse's fuller testimony given before Sibley and then simply chose, in the interest of time and wear on his writing hand, not to repeat what Sibley had already done. In that case, Brown would have been most interested in uncovering new information and made that the focus of his questioning of Alphonse Gervais.

On the other hand, the brief deposition in Brown's casebook may have been the only testimony Alphonse ever gave. It's possible that the incriminating evidence Alphonse described to Williams later in his life was discovered after Brown conducted his hearing on November 1, 1839. In other words, after Phelan was arrested on October 31 and later detained in the Fort Snelling jail (which Williams confirms), it's possible that a further police investigation was conducted, perhaps by the county marshal, which uncovered the bloody clothes in Phelan's cabin that Alphonse mentioned. All that evidence, including a separate police report, could have been packed up and eventually sent to Prairie du Chien, only to be lost with the rest of the court records later. If that was the case, it would help explain why Brown's casebook seems incomplete and his questions to Alphonse Gervais seem so limited. In any case and in fairness to Phelan, because Alphonse Gervais told his story to Williams decades after the fact and not sworn under oath, it doesn't carry the weight of the evidence derived from the sworn testimonies in Brown's casebook.

## Summing Up the Testimony

Returning to the sworn testimonies of Stephen Scott and John Foy, there are a few additional points to consider from the last climatic part of their story. First, Scott testified that Phelan specifically told him that Sergeant Hays had "put on his best clothes" before he had taken him across the river. Phelan never said why Hays would wear his "best clothes"—the "blue coat and oxford grey pantaloons" he described earlier—to hike to the Indian village. Consider the limited window of time that Phelan had on that Friday morning to perform the many actions that he either claimed he did, that other witnesses testified he did, or that we have logically deduced that he did. Add to that long list that Phelan had to wait, presumably, for Hays to put on best clothes (and remember that according to Williams, Hays was "exact in his dress") before they paddled across the river. Additionally, Mrs. Gervais testified that when Phelan visited their cabin on Friday afternoon, September 6, he told her that an employee of fur trader B. F. Baker had stopped by the cabin in the morning and offered Sergeant Hays a ride downriver to Kaposia, and that Hays declined. Then, according to Mrs. Gervais, "when the man left the house, Hays accompanied him up as far as the hill, after which he returned, breakfasted, dressed himself and then Phelan had went with him across the river."[58]

Now we can better appreciate the significance of Mrs. Gervais' anecdote about Sergeant Hays and the unnamed river traveler. If her recollection was correct, Phelan told her that he was visited by a river traveler on the same morning that he hiked home from Evans' cabin, and that the visitor spent some time at their home. Since we have reasonably established that Phelan's window of time to hike from Evans' cabin to his and then transport Sergeant Hays across the river and return home, before the arrival of Scott and Foy, was an hour or less, how could he have had any time to receive a visitor before Hays departed? The very idea that Phelan could make a thirty-minute hike, a thirty-minute canoe ride, a three-block walk from his cabin to his landing, and also wait for a man to dress and eat breakfast, and receive a guest and converse for a few minutes before the guest departed and walked down the hill to the river, all in sixty minutes or less, is preposterous.

One question remains concerning Scott's dramatic discovery of "a body of blood" and "trampled down" brush with "drops of blood

Brown never mentions the discovery of bloody clothes found under the floor board of Phelan's cabin that Alphonse Gervais reportedly told Williams about many years later. Thus, the theory that Alphonse might have included that information in an earlier deposition taken by Sibley is no longer plausible because Brown would have surely made some mention of it in his summation. If any bloody clothes were found in Phelan's cabin, Brown's summation is clear evidence that they were found after Brown recorded his findings. Given what Brown has included in his summation, we can draw only two conclusions about William's bloody clothes report: either Williams got the story wrong—by his own carelessness or lack of integrity, or by the faulty, distorted, maybe even dishonest memories of his sources—or those bloody clothes were found after November 1, 1839.

But even without any evidence of bloody clothes found at Phelan's cabin, Brown concluded confidently that Phelan "committed the murder." It must be acknowledged that Brown had access to information that was never recorded: unlike modern investigators of the case, who can only read the testimonies of witnesses—long dead and mostly forgotten—Brown had the advantage of actually seeing and hearing live witnesses deliver their testimonies. Given his reputed talent as a "close observer of men," we can assume Brown would have observed Edward Phelan closely—looking him in the eye, reading his body language, and listening to the telling tone of his voice. All these observations would inform his impressions of Phelan's honesty and his judgment of Phelan's guilt.

The frontier justice of the peace had additional advantages in evaluating the evidence. As a veteran fur trader and experienced canoeist in the local waters of the Mississippi, he was especially qualified to assess the issue of canoe travel times, particularly the plausibility of Phelan's being able "to cross and re-cross the river in the time allotted by the witnesses." Brown's conclusion that Phelan did not have enough time to paddle Hays across the river on the morning he claimed he did is significant.

Brown's third concluding point, that "[Phelan's] telling Mrs.

on the herbage," down at the river bottom about seventy-five yards from Phelan's Landing on the morning of September 6: Was this the same spot where Bartholomew Baldwin saw "grey hairs" on "beaten down" herbage, on a trail "some distance above where the body was found" on September 30?[59] That intriguing question is impossible to answer with certainty. Unfortunately the record is imprecise about where exactly Baldwin saw that possible evidence of where Sergeant Hays' body was dragged to the river or, maybe later, dragged out of the river. Remember, Baldwin was drawn to that spot when an Indian told him that his son had seen a body there, instead of further down river where the army investigators found it. All we know from Baldwin about the location of that spot is that it was "above where the body was found."[60] Hays' body was found somewhere in or along the river "near Carver's Cave," another imprecise location, but in the days before roads and even survey lines marked the local wilderness, it was difficult to give precise locations.[61] "Some distance above" Carver's Cave could be almost anywhere upriver to Fort Snelling, but Baldwin seems to imply that it was specifically in between Carver's Cave and Phelan's Landing. It is quite possible that the trampled brush with gray hairs on it that Baldwin saw along a river trail was the same place, seventy-five yards from Phelan's Landing, where Scott saw the body of blood twenty-four days earlier. That would certainly tie the story together neatly, but unfortunately there is no way of absolutely proving that the two sites were the same. Yet in light of Scott's powerful testimony, Baldwin's discovery of gray hairs on trampled brush more than three weeks after Hays' murder now seems less important. Indeed, finding a large pool of fresh blood, seventy-five yards from Phelan's Landing, on the very morning Phelan claimed he transported the murder victim across the river, clearly trumps almost any evidence found weeks later.

# CHAPTER SIX

## Phelan's Mysterious Trial
## and an Analysis of Arguments for His Defen

Now that we have presented testimony from the twelve witne
that appear in Joseph R. Brown's casebook, it is time to give Jus
Brown's conclusion. Given the number of witnesses, the lack of
ity of some of their testimony, and the several confusing points of
case, one would expect Brown's summation to be rather lengthy.
prisingly, his summation is quite brief. He reduced all the testim
to four concise concluding points:

> First, [Phelan] had not sufficient time to travel from Evans house to
> his own, go to the shore and cross and recross the river in time allot
> ted by the witnesses. 2nd, at the time Scott spoke to him of the blood
> in the [river] bottom, he had a calf lost, which he thought the Indians
> had killed, because Hays had gone to the village to endeavor to find
> the meat, yet he answered Scott that the blood could not be from their
> cattle. Had he really had a calf lost the circumstances of the blood in
> the bottom would have convinced him that it was the blood of his cal;
> I therefore consider the affair of the calf a fabrication. 3rd, his telling
> Mrs. Jervais and others, that Hays had probably gone to Mr. Mooers
> was calculated to prevent a strict search for deceased. 4th, I conceive
> the night he went to Evans was the night he committed the murde
> and that in all probability he was fresh from the deed when he went
> there. What was he doing with a canoe paddle when searching for a
> calf on land?[1]

Jervais[sic] and others that Hays had probably gone to Mr. Mooers was calculated to prevent a strict search for deceased," is an interesting deduction. Brown apparently believed that Phelan fabricated
the story about Hays going to Hazen Mooers' trading post fifteen
miles downriver for a calculated reason. Given the time it would take
to travel to Mooers' place and back, no one would question Hays'
absence for some time. The more time Phelan had before Hays was
discovered to be missing and a search was conducted, the more time
evidence of a crime would disappear, or could be disposed of.

Interestingly, Brown did not reference Genevieve Gervais' testimony about Phelan's odd reaction when she informed him that
Brown himself, who had just arrived from Grey Cloud Island, was
next door at the Perry house. According to Mrs. Gervais, "Phalen
replied that if his clothes were not so bad he would go, but he did not
like to go as he was."[2] Brown gave Phelan a chance to respond specifically to Mrs. Gervais' testimony, recording that "the prisoner here
denied the whole evidence, saying he never had told her anything of
the kind." Phelan also notably added that Hays "never contemplated
going anywhere else but to Little Crow's Village."[3]

However, Phelan's friend William Evans gave testimony that
directly contradicted Phelan on that point:

> *Three or four days afterward [September 8 or 9] I saw Phalen at his*
> *own house; he told me his partner had gone to Little Crow's Village*
> *and had not returned. Said he supposed the cause was that he had*
> *gone down to Mr. Mooers' or thereabouts.*[4]

Phelan's inconsistencies here are glaring. After being confronted
with Mrs. Gervais' testimony, Phelan not only denied her "whole"
account —which included his reported reference of Hays probably
being at Hazen Mooers—he also added that Hays "never contemplated going anywhere else but to Little Crow's Village." If he knew
that Hays "never contemplated going anywhere else," why did he
specifically tell Evans, on or close to the same day that according to

Mrs. Gervais he told her that Hays "probably had gone to Mr. Mooers"—that he "supposed" Hays "had gone down to Mr. Mooers"?[5]

Surprisingly, Brown never commented on these inconsistencies, nor did he touch on the issue of motive. His final note about the case reads:

> *Nov. 4—appointed John McCormack special constable for the purpose of conducting Phalen to prison at Prairie du Chien. He took him down on board the steamboat "Detroit." The recompense McCormack was to receive was the fees of a regular constable in such cases, and the passage of the prisoner, which was agreed to be twelve dollars.*[6]

We can deduce from this final note that after the November 1 hearing, Phelan was detained at the Fort Snelling guardhouse, as Williams reported, until Constable McCormack (of whom virtually nothing is known) escorted him by steamboat to the Crawford County jail at Prairie du Chien. Maybe McCormack was the one who found those bloody clothes?

## What Happened in Prairie du Chien?

What happened to Phelan at Prairie du Chien is a mystery. We know he was transported there in early November 1839 for a grand jury hearing. But whether he was indicted and later brought to trial is unclear. Williams reported that "Mrs. Gervais and William Evans were two witnesses who were subpoenaed to go to Prairie du Chien at the trial the following spring and give evidence against Phelan."[7] Williams' phrase "at the trial the following spring," suggests that Phelan was in fact indicted for murder and then brought to trial on that charge in the spring of 1840, although Williams later speculated that maybe only a grand jury hearing was held.

The records of St. Gabriel Catholic Church in Prairie du Chien reveal that Basil Gervais was baptized there on May 10, 1840, which confirms the family legend that Mrs. Gervais, the baby, and one of her older sons (Alphonse?) traveled all the way (in a canoe) to the church in Prairie du Chien to have the baby baptized.[8] It stands to reason that she may also have been in town to appear as a witness in the trial. If an older son helped her canoe there, as the family story goes, then it is highly likely that the son would have been Alphonse, the only Gervais child who was a witness in the case.

If Williams was correct that Phelan had a court hearing in the spring (May?) of 1840, then Phelan would have been detained in the county jail from early November 1839 until at least late May 1840. That jail, known as "the dungeon," still exists in the rustic basement of the old, stone Crawford County Courthouse, at Prairie du Chien, Wisconsin. The exact age of the historic courthouse is not known, but according to some records, at least part of it dates back to 1834.[9] Thus, it is likely that the only place where Phelan spent all his time during the entire duration of his confinement and trial at Prairie du Chien was in the building that still stands today as the Crawford County Courthouse, in the center of Wisconsin's second oldest town.

Unfortunately, sometime after Phelan's supposed trial at that stone courthouse, all records of the murder case were mysteriously lost. What happened to them is as big a puzzle as the murder case itself. The Crawford County Courthouse has criminal court records stored in its vault that date back to the early 1830s. But strangely the casebooks for the years 1839 and 1840 show no record of any case involving Edward Phelan, no record of a grand jury hearing, and no record of a trial.[10] Is it possible that Phelan was never at Prairie du Chien, and that the whole story of a court hearing there was a myth of St. Paul history? No, in fact we know from reliable evidence that Phelan was definitely incarcerated at Prairie du Chien from November 1839 to at least May 1840, and that sometime during that period there were court proceedings—a grand jury hearing at the very least, but presumably also a trial.[11] So what happened to the records of those important proceedings? A good guess is that they got lost in the transition of changing the jurisdiction of St. Paul from Crawford County to the new St. Croix County. St. Croix County, as noted earlier, was created by the Wisconsin Legislature, thanks largely to the efforts of Joseph R. Brown, in January 1840, and after a vote by the new county's residents on August 3, the county seat was established at Joseph R. Brown's new home (called "Dakotah"), at the head of Lake St. Croix, just north of present downtown Stillwater.[12] Perhaps after Phelan's trial in May or June of 1840, officials reasoned that the records of the proceedings should be filed in the new county where the murder case originated, and they were simply shipped back to Joseph R. Brown—who himself was in the transition of removing his headquarters from Grey Cloud Island to Lake St. Croix—and somewhere along the way the records got lost. Yet even if the records made it safely to Lake St. Croix, there was no courthouse there to properly store documents, only Brown's rough log cabin.

It is frustrating to contemplate the wealth of interesting information those lost records would contain, and how much light they might shed on the many questions posed by the limited evidence preserved in this case. Added to that frustration is the fact that no local newspaper had been established yet to chronicle Phelan's trial. The closest newspaper to Prairie du Chien in 1839 was the *Wiskonsan Enquirer* [sic], published in Madison, 102 miles away. One such question the lost records or a news account might have answered is what sort of legal counsel was available to Phelan. Neither J. Fletcher Williams' interviews nor Joseph R. Brown's casebook give any hint about who served as Phelan's lawyer. Given his limited financial resources and the fact that he was a military veteran, it is probable that some officer at Fort Snelling with knowledge in the law, or later someone at Fort Crawford in Prairie du Chien, offered his services. In 1839, when the Gervaises, Perrys and other east bank settlers encountered legal problems over the legitimacy of their land claims, Fort Snelling's Colonel Samuel Stambaugh served as their lawyer.[13] Whoever Phelan's lawyer was, he proved successful; Phelan was never convicted of the charges against him. Incidentally, we do not even know what those specific charges were. Was he charged with first- or second-degree murder, or something else?

Given the potentially strong case against Phelan, one can only speculate about the line of defense his lawyer used to win his acquittal. Brown's casebook alone provides a few defense witnesses. William Evans—Phelan and Hay's neighbor and comrade from the army—who Williams said was supposed to give evidence "against Phelan," could have been turned into a witness for the defense. Although Evans would have had to testify that he saw Phelan carrying a canoe paddle Thursday evening, he also had helpful testimony for Phelan's defense. In his testimony before Justice Brown, Evans impressively defended Phelan's relationship with Sergeant Hays:

> Have known Phalen and Hays some time and have seen them frequently since they have lived together. Am not aware of their having any quarrels or disputes. [14]

Bartholomew Baldwin and Ben and Alphonse Gervais also confirmed Evans' point. Again, Alphonse Gervais stated:

> Have been in the habit of seeing Phalen and Hays frequently. Never saw any sign of dispute or ill feeling between them. Do not know of them ever having quarreled. [15]

If there was a trial in Prairie du Chien, and if Alphonse Gervais testified as a witness, we can only wonder if he provided any new incriminating evidence against Phelan, relating perhaps to the perplexing matter of the bloody clothes found in Phelan's cabin.

## The Unresolved Question of Motive

What Phelan's lawyer could have drawn from these and possibly other witnesses was evidence to support an attack on the question of the murder motive, an issue that Justice Brown neglected to cover in his summation of the case against Phelan. A prosecutor's common maxim is that in order to prove a defendant guilty of murder you must establish that he had the "motive, means, and opportunity" to commit the crime. Brown certainly covered two of those three essentials.

The "means" was the canoe paddle that witnesses saw the muscular Phelan carry into Evans' house Thursday evening September 5. The "opportunity" was the fact that Phelan lived with Sergeant Hays in virtual isolation and had the opportunity to kill him almost any time before he disappeared, but especially on Thursday evening, sometime before Phelan unexpectedly arrived at Evans' house. But what about Phelan's motive for murder? Although throughout American history many defendants have been convicted of murder without the prosecutors clearly proving the motive for the crime, the murder motive is typically a key factor in determining why a crime was committed and why one particular suspect was the most likely perpetrator of the crime. In the case of Edward Phelan, his motive for murdering Sergeant Hays has not been clearly established.

Major Taliaferro was the first to suggest the money motive. "Hays had money" and Taliaferro surmised that Phelan wanted it.[16] Based strictly on Brown's cross-examination questions to Phelan, McPhail, Baldwin, and Ben Gervais about Hays' "money matters," it would seem that Brown, too, suspected money as the main motive. But testimonies make clear that Sergeant Hays had left two hundred dollars, presumably most of his money, in the care of Lieutenant McPhail at Fort Snelling. If money were his motive, how did Phelan expect to get it from McPhail after Sergeant Hays' death? That question undermines the theory that money was the motive. However, one could expand the money motive to include other valuable assets that Sergeant Hays owned and Phelan might have coveted—mainly his land and cattle. Significantly, there is solid evidence that after Phelan was acquitted, he returned to his claim and tried hard to take possession of Hays' land claim. (That interesting story will be covered later.) There is also evidence that suggests that Phelan ultimately did acquire Hays' cattle. According to the St. Croix County Tax Assessment records for 1847, Edward Phelan owned twelve head of cattle, valued at $240. That might not be impressive by today's standards, but in 1847 those figures made the still single and sole proprietor Edward

Phelan one of the largest cattle owners in St. Paul.*[17] It is not unreasonable to suspect that some of those twelve cattle were once the property of Sergeant Hays.

In light of this evidence, the expanded motive of obtaining Sergeant Hays' property becomes plausible. But, of course, the prosecutor at Prairie du Chien did not have the benefit of knowing what Phelan's future actions would be when he returned home. If the prosecutor in Prairie du Chien believed that Phelan's motive was the desire for Sergeant Hays' property, money included, then logically he would have charged him with first-degree (premeditated) murder, which in 1840 Wisconsin was a hanging offense. (Wisconsin did not abolish the death penalty until 1852.)[18] It is, of course, a logical deduction that if the reason Phelan murdered Hays was to acquire his property then he had to do it with some premeditation.

But a premeditated murder begs some questions. What kind of premeditated plan would lead a mud-spattered Phelan to stumble into Evans' house on the night of the murder, carrying a canoe paddle? What kind of premeditated plan would have Phelan spend the night at Evans' house, when his alibi was that he transported Hays across the river the next morning? If he committed the murder, either Phelan did not have a very good plan, or he somehow botched it, or something outside his control subverted it. Or, he did not kill Sergeant Hays with premeditation. Maybe he had planned to lure Sergeant Hays away from the cabin, kill him quickly and return before dark, but something went wrong and he stumbled around in the dark until he found Evans' cabin. Maybe once inside Evans' cabin he simply decided to stick with his planned alibi about escorting Sergeant Hays across the river in the morning. Or, maybe he thought that visiting Evans that night would somehow enhance his alibi. Maybe he felt he needed Evans as a witness to support his story about the lost calf and Sergeant Hays' intent to go to Kaposia the next morning to

---

* The area surrounding Phelan's claim on the river was officially named St. Paul in 1841.

look for it. Showing up with the canoe paddle (assuming that was the murder weapon), however, doesn't seem very smart or premeditated.

All of those scenarios are certainly possible but so is the theory that Phelan killed Sergeant Hays impulsively, without premeditation. Consider the condition of Sergeant Hays' body: Emerson said that it was "mutilated in a shocking manner—the bones of the face were broken into several pieces, as if done with some mighty weapon."[19] McPhail reported that Sergeant Hays had come to his death "by blows inflicted upon the face with some heavy weapon, breaking both jaw bones, upper and lower, also the temple bone, together with the cheek and other bones belonging to the face."[20] Those descriptions suggest that Sergeant Hays was attacked by a frontal assault. The blows were "inflicted upon the face" and several bones were broken "belonging to the face." In other words, Sergeant Hays' murderer did not attack from behind but looked straight at him and clubbed him violently and repeatedly in the face. That mode of brutal face-to-face over-killing could have been premeditated, and the world has seen many such vicious, sadistic murderers who could do such violence. Perhaps Phelan was such a killer. But such an excessively violent, face-to-face attack is more of an indication that the murder was a crime of passion. If Phelan did kill his partner with that canoe paddle, the medical evidence strongly suggests that the murderer would have been compelled to look the victim in the eye before he struck the first blow.

Here is the question: If Phelan did plan the murder of Hays strictly for the motive of acquiring his wealth—it was nothing personal, he just wanted Hays' land, cattle, and money—then why would he kill him so brutally? Given the force of the blows to Hays' head, it would have been almost impossible for the killer to avoid being splattered with blood. Again, if Phelan had planned the murder, couldn't he have thought of a cleaner way of killing the victim? Wouldn't it have been easier, cleaner, and less unsettling for Phelan to simply club Hays in the back of the head when he wasn't looking and then drown him in the river? Then, if the body was found, the death might be passed off as an accident. It's possible that Phelan originally planned to kill Hays cleanly and easily but something went wrong. Maybe Hays turned around just as Phelan was about to club him— and the killing evolved into a brutal head battering.

The medical evidence all points to the greater likelihood that Sergeant Hays was murdered in an act of anger or rage, not as an act of cool, deliberate premeditation. But then two obvious questions arise. If Phelan murdered Sergeant Hays in a rage, what was he angry about? What could Sergeant Hays have done to provoke such rage?

Williams described Hays as an "honest, good, courteous, old gentleman," who "impressed everyone who met him favorably"—and "every one of the earliest settlers of Saint Paul who knew John Hays speaks of him with unqualified praise."[21] The man Williams described certainly does not seem like the type of person who would provoke someone to extreme anger. Furthermore, William Evans, Ben Gervais, and Alphonse Gervais all testified under oath that in the many times they saw Phelan and Sergeant Hays, they never observed them quarreling or showing any signs of ill feeling.

However, this testimony doesn't mean as much as it seems. Just because Sergeant Hays was well liked by the other settlers, who never lived with him, doesn't mean that as a housemate he didn't do things to anger his partner. Williams mentioned that Sergeant Hays was "something of a martinet in discipline, precise and exact in his dress, bearing and actions," and was "a man of exactly the opposite characteristics as the ruffianly Phelan."[22] It is also relevant that Hays had been a sergeant in the army. Men don't rise to the rank of sergeant by being amicable, passive, easy-going fellows. Surely Sergeant Hays was a man with leadership skills who was not afraid to assert himself. Indeed, for a veteran sergeant like Hays, barking orders to privates like Phelan was an inherent part of his job. The martinet sergeant, who was "precise and exact in his dress" and used to giving orders, might easily have incited resentment in the reputedly rough private from the slums of New York. What's more, Phelan and Hays were sharing the cramped quarters of a "little log shanty"; friction seems likely between two men of different ages, different rank, different personalities and from different regions of the same country (Ireland). The proverbial phrase "familiarity breeds contempt" is perhaps even more true for two guys crammed together in an isolated little shanty for over four months.

The testimony from Evans and Ben and Alphonse Gervais that they never witnessed friction between Phelan and Hays is also not as strong as it seems. Just because Phelan and Sergeant Hays never reportedly quarreled in public doesn't mean that they didn't have disputes in private. It is not uncommon in cases of domestic violence, murder included, to find shocked neighbors of the couple involved in the violence expressing their bewilderment that such a thing could happen because "they always seemed to get along so well." Perhaps that was the situation with Phelan and Sergeant Hays. They kept all their arguments private. Thus, presumably when a neighbor came over they set aside their disagreement and put on the public face of domestic harmony.

But at least one dispute between Phelan and Hays was reported in the testimonies before Justice Brown. Stephen Scott and John Foy both gave accounts of a disagreement between Phelan and Hays over the digging of a root cellar. Phelan had told them that Hays wanted to throw the dirt up the hill and Phelan wanted to throw it down the hill. That hardly seems like the type of quarrel that would provoke a murder. Nevertheless, that reported dispute is a clue that Phelan and Hays did not always get along as harmoniously as Evans, Ben Gervais and Alphonse Gervais characterized it. It is at least possible that the little dispute over where to throw dirt escalated into an angry confrontation that ended in a brutal assault perhaps even with a shovel being used as a weapon. Or, the dirt dispute may have been one episode in a series that had the cumulative effect of producing a long-simmering rage. In other words, it wasn't just one thing that set off Phelan's temper but a four-month long accumulation of resentment and irritation that finally reached a boiling point, presumably sometime on that fateful Thursday of September 5, 1839. There was also the speculation that Phelan resented Sergeant Hays' plan to "buy an Indian girl."

## A Later Account from Mrs. Gervais

There is one additional piece of evidence, albeit a questionable one, that suggests that Phelan and Hays were not really compatible housemates. J. Fletcher Williams interviewed Genevieve Gervais decades after the murder and reported a revealing anecdote:

> *Mrs. Gervais, whose memory is remarkably clear for one so aged, says, among other things, that a short time before the murder of Hays, she asked how he and Hays got along. "Very badly," replied Phelan. "He is a lazy good-for-nothing. But never mind (he added with a wicked look), I'll soon be rid of him."*[23]

Like her son Alphonse, Mrs. Gervais makes a sensational accusation against Phelan that she never offered in her sworn testimony before Justice Brown on November 1, 1839. Directly quoting Phelan's complaint that Sergeant Hays was lazy and specifically predicting that "he'll soon be rid of him" is a powerful indictment of Phelan that would not have been lost on Justice Brown. If Mrs. Gervais' story is true—if Phelan did make that incriminating comment to her—then why didn't she include it in her testimony when she was under oath before Justice Brown? The fact that she didn't include this anecdote in her testimony on November 1, 1839 doesn't prove that her later story to Williams is false. Like her son Alphonse's late story about bloody clothes under Phelan's floorboards, it is possible that Mrs. Gervais never testified about Phelan's self-incriminating comment because she was never asked. Two points stand out in Mrs. Gervais' testimony: first, her testimony is long and second, it focuses exclusively on the conversations she had with Phelan on Friday, September 6 and Sunday, September 8, 1839. Brown may have been so focused on the conversations of those two dates, both of which were significant, that he forgot to ask her about any other relevant conversations she had with Phelan. Her testimony never touches on the subject of Phelan and Hays' relationship. In other words, there is no sign there that Brown questioned her about that. On the other hand, the shorter testimonies of Ben and Alphonse Gervais indicate that Brown directed them to comment on their perceptions of Phelan and Sergeant Hays' relationship. The exchange between Phelan and Mrs. Gervais "a short time before the murder" that she reported to Williams later in her life may well have taken place; her testimony about the conversations on September 6 and 8 does not contradict it. But it is a problem that thirty years passed before she divulged this story to Williams.

Furthermore, Mrs. Gervais' new information does not square with the old testimonies of her husband Ben Gervais and her son Alphonse. As previously mentioned, both husband and son testified that Phelan and Sergeant Hays got along well. Why would Mrs. Gervais' impression contradict her husband's and son's? Maybe she knew something her husband and son did not. Her husband Ben made it clear in his testimony that during her conversation with Phelan on September 6, he was outside the cabin for most of the time. It's possible that Mrs. Gervais spoke to Phelan alone on other occasions as well, and that sometime during their other talks Phelan made the comment about Hays—or something quite similar—to Mrs. Gervais that she later reported.

It's also possible that Mrs. Gervais gave an account of that exchange with Phelan before the Prairie du Chien court in May 1840. A prosecutor in that proceeding would likely have posed more in-depth questions than Brown did about her knowledge of Phelan. And a defense lawyer for Phelan would have cross-examined her vigorously about what she said, or failed to say, in her testimony before Justice Brown. He also might have explored the possibility that Mrs. Gervais was prejudiced against Phelan and that bias might have distorted her perception of him. He would certainly have questioned the plausibility of Phelan's being so foolish as to openly admit to her that "soon" he was going to "be rid of him." He also would likely have exploited the fact that Mrs. Gervais was "hard of hearing." He also could have suggested that Phelan's words actually meant that he would "be rid of him" soon only because Sergeant Hays was planning on moving out "soon." Clearly, Genevieve Gervais would have been an important, interesting witness in the Phelan trial, and she is, without a doubt, an important, intriguing character in this perplexing murder case.

Whatever the line of defense was, Phelan's lawyer succeeded; Phelan was acquitted and spared the fate of being hanged or sent to prison. The defense is even more impressive when you consider that Phelan's lawyer was missing two compelling witnesses: James Thompson, the former slave who beat Phelan in the "Battle for the Pig," and August Larpenteur (1823-1919), an early St. Paul fur trader who helped lay out the city of St. Paul and who later became the namesake of Larpenteur Avenue, and who was also the longest surviving pioneer of St. Paul. Both Thompson and Larpenteur were convinced that Phelan was innocent of murdering Sergeant Hays, and they believed they had strong evidence to prove it.

## Thompson's Story of a Deathbed Confession

Thompson's intriguing information, like the story of the Battle for the Pig, comes from the pen of Thomas Newson, who interviewed him when the former slave was about eighty-five years old and who published the account in *Pen Pictures* (1886)

> *It has been generally believed that Phelan killed Hays, his partner, but Mr. Thompson sets the matter to rest very decidedly by stating unequivocally, that an Indian by the name of Do-wau, the singer, killed him, and when fatally shot at the battle of Kaposia this Indian, just before he died, admitted the deed.*[24]

The battle of Kaposia that Newson refers to is the surprise attack that about one hundred Ojibwe warriors made on the outskirts of Little Crow's village (Kaposia) in September 1842. In this memorable battle—which caused the deaths of at least eighteen Dakota (including Wabsheeda, the man who first informed Taliaferro that his

sons had found Hays' body) and about ten Ojibwe—Dakota warriors drove retreating Ojibwe down the gorge of a creek that later
became known as "Battle Creek."[25]

Thompson's claim of a Dakota's deathbed confession of Sergeant
Hays' murder is certainly a bombshell that could blow apart the murder charge against Phelan. But like so much evidence in this enig-
matic case, Thompson's story raises as many questions as it answers.

Thompson would seem to be a credible source. He knew Phelan
well, he lived in the area, and he had a family relationship with the
local Dakota, a critical factor because his family was likely the source
of the story. Thompson was married to a Dakota woman from Kaposia even before he was liberated from slavery. The name of that Dakota
wife was never recorded by Alfred Brunson, the Methodist missionary who purchased Thompson's freedom in 1837. But other sources
show that she was the same Dakota wife that Thompson told Newson he married in 1848, the year that St. Paul's first Protestant church
was organized. They were married until their deaths four days apart,
thirty seven years and nine children later. In other words, like so
many couples who lived in the wilderness, she and Thompson may
simply have had a common law marriage until they could have a
church wedding several years later.[26] The 1850 Minnesota Census
for Ramsey County shows that the wife of Thompson, who Newson described as "a full-blooded Indian," was a thirty-three-year-old
woman named Mary and that she and Thompson already had, two
years after their marriage, two children living in their household:
twelve-year-old Sarah and seven-year-old George.[27] Other evidence
reveals that many years earlier, before the birth of Sarah, Mrs. Mary
Thompson had been either the wife or mistress of a Fort Snelling
officer, Lieutenant Williams.[28] Interestingly, Newson only referred to
Thompson's wife Mary as "the mother of Mrs. Odell." Mrs. Odell
was Elizabeth Williams Odell, the daughter of Mary and Lieutenant
Williams, and the wife of former Fort Snelling soldier, Thomas Odell,
who built a trading post (the "first building in West St. Paul") in 1850

in the vicinity of present-day Humboldt Avenue and Congress Street in what is now the West Side of St. Paul.[29]

Most of the evidence suggests that either Thompson's wife Mary, his son-in-law Thomas Odell, or his stepdaughter Elizabeth, or all three or some combination of them, were the main source of Thompson's story about the Dakota who confessed to the Hays murder after the battle of Kaposia. In his account of that historic battle, J. Fletcher Williams specifically mentions that "Mrs. Thomas Odell, then Miss Elizabeth Williams, a half-breed girl," was close enough to the battle to hear the opening gunfire. According to Williams, young Elizabeth "was a pupil at the Red Rock mission" at the time of the Ojibwe attack.[30] The Red Rock mission was the Methodist mission house, founded by Thompson's liberator Alfred Brunson in 1839, that stood across the Mississippi from Kaposia, below Pig's Eye Lake, in present-day Newport. Williams' account of the Battle of Kaposia concluded with some revealing and relevant information.

> *When the Chippewa first made the attack a messenger was sent to Fort Snelling with the intelligence. It was the policy of the Government to prevent and punish these inter tribal carnages, and Major Dearborn at once dispatched a party of soldiers...to Kaposia to stop the conflict. The party came down below Pickerel Lake in boats, and thence across by land, but did not arrive until after the conflict was over. Thomas Odell, now of West Saint Paul [now the city's West Side], was one of this party. I am indebted to him and his wife for many of the minor incidents of this strange affair.[31]*

Thanks to Williams, we know that Thompson's son-in-law, Thomas Odell, was one of the first non-Indians to view the scene of the battle when it ended. If there was a mortally wounded Dakota warrior who confessed to the murder of a white man, Odell would have been in the right place and time to hear it. Whether there was such a confession and whether Odell witnessed it is not known; if there was, Odell would have at least been close enough to that death drama to soon hear about it. Was Odell then the main source of Thompson's story? The evidence seems to suggest it. But what about other family members?

We do not know the whereabouts of Thompson's wife Mary on the day of the 1842 battle. We might assume she was in St. Paul with her husband but it is also possible that she was at Kaposia visiting family. If she was at Little Crow's village that day, she would have seen the battle from across the river, since the Ojibwe attack and ensuing battle took place on the east shore, around Pig's Eye Lake, and the Dakota ultimately drove the retreating Ojibwe farther east. If Mary was at Kaposia that day, it's possible she could have heard firsthand about the deathbed confession. However, a much more likely scenario for Mary would be her visiting Kaposia not before the battle but after it. One can imagine how she would have reacted when she heard the news in St. Paul that several Kaposia villagers had been killed and wounded in an Ojibwe attack. Naturally she would have been most concerned about all her relatives and friends at Kaposia— and so it would have been understandable for her to go down there as soon as she could to provide aid and comfort to her people. If that was what happened then maybe Mary learned of the alleged confession at that time.

Thanks again to Williams, we know that Mary's daughter Elizabeth was at the Red Rock mission, downriver from the fighting. Although Elizabeth Odell provided Williams with information about the battle, census records show that she would have been only six years old in 1842. Given her young age and the fact that although she was close to the battle scene she was not at the battlefield, it is unlikely that Elizabeth was the original source of Thompson's story. But the fact that Elizabeth was at Red Rock at the time of the battle might be a clue as to her mother's whereabouts in September 1842. Maybe Mary Thompson was temporarily staying at Red Rock at that time to be near her six-year-old daughter.

But where was James Thompson himself during the battle of

Kaposia? Presumably he was living somewhere in present-day St. Paul, but he could have been almost anywhere since no one ever recorded where he lived during the early 1840s. Apparently between 1848 and 1849 he was living close enough to Rice Park to spend several months near the corner of Market and Fifth Streets, helping to construct the Market Street Methodist Church, the first Protestant church in St. Paul. According to Newson, Thompson helped build that historic church and "furnished 2,000 feet of lumber" and "made out of the logs taken from the river 1,500 shingles for the roof and then gave a lot which he owned towards paying for the church."[32]

We already know that Thompson had deep roots with the Methodist Church, going back to Methodist missionary Alfred Brunson's purchase of his freedom and his work as an Indian interpreter and carpenter at Kaposia. Given his ties with the local Methodists, it is not inconceivable that in September 1842 Thompson may have been down at the Red Rock mission, where his stepdaughter Elizabeth was in school, perhaps doing some carpentry work, or helping out as an Indian interpreter, when the battle of Kaposia broke out. If he was there on that day—and that is a big unproven if—then he, himself, would have been close enough to the battle to hear the opening gunshots. Just maybe then, he would have been moved to rush up to Kaposia to check on the safety of his in-laws. Perhaps, if Mary was with him at Red Rock, she would have joined him in the trek to Kaposia, or at least encouraged him to go there. In other words, it is not beyond the realm of possibility that Thompson himself was a direct observer of some, or even all of the events he related in his sensational story.

And that possibility would not change if Thompson had been in St. Paul at the time of the battle because the scenario we gave previously for his wife Mary might also apply to him. Hence, when St. Paul got the news of the terrible bloodshed at Pig's Eye Lake, perhaps his wife encouraged him to go down and help the victims. Thompson "ran the first ferry boat in St. Paul" and would have had been able to row or paddle to the battle scene to help the wounded, among whom could have been the alleged confessing murderer.[33]

What then can we conclude from all these deductions and specu-
lations? Not much, other than the following points:

- Thomas Odell was the only Thompson family member
  who was proven to be close to the time and place where
  the alleged Indian confession of murder occurred.
- Although there is no direct proof, it is at least circum-
  stantially possible that Thompson's Dakota wife Mary, and
  even Thompson himself, could have also been direct witnesses to the alleged confession, or had close connections
  to the people who were.
- It is less likely that Thompson's stepdaughter, Mrs. Elizabeth Odell—who was only six years old and not at the
  battlefield in 1842—was a direct witness to the alleged
  Indian confession.
- One plausible part of Thompson's Indian confession story
  is the fact that Thompson and his extended family had
  not only close ties with the Kaposia village, but at least
  one member of the family, Thomas Odell, was documented to be at the very place and at the very time that
  the event related in the story occurred.

  Aside from his stint as a whiskey trader, nothing in
  James Thompson's known life would lead one to question his credibility. Other than his supposed friendship
  with Phelan, which we know about only from Newson's
  brief mention in his account of the Battle for the Pig,
  there is no reason that Thompson would invent the story
  of the Indian's deathbed confession, especially when he
  himself was near his own deathbed at the time Newson
  interviewed him. Thompson died in 1884, the same year
  Newson wrote his book.

In addition to the credibility of Thompson's family background,
the other plausible part of his story is its specificity. He didn't vaguely

say that some Indian somewhere, sometime confessed to killing Sergeant Hays; he specifically said that an Indian named "Do-wau, the Singer," who was wounded at the battle of Kaposia, confessed to killing Hays. Although that level of detail does not by itself prove that the story is true, it certainly enhances its believability.

Unfortunately, no eyewitness account of the battle of Kaposia was ever recorded; there is no way to verify whether any "fatally shot" Dakota confessed to anything "just before he died." Again, Thompson's story raises more questions than it answers: Who exactly was Do-wau, the Singer? Who exactly heard him confess to murder? What exactly did he say in that supposed confession? It is frustrating that such critically important evidence is so empty of elaborating details. Without knowing exactly what Do-wau confessed to, it is difficult to assess it. What if he confessed only to killing some white man years before? Such a confession would not be proof that he confessed to killing Sergeant Hays. He conceivably could have killed some unknown drifter, or any one of a number of deserting soldiers, who disappeared from Fort Snelling over the years and whose body was never found. With respect to the possibility that he had killed a Fort Snelling deserter, then his confession could have even included a reference to the victim being a soldier. It would then be understandable that a listener to that confession might have jumped to the conclusion that the soldier was Sergeant Hays. On the other hand, if he specifically confessed to clubbing Sergeant John Hays to death—the white farmer with gray hair and a long nose—in the fall of 1839, or three years before the battle of Kaposia, then that would be the end of the murder mystery and Edward Phelan would be exonerated. But again, we do not know exactly what Do-wau said. In fact, Do-wau's confession could be nothing more than what we today might call an "urban legend," or in the vernacular of Thompson's time, a local legend. In other words, there may have been a dying Do-wau but he never really confessed to killing Hays. He did perhaps utter something vague about a white man, or a killing, but nothing clear or specific. However, as his last words were retold from person to person and eventually passed on to the Thompson family, so many embellishments were added, that now Do-wau's vague words had turned into a clear confession that he had murdered Sergeant Hays. All these scenarios are possible but none can be proven—so where does that leave us? Frustrated and confused—but we have more evidence to consider.

## Larpenteur Sides with Thompson

Intriguingly, August Larpenteur provides some additional evidence that supports Thompson's story. Although Larpenteur knew Phelan and had much to say in support of his innocence, there is good reason that he never testified at any hearing or trial. August Larpenteur did not move from St. Louis to St. Paul until September 15, 1843, four years after Sergeant Hays' murder. Nevertheless, Larpenteur's work in the fur trade in the 1840s brought him in close contact with the local Dakota, and through this relationship he learned something that convinced him that Phelan was not the one who killed Sergeant Hays. Fortunately for St. Paul history, Larpenteur lived to be ninety six, longer than any other St. Paul pioneer and devoted much of his later years to sharing his memories of early St. Paul with anyone who was interested. On September 12, 1898, he stood before a meeting of the Minnesota Historical Society and read a lengthy paper entitled "Recollections of St. Paul." Included among his remarks were some interesting and revealing comments about Edward Phelan and the murder charges against him.

> *Edward Phelan (or Phalen) was one of those simple, plain, uneducated Irishmen…One morning in September, 1839, Hays was missing. The body was recovered in the river near Carver's Cave. Phelan was arrested, taken to Prairie du Chien, then remained in prison for over six months, was tried and acquitted. He never killed Hays; the Indians have told me since that Hays was not killed by Phelan. They always spoke to me as though they knew who did kill*

*him ... Old Phelan was human. He took his toddy, too, but he would
not injure a hair of your head while I knew him.*[34]

What can we fairly deduce from the recollections of this sev-
enty-five-year old pioneer made almost sixty years after the murder
of Hays? Larpenteur claimed that Phelan "would not injure a hair
on your head while I knew him," but the earliest Larpenteur could
have known Phelan was three years after Phelan returned from his
murder acquittal, after spending six months in the Prairie du Chien
jail. By that time Phelan might have been a somewhat changed man,
perhaps a little less aggressive than he might have been back in 1839.
Nevertheless, Larpenteur's defense of "Old Phelan" was one of the
few times in recorded history that someone said something positive
about Edward Phelan.

The key part of Larpenteur's remarks was his assertion that Phelan
"never killed Hays." Most significantly, he claimed that the Indians
told him that "Hays was not killed by Phelan," and though they never
divulged who had killed Sergeant Hays, "they always spoke as though
they knew who did kill him." Although Larpenteur repeatedly used
the general term "Indians," there is no question that he was referring
specifically to the Mdewakanton Dakota band from Little Crow's
Kaposia village; they were the only Indians he regularly traded with,
and Dakota was the only Indian language he understood.[35]

The significance of Larpenteur's claim is that James Thompson
was not the only early St. Paul settler who attributed the death of
Sergeant Hays to the local Indians. His account suggests that Indians
themselves implied to him that they knew who the killer was, and it
wasn't a white man. Larpenteur never said a word about a Dakota's
confession to Sergeant Hays' murder even though he specifically dis-
cussed the battle of Kaposia in his "Recollections," but his account
doesn't contradict Thompson's story. Larpenteur's impression that
the local Dakota knew who killed Hays coincides with Thompson's
belief that a local Dakota (Do-wau) confessed to the murder in 1842.

CHAPTER SIX

Larpenteur, of course, was in St. Louis in 1842 and nowhere near the Dakota. His first "chance to see a live Indian" didn't come until after he arrived in St. Paul in September 1843. By November, however, he apparently acquired "sufficient knowledge of the [Dakota] language to get along nicely with them in trade, and in a couple of years become quite proficient."[36]

Larpenteur's conversations with the Dakota about Sergeant Hays' murder must not have occurred until at least November 1843, fourteen months after the 1842 battle of Kaposia, and four years after Sergeant Hays' death. Based on what Larpenteur said, and what he did not say, in his "Recollections" (which were partly his autobiography), it seems that he was not personally close to James Thompson. If he had been, Thompson surely would have told him the story of Dowau's confession—and Larpenteur likely would have repeated it in the "Recollections."

What should we make of August Larpenteur's remarks as a defense of Edward Phelan? How credible is St. Paul's longest surviving pioneer and how trustworthy are his recollections? Like Thompson, there is little in Larpenteur's known life to cause one to question his honesty and the general truthfulness of his stories. It would appear that Larpenteur, a native of Baltimore and descendent of a French soldier in Napoleon's army, was a frank, articulate, honorable man, with a slight flair for the dramatic, who knew what he was talking about when he spoke about early St. Paul. His remarks about the local Dakota were clearly drawn from his first-hand experiences as a fur trader and as a resident of a frontier river town which, before the Dakota were removed to a reservation in 1853, was always "thronged with Indians." Even as late as 1849, visiting writer E.S. Seymour described St. Paul as,

*near the dividing line of civilized and savage life. We can look across the river and see Indians on their own soil. Their canoes are seen gliding across the Mississippi, to and fro between the savage and civilized territory. They are met hourly in the streets.*[37]

Unlike James Thompson, however, Larpenteur had no family connections to the Dakota. He did not marry a Dakota woman, like so many other fur traders did, but instead married St. Paul's first German immigrant, Mary Presley, in 1845, the sister of Bartlett Presley, who later helped found and develop the St. Paul Fire Department.[38]

Interestingly, in Larpenteur's "Recollections" he recalls a revealing and relevant incident of one Indian's violent attack on him and Mary in his St. Paul home.

> *It was a dark and dismal night. My wife had retired. I was about closing up. There were embers aglow in the fireplace, when a knock was heard at the door. We were alone. I opened the door, when an Indian came in, seating himself by the fire. I was in hope that after he had warmed himself he would get up and go away. I entertained him as well as I could, but he became very abusive, and before I could think he drew his knife and was in the act of making a plunge at me, when my wife in her white sleeping gown appeared in the door, thus diverting his attention, which gave me the opportunity of grabbing his hand in which he held the knife, and disarming him. I was his equal then. I left him a fit subject for the cemetery, and threw him over the bluff. Next morning he crawled up and came into the house, and I assisted him to perform his ablutions and gave him a good brekfast. We parted friends, and were friends ever thereafter. Such scenes as these were not infrequent to wives and mothers of the pioneers of Minnesota.*[39]

This dramatic story is filled with telling tidbits, though it should be acknowledged that it was only Larpenteur's version of an incident, and told nearly fifty years after it occurred. Assuming the story is essentially true, it shows once again that unsuspecting settlers were occasionally violently attacked by the Dakota, seemingly without provocation. (Recall the incident when nine or ten Dakota broke into Vetal Guerin and Adele Perry's cabin.) What is striking in Larpenteur's story is both the seriousness of the attack—the Dakota lunged at Larpenteur with a knife—and how seemingly unprovoked it was. According to Larpenteur's account, he and his wife had done nothing to incite the Dakota to violence. Indeed, according to Larpenteur, far from provoking him, Larpenteur returned rudeness with courtesy by permitting the intruder to warm himself by the hearth and then "entertain him as well as [he] could."[40]

This incident relates to the issue of motive: the apparent lack of motive in this case of the attempted murder of Larpenteur might apply to the actual murder of Sergeant Hays. What motive did any Dakota have for attacking Larpenteur, or attacking and killing Hays? Ben Gervais testified that Phelan reported that the missing calf returned shortly after Sergeant Hays had left his land; hence, it hadn't been stolen and thus there wouldn't have been any altercation between Hays and the Dakota over the return of the stolen calf. Therefore, what reason did any Dakota have to kill Hays? But Larpenteur's anecdote about the knife-wielding Dakota reveals a different perspective on the issue of motive. The attack on Larpenteur—and for that matter, the attack on Vetal Guerin—shows that in some cases there is no understandable motive behind acts of human violence. Had Larpenteur's assailant been interviewed, he might have revealed his motive, and it might have been understandable. Perhaps he had a dispute with Larpenteur, or maybe he was just a thief who was willing to kill a white settler and take what he wanted. Or, maybe he resented whites in general, perhaps fur traders in particular, and took it out on Larpenteur (what would be known today as a racially-motivated hate crime). In any event, we have no way of knowing the Dakota's reasons were for attacking Larpenteur without a record of his version of events. The Dakota, like all pre-modern American Indian tribes, did not have a written language, and from the standpoint of Larpenteur, Guerin, and a number of other local settlers who reported incidents of Dakota attacks, there was no motive for attack or violence that they could understand. In most cases, the search for convincing, conventional motives for Dakota assaults on local settlers is as futile as the search for written testimony from local Dakota.

Larpenteur's story of being almost knifed to death by a Dakota in his "Recollections" provides some additional evidence for Phelan's defense: the story simply confirms the fact that sometimes some Dakota would assault local settlers for no apparent reason. That, as any of Phelan's defenders might argue, was exactly what could have happened to Sergeant Hays.

Larpenteur's story also reveals something about the storyteller. Apparently August Larpenteur was not just physically quick, strong, and tough—he overpowered his assailant and threw him over the cliff—but his moral character was remarkable. He forgave his assailant the next morning, fed him breakfast, and went on to become his life long friend. Larpenteur's quick forgiveness and generosity toward his would-be killer was extraordinary behavior for a victim of an assault. In today's world that would be incredible. But the frontier fur trading world was a strange one. A fur trader like Larpenteur, who was largely dependent on the Dakota for his livelihood, may have learned a level of tolerance toward his native partners that people outside the fur trading business or the frontier world would not understand. It is not unreasonable to be a little skeptical about Larpenteur's story, but that episode and the rest of his "Recollections" clearly reveals one salient character trait: August Larpenteur was not prejudiced against the Dakota. His lack of prejudice toward the Dakota is critically important in assessing the accuracy of his accounts of the one Dakota who tried to kill him, and particularly those Dakota who insinuated that Sergeant Hays' killer came from their band. In other words, they cannot be dismissed as the words of someone who was predisposed against the Indians.

In the final analysis, August Larpenteur would have been a credible defense witness for Edward Phelan. Even though his account of the Dakotas' intimation about Hays' murder lacked elaboration and context which does raise questions, it could stand by itself as sound support for the theory that John Hays was killed by one or more local Dakota. Joined with Thompson's story of the Dakota who confessed to the murder, the two accounts together make that theory even more compelling.

CHAPTER SIX

## Revisiting James Clewett

Is there anyone else that would further corroborate the allegation that Sergeant Hays was killed by one or more local Dakota? There is, and he is not a new witness. J. Fletcher Williams, who was himself convinced that Phelan was the true murderer of Hays, dutifully acknowledged that fur trader James Clewett—one of the canoeists who gave damaging testimony against Phelan in 1839—told him that he also had reason to believe that an Indian murdered Hays. It gets better for Phelan: Clewett's account has striking similarities to James Thompson's sensational story.

> J. R. Clewett says he thought, at the time, the Indians had committed the murder; and that one Indian, a few years afterward, just before his death, confessed that he was the murderer of Hays; also, that some of the Kaposia Indians used to assert that a brother of Little Crow had committed the act.[41]

Here we have another local fur trader, who by definition would have been very familiar with the local Indians, essentially supporting the claims of both Thompson and Larpenteur, and even adding a new important detail of his own. Clewett's statement confirms Larpenteur's story that local Dakota more or less admitted that Sergeant Hays' murderer was from the Kaposia village. More significantly, his statement supports Thompson's claim that a Dakota confessed to the murder "a few years afterward, just before his death." Although he did not mention the battle of Kaposia, or name the confessing killer as "Do-wau"—key details in Thompson's story—he did say that "some of the Kaposia Indians used to assert that a brother of Little Crow had committed the act."

It is not clear whether Clewett was giving one or two different accounts of who the murderer was. Was he saying that he heard one account that "one Indian, a few years afterward, just before he died, confessed that he was the murderer of Hays," and then later heard a

106

second story that "a brother of Little Crow had committed the act"? Or was his account simply a progression of information about only one alleged killer, a brother of Little Crow, who was the same Indian who "confessed that he was the murderer of Hays"? In either case, it is critical to know if there is any evidence, outside of the Thompson and Larpenteur sources, that could verify any of the information that Clewett revealed, in particular, whether Little Crow had a brother who had died at, or close to the time of, the battle of Kaposia?

Gary Clayton Anderson, the foremost modern scholar of the most famous of the Little Crows—Ta-o-ya-te-du-ta, the leader of the Dakota Uprising of 1862 (one of the bloodiest Indian rebellions in American history)—has researched the genealogy of the Little Crow dynasty. First, there is no doubt that the Little Crow Clewett refers to was the famous leader of the uprising—who Anderson calculated was born at Kaposia about 1810 and was the oldest son of Chief Big Thunder. According to Anderson, Ta-o-ya-te-du-ta (His Red Nation, or Little Crow after 1846), "had ten half brothers, and ten half sisters."[42] Two of those half-brothers were reportedly "killed during a raid on the Ojibway in 1841."[43] Although that 1841 raid was not the 1842 battle of Kaposia, they were directly connected. The 1841 Dakota raid on the Ojibwe, which occurred at Lake Poke-gama near present-day Pine City, provoked the Ojibwe to retaliate by raiding Kaposia the next year. (The Dakota would argue that their raid on the Ojibwe was retaliation for an earlier Ojibwe attack on some Dakota.) Return Ira Holcomb—the first historian of Minnesota to publish in the twentieth century and an excellent source of choice detail—noted that those two half-brothers of Little Crow were killed by Ojibwe snipers about a mile above St. Croix Falls when the Dakota were en route to Pokegama, in May 1841.

*Their names were Tah Mahzah Waukon, or His Spirit Iron and Dowan, or Sing; the latter was also called the Left Hand. They were half brothers of Tah-o-yah-te-Dou-tah, or the Little Crow of 1862.*[44]

107

Perhaps now some of the pieces of the puzzle are coming together. Most significantly, this account corroborates exactly what Clewett said: that Little Crow had a brother (actually two brothers) who died a few years after Hays' murder. Moreover, that brother was known as "Dowan, the Sing," and this name is clearly a variant of the name "Do-wau, the Singer" that Thompson gave to the confessing Dakota murderer in his story.

Holcomb's evidence appears to verify much of what Clewett told Williams. Drawing together the information from Anderson, Holcomb, Clewett, Thompson, and Larpenteur, we can make the following logical deductions:

- A brother of Little Crow (and son of Big Thunder) named "Do-wau" or "Dowan"—the "Singer" or the "Sing"—was killed, along with another brother, by two Ojibwe snipers in May 1841 while a Kaposia war party was en route to attack the Ojibwe at Lake Pokegama on the Snake River, roughly seventy miles north of present-day St. Paul.

- If Do-wau the Singer was the "fatally shot" man who Thompson claimed confessed to Hays' murder, then that confession could not have taken place at the 1842 battle of Kaposia, because it is documented, not just by Holcomb but also by Neill, that he died more than a year before and over fifty miles away from the Kaposia battle site.

- Since Do-wau did not die at the battle of Kaposia, then any notion that Thompson, his wife, or his son-in-law Thomas Odell could have been close enough to the mortally wounded warrior to hear his dying words is not plausible. According to Holcomb's elaborate account of the "Attack on Pokegama," the only witnesses to the death of Do-wau were his fellow Dakota warriors. The earlier theory that at least one member of the Thompson

family, Thomas Odell, could have been close by the supposed death scene of Do-wau is no longer valid.

- If Do-wau did confess to killing Sergeant Hays, then only
warriors from Kaposia could have heard it. Thus, one or
more of those warriors had to be the source of the dying
confession story—although the original details may have
differed greatly from what was later reported. In other
words, it was local Dakota, not white witnesses, who
originally spread the story of Do-wau's dying confession
of Sergeant Hays' murder, however distorted it may have
become.

- Since one key detail in Thompson's story—that Do-wau
was "fatally shot at the battle of Kaposia"—is demonstra-
bly false, then the detail that Do-wau confessed to Sergeant Hays' murder may also be incorrect. Although the
close connection of the two raids—Kaposia and Pokegama—makes the mix-up of the two more understandable, the mistake lessens the credibility of Thompson's
story. One of the story's most compelling features was its
inclusion of identifying details. The fact that one of those
details is false seriously undermines its credibility.

One more point to ponder: does the new information about the
sons of Chief Big Thunder and half-brothers of Little Crow shed any
light on Phelan's story of the alleged confrontation between Sergeant
Hays and a reckless, gun-firing young Dakota at their cabin shortly
before his murder? Phelan had told Henry Sibley "a few days after"
Sergeant Hays' body had been found that "one young Indian came to
the house about two months ago and was taking aim with his gun at
things in the house." According to Phelan, Sergeant Hays "told him
to stop" but the Indian ignored the warning and took "aim at a looking glass in the house." Sergeant Hays ultimately had to grab the gun
away from the young Indian and force him out of the house. Though
Sergeant Hays did return the gun to him, he angrily "told the Indian

if he came back he would club him." Then either Sergeant Hays or Phelan, or both, "followed the Indian up the hill and saw him load his gun and he threatened to tell Waultietankaa [Wakinyantonka—Chief Big Thunder] about it." Phelan described the unruly, threatening Dakota as "a very young man, about eighteen years of age."[45]

If Phelan's story was true, it could be possible that the unruly, eighteen-year-old gun-shooter was one of Chief Big Thunder's sons. The young Dakota was quick to invoke Big Thunder's name ("he threatened to tell Waultietankaa [Wakinyantonka—Chief Big Thunder] about it"), and Big Thunder had at least ten sons. It would work wonderfully for Phelan's defense if Dowan and the unruly young Dakota in Phelan's story were one and the same. The statements of Thompson, Larpenteur, and Clewett would then fit nicely into Phelan's account that a brash, bold Dakota confronted Sergeant Hays in the summer of 1839. Imagine how well the evidence would tie together if that same Dakota was the killer of Sergeant Hays and the brother of Little Crow who Thompson called "Do-wau," and who Clewett said confessed to the murder "just before his death." However, the evidence is too scant to verify a connection between the young Dakota in Phelan's story and the brother of Little Crow named Do-wau or Dowan. And there is no way to prove the truth and accuracy of Phelan's story about the Dakota from Little Crow's village who visited their cabin in the summer of 1839.

## Sibley's Perspective and the Plausibility that Indians Killed Hays

Despite what James Clewett told him about an Indian confession, J. Fletcher Williams was convinced that Edward Phelan murdered Sergeant Hays. Why did Williams disregard Clewett's seemingly credible statement and reject the theory that someone from Kaposia had killed Sergeant Hays? Apparently Williams was more impressed with the information Minnesota's most prominent fur trader, Henry Sibley, gave him. Sibley told Williams that it would have been "impossible" for any local Dakota to kill Sergeant Hays and keep it a secret from him. "Had any Indian committed the act he (Gen. S.) would certainly have found it out."[46] Sibley's confidence may have been warranted. He certainly knew the Dakota very well and had family connections to them through his first wife, Red Blanket Woman, who bore his first child in August 1841.[47]

Sibley was well respected by the Dakota. Minnesota pioneer William LeDuc recalled Sibley's close relationship with the Dakota. "He was the 'Great Trader' of the Indians…and adopted into the Sioux tribe the language of which he spoke as well or better than the Indians." LeDuc also noted that Sibley was "a good friend of Little Crow" (or Big Thunder), the Chief of the Kaposia village. In fact, LeDuc claimed that when the old chief was dying, one of his last requests was to see his friend Sibley and then tell his people that they should "listen to his advice and follow his directions" and especially remember to "never quarrel with the whites." (Big Thunder died in October 1845 from an accidental gunshot wound.)[48]

But it still may seem a bit presumptuous of Sibley to insist that no murder by a Kaposia Dakota could have been kept hidden from him. His Dakota wife was not from Kaposia but came from Black Dog's village, located on the Minnesota River at Black Dog Lake in present-day Eagan.[49] Moreover, Sibley's responsibilities as the regional coordinator of Minnesota's Dakota trade forced him to deal not just with Kaposia, but with over a dozen other Dakota villages, stretching from present-day Winona to Lake Traverse and Big Stone Lake on the South Dakota border. The time Sibley devoted to the affairs of Kaposia was limited and maybe no more than the time he devoted to the other villages close to his Mendota home, like Black Dog, Good Roads (in present-day Bloomington), and Tintontowan—or Shakpays (at present-day Shakopee). Maybe incidents occurred at Kaposia that Sibley didn't know about—perhaps even a murder? Sibley might have responded that he never pretended to know every incident at the Kaposia village. His only claim was that he "certainly" would have known about any extremely serious crime, like the murder of an innocent white man.

But Sibley's strong skepticism that the local Dakota were involved in Sergeant Hays' murder did not stem from a romantic notion of the Dakota as "noble savages"—gentle, peace-loving people who would kill only in self-defense. Years later, on February 1, 1856, at an annual meeting of the Minnesota Historical Society,* Sibley himself recounted instances of Dakota murdering Fort Snelling soldiers and concealing their bodies. Sibley's remarks, read from his paper entitled, "Reminiscences; Historical and Personal," are particularly relevant to the Hays' murder. But whether they help or hurt Phelan's defense is another paradox to unravel.

> *A number of American soldiers, supposed by their officers and comrades to have shamefully deserted their colors, had in reality been ruthlessly slain, and their bodies concealed by Dakota bands. Several of such cases were brought to light in after years by the traders, and avowed by the Indians themselves. One soldier was shot, and his body secreted near Lake Calhoun—another was disposed of in like manner, about two miles below Mendota—and I myself discovered the skeleton of a white man, not far from my present place of residence, which bore the mark of a bullet in the skull, and which was recognized as the remains of a soldier by the strips of clothing found in the immediate vicinity. On one occasion, Alexander Faribault, while descending the Mississippi in a boat in company with others, found at the head of Lake Pepin, four dead bodies of soldiers, partly devoured by birds of prey. The fate of these men elicited but little sympathy, for they were engaged in an attempt to desert when they were set upon and butchered, by certain Dakotas of the Red Wing Band.*[50]

Here we have even more evidence of Dakota inflicting violence on white people, only this time the violence is murder and the victims were Fort Snelling soldiers—as Hays once was. These vivid

---

*Sibley was a great preserver and promoter of Minnesota history and spent the last twelve years of his life serving as president of the Minnesota Historical Society.

accounts can cut both ways. So many reports of Dakota violence against whites during Minnesota's frontier era strengthens the theory that Sergeant Hays could have been killed by one or more Dakota. After reading Sibley's account of the many bodies of murdered soldiers found up and down the river, it is easy to imagine that Sergeant Hays, walking alone downriver to Kaposia, could have been killed by one or more of the villagers. Their motive, whatever it might have been, is less important than the established fact that the Dakota did kill white people and try to hide the crime.

On the other hand, the murder of several white soldiers by Dakota strengthens the theory presented earlier concerning an alternate meaning of Do-wau's dying confession. Do-wau may have confessed to murdering a white soldier, but the soldier may have been a deserter, or someone other than John Hays. If that was the case, then consider how the evidence would fit together, without the necessity of assuming that anyone lied: Do-wau confesses to killing a white soldier (one of the deserters) but the Dakota warriors who hear it wrongly conclude that he was referring to Sergeant Hays. Those warriors then tell other Kaposia villagers what they believe to be the truth: that Do-wau confessed to Hays' murder. The story spreads and fur traders like James Clewett and August Larpenteur honestly pick up their versions of the story, and James Thompson's Dakota wife and Dakota stepdaughter honestly pick up their version of the story. None of the sources of the story (who all seem credible) were deliberately lying; they were honestly passing on misinformation. In the case of Thompson, putting Do-wau's death scene at the wrong place and time was an honest mix-up that could have been introduced not by Thompson, but by the writer who interviewed him, Thomas Newson.

One final point on the dead soldiers Sibley reported: Sibley mentioned that "one soldier was shot…and then another disposed of in a like manner" and yet another "bore the mark of a bullet in the skull." Although he never specified whether the other bodies also had "bullets in the skull," the fact that three soldiers were shot shows that at least three victims of the Dakota were killed in a much different way than was Hays. Hays was clubbed to death by repeated blows to the face. Even though there is ample evidence of the Dakota clubbing and hacking their enemies to death (the tomahawk and war club were ancient weapons), the Dakota clearly had a preference and fascination for firearms, weapons they had traded for since the late seventeenth century. (Phelan's story of the gun-firing Dakota is an illustration of that point.) One might argue that the condition of Hays' body—no bullet wounds, and only a battered face, with no indication of scalping and no cuts on the rest of the body—indicated it was not a Dakota killing. And that raises the question: how did the Dakota customarily kill their enemy?

According to Presbyterian missionary Samuel Pond, who knew the Dakota intimately and was one of Minnesota's best authorities on the tribe, there were different ways and means of killing their enemy and treating their bodies, depending on the situation.

> *[The Dakota] very rarely, if ever, tried to prolong the agony of those that they killed, but dispatched them at once and cut their dead bodies to pieces…It was considered unmanly to shoot women and children, unless they were likely to escape by flight; and unless they chose to take them captives, they commonly killed them with knives, spears, war clubs, or hatchets. To seize a man who was not wounded and kill him with a knife, was considered an act of bravery worthy of the highest applause, and the Dakotas sometimes needlessly lost their lives in attempting to kill wounded men with knives and clubs.*[51]

Pond also respectfully explained the Dakota tradition of taking the scalps of enemy dead.

> *The scalps of the slain were always taken if possible, for if these trophies were not secured no honors were awarded. Nothing but the scalp was received as proof that an enemy had been killed, for if any other evidence had been admitted there would have been danger of imposition or exaggeration, when the war party was very small. When they*

*were hard pressed by the enemy and had no time to take the whole*
*scalp, they might seize a lock of hair and cut off a piece of skin with*
*it...In scalping a female, the Dakotas took only that part of the skin*
*of the head on which the hair grows; but from a man they took the*
*skin of the whole head, except the nose and upper lip, the skin of the*
*cheeks and chin being taken with the ears also attached to the scalp.*
*It took some time to scalp a man properly; and if they dared not stay*
*where one was killed long enough to do it, they cut off the head and*
*carried it with them till they had leisure to take off the scalp.*[52]

Based on Dr. Emerson's report, it was clear that Sergeant Hays'
body was neither scalped, shot, nor "cut to pieces." That might be
evidence that Sergeant Hays was not killed by Dakota. However, Sibley never mentioned that any of the dead soldiers, who he said were
killed by Dakota, were scalped. If those soldiers were only shot, why
didn't their Dakota killers follow the tradition of scalping them? One
plausible answer is that the Dakota traditionally took the scalps of
their enemies, above all the Ojibwe, and the whites were not considered their enemies at that time. Indeed, due to a series of treaties the
Dakota had with the U.S. government, gifts and services provided to
them by the Indian agent and Christian missionaries, and the close
relationships and blood ties they had with the fur traders, the Dakota
generally considered the whites of the region their friends and allies.
Although the relationship between the two peoples was far from perfect and had its tensions, the Dakota were dependent on the whites
for their trade goods—guns, knives, iron hatchets, iron traps, woolen
blankets, etc.—that were increasingly considered necessities. The
Dakota also had realistic respect for the awesome power of the United
States military, impressively represented by Fort Snelling. In other
words, killing a white was not like killing an Ojibwe to the Dakota.
Indeed, if a Dakota killed a white, he probably would have been rep-
rimanded by his chief. Furthermore, the scalp of a white man would
not be a prized trophy like the scalp of an Ojibwe would be, but only
evidence of a crime. The leaders of the local Dakota knew all too

well that the killing of one white man might lead to white retribution on their entire village. Hence the Dakota who killed the white soldiers were probably not just hiding the killings from the whites but also from their fellow Dakota. It is relevant to note that it was a local Dakota, "directed by his chief," who first reported the discovery of Sergeant Hays' body to Major Taliaferro, telling evidence that the local Dakota did make efforts to maintain a friendly, cooperative relationship with the whites. But it might also be a clue that they weren't the ones who killed Hays.

What all this means is another enigma: Sergeant Hays' body did not bear the signs of a Dakota killing but that still doesn't necessarily mean that he was not killed by a Dakota. We have already explained why a Dakota might not have scalped him. But a rogue Dakota might well have bashed in Hays' face with a war club or even a canoe paddle. After all, Phelan was not the only one who had a canoe paddle.

So far we have considered only two suspects in the murder of Sergeant Hays: Edward Phelan and some Dakota Indian. But are there any other potential suspects? Although it's possible that some other settler, soldier, trader, or traveler could have committed the murder, there is no direct evidence to support that theory. Historians Helen and Bruce White meticulously calculated the entire non-Indian population of the Fort Snelling region for 1838 and reported the following interesting statistics: "231 enlisted men and 12 officers, as well as a handful of servants and washer women" residing inside the fort; and "365 civilian non-Indian people, some settlers, some involved in the fur trade, others working for the Indian Department" residing outside the fort (which could be as close as Mendota and as far as Lake Pepin and Lake Traverse).[53] In other words, there were roughly six hundred non-Indian people living in the greater Fort Snelling region (present-day southern Minnesota) at the time of Sergeant Hays' murder. Although in theory almost any able bodied man in that group could have been a potential suspect, realistically only a tiny number of them would have had the motive, means, and opportunity, not to mention the deviant moral character, to actually commit that brutal murder.

## Are There Any Other Suspects?

The only local settler aside from Phelan who was reputed to have a deviant character was the infamous Pierre "Pig's Eye" Parrant. Indeed, Parrant almost matches Phelan in the conspicuously negative way he was depicted by Minnesota historians. J. Fletcher Williams, the first writer to vividly describe Parrant, presented a very unflattering picture of him:

> *He bore not the most enviable character ... Parrant's personal appearance may have formed the estimate of his character. He was a coarse, ill-looking, low-browed fellow, with only one eye and that a sinister looking one—[which was] marble-hued, crooked, with a sinister white ring glaring around the pupil, giving a kind of piggish expression to his sodden, low features ... He spoke execrable English. His habits were intemperate and licentious.*[54]

Other writers conformed to Williams' low opinion of Parrant. Thomas Newson called him "an ugly looking fellow but no doubt brave....a Canadian voyageur, with a bad reputation and sinister features."[55] The Rev. Edward Neill described Parrant as "ignorant and overbearing—he loved money more than his soul."[56] Colonel John Hankins—a writer from New York who traveled to St. Paul in 1867, did some research on Parrant and then published a semi-fictional history of the city two years later—concluded that Parrant was "a rum fiend...a frontier rum seller. He had a miserly heart and loved nothing better than gold."[57] Christopher C. Andrews, author of *History of St. Paul, Minnesota* (1890), wrote that "Pierre Parrant was a lawless fellow who felt the chief end of man was to drink and sell whiskey."[58]

If this was a work of fiction the "sinister looking" Pig's Eye Parrant would be the perfect character to cast as the alternative suspect in the Hays murder mystery. But whether Pig's Eye was a viable suspect in the murder of Sergeant Hays is open to question. Conveniently for Phelan, Parrant was Phelan and Hays' nearest neighbor at the time of the murder. According to Williams, Pig's Eye moved from Fountain Cave to "what is now the foot of Robert Street" and built "a hovel in which to reside and carry on his liquor trade" in May 1839 after defaulting on a ninety dollar loan in which his saloon was collateral.[59] Thus, at the time of Sergeant Hays' disappearance (September 6), the "licentious" Pig's Eye Parrant was living about seven blocks downriver from Phelan's Landing. Was Pig's Eye's close proximity to Phelan and Sergeant Hays' home enough evidence to consider him a valid suspect in Hays' murder?

Though it was undisputed that Parrant had a "bad reputation," one man who actually knew him defended his character. Ironically, he was the same pioneer who defended Phelan—August Larpenteur:

*The only offense I could charge him with if it could be called an offense, was that he sold whiskey. Well tell me who didn't? His word in a deal was as good as any other man's whose word was good at all.*[60]

Unlike the historians who depicted Phelan as a big, "bad," "ruffian," no historian ever depicted Parrant as being a "dangerous person"—someone really "cruel, revengeful" and "wicked."[61] Though as a young voyageur in Canada he once reportedly got into a knife fight that cost him an eye, there is no evidence that Parrant ever engaged in violence after he moved to present-day Minnesota as a middle-aged whiskey trader around 1830. According to Williams, he was "probably sixty years of age" in 1838.[62] Aside from Major Taliaferro and some officers at Fort Snelling, who all denounced his liquor trading, there is no evidence that he had any serious dispute or quarrel with any non-Indian in the region, except for one claim dispute he had with Michael LeClaire in February 1840 that was peacefully settled.[63] Moreover, there is also no evidence that Parrant ever had any dealings with Sergeant Hays, let alone disputes with him. Given

Pig's Eye's notorious reputation, investigators at the time—and historians who later interviewed those knowledgeable about the murder case—would have automatically suspected him if there had been even the slightest evidence against him, and historians would have reported it. The fact that his name is never mentioned as a suspect by any writer who wrote about the murder of Sergeant Hays is telling. Equally telling is that none of the witnesses who testified at Justice Brown's inquiry ever mentioned Parrant, or even hinted that the old whiskey trader had any connection to Sergeant Hays' murder.

Henry Sibley and Joseph R. Brown—the only known investigators of Hays' murder—were responsible for investigating all plausible suspects. We can only assume that their focus on Edward Phelan as the prime suspect was not an irresponsible rush to judgment. How thoroughly they investigated the murder is of course not known because, outside of Brown's casebook, all the records of the murder case have been lost, and we can only speculate about the scope and thoroughness of Sibley and Brown's investigations. J. Fletcher Williams did state that Sibley "carefully sifted the evidence" before reaching his "no doubt" conclusion of "Phelan's guilt."[64] Whether Sibley's "carefully sifting the evidence" included a consideration of potential suspects other than Phelan is unclear. But it is not unreasonable to assume that it did.

Being a historian inherently involves having some degree of trust in what dead people tell us. In the end, we have to ask ourselves how much we trust J. Fletcher Williams as an honest and competent historian and how much we trust Henry Sibley and Joseph R. Brown as honest and competent investigators. If we trust Williams, it is significant that he reported only two murder suspects: Edward Phelan—who he said "of Phelan's guilt no one who was a resident in this vicinity had any doubt"—and "a brother of Little Crow," who he said Sibley completely rejected as the murderer. And Phelan himself stated that he was "not aware that [Hays] had any difficulty with any white man."[65]

# CHAPTER SEVEN

# Who Killed John Hays? Following the Evidence to a Logical Conclusion

In light of all the available evidence relevant to the question of who killed Sgt. John Hays, only two explanations are plausible. Either Edward Phelan killed Hays, or he was killed by local Dakota. Any theory that Phelan and an Indian or Indians collaborated in the murder of Hays is simply not plausible. The key to solving the mystery— if it can be solved at all—is to determine which explanation has the greater capacity for integrating all the evidence together, especially those statements that seem to contradict each other. It all comes down to following the logical consequences of each explanation and then seeing which one ends up as the most reasonable. This case—with all its missing documents, unrecorded evidence, conflicting statements, confusing testimonies and not even one direct statement from any local Indian—poses an extraordinary challenge. To borrow a phrase from Winston Churchill, it is "a riddle, wrapped in a mystery, inside an enigma." Nevertheless, if we are patient and persistent in our use of logic and common sense, we should be able to determine which explanation of Hays' murder is more reasonable.

Let us explore the logical consequences of each explanation. Since more time has been spent considering the evidence against Phelan—the case for believing that he alone killed Hays—we will start with the alternative explanation of the murder. If a Dakota (presumably Do-wau) killed Hays, then Phelan was innocent of the murder. If Phelan did not kill Hays, he would have no discernible reason to make up a story about his activities or whereabouts the last time he saw Hays. An innocent person might lie to protect a loved one but Phelan, a bachelor, had no loved ones around to protect. An innocent Phelan would have had no reason to lie about a lost calf or about transporting Hays across the river to look for it on the morning of Friday, September 6, 1839. If Phelan were innocent, then it would have to be generally true that Phelan did in fact transport Hays across the river on that Friday morning after he walked home from Evans' house, and that Hays was killed sometime later, presumably on the west side of the river, on his way to Kaposia. If that is the case, then those events must be reconciled with the sworn statements of Stephen Scott, John Foy, Henry Mencke, and James Clewett.

However, those statements contradict key parts of Phelan's account. If Phelan told the truth about what he did that morning, then we must conclude that Scott, Foy, Mencke, and Clewett were either lying or just honestly mistaken—but very mistaken—about what they remember they saw and did that morning. The fact that they all told essentially the same story— that they did not see Phelan canoe "across" the river that morning as he claimed and that it took two of the men (Scott and Foy) no more than an hour, and maybe less, to canoe to his landing after leaving him at Evans' house—makes it unlikely that all those men were deliberately lying. To believe that they were lying is to believe that this motley group of frontiersmen—two lumbermen, an English fur trader, and a Germanic liquor dealer—somehow conspired together to tell the same basic false story. What motive would they have for lying under oath?

But if the four men were not lying, and if Phelan also was not lying, then we must assume that they each made honest mistakes in their recollections of time and/or their memories of events. Their recollections of time are, of course, quite critical. Earlier we covered in detail the seemingly impossible time problem Phelan would have had in order to perform all the necessary tasks we have established he had to do on the Friday morning he walked home from Evans' house and then supposedly canoed Sergeant Hays across the river.

Phelan would have needed far more time to do those tasks than Scott, Foy, Clewett, and Mencke collectively gave him. Assuming Phelan did take Sergeant Hays across the river that Friday morning, is there a way to expand the time estimates of the witnesses in order to give Phelan more time to do those tasks and make the "seemingly impossible" possible? In other words, can we maximize the minutes Scott and Foy took to go from Evans' house to Phelan's Landing, and minimize the minutes Phelan needed to do tasks he said he did after he left Evans' house? The Friday morning travel time of Scott and Foy is, of course, critical because they were the witnesses who actually saw Phelan canoeing the river (but not crossing it), beaching his canoe at his landing and then walking back to his cabin, supposedly only about an hour or less after they had left him inside Williams Evans' house.

## Constructing Scott and Foy's Maximum Timeline

Let us start at the place where Phelan, Scott, and Foy all began that fateful morning: William Evans' house. It is an undisputed fact that Phelan, Scott, and Foy all had breakfast together with William Evans inside his home early Friday morning, September 6, 1839, and that after breakfast, Scott and Foy left Evans' house before Phelan did. Evans testified that Phelan left his house "probably a few minutes after" Scott and Foy did. It is also well established that Phelan walked approximately a mile and a half back to his cabin, while Scott and Foy canoed roughly the same distance to Phelan's Landing. Next, let's see if we can add some more minutes to Scott and Foy's travel time. What follows may at times seem tedious, but it is necessary detective work if we want to solve this murder. Neither Scott, Foy, nor any other witness mentioned how long it took them to walk from Evans' cabin to Evans' Landing on the river where their canoe was beached. In fact, we do not know the distance between Evans' house and his landing because we don't know the precise location of either place. The only source that mentions the location of Evans' house is J. Fletcher Williams, who notes only that it was "on Dayton's Bluff, near the Dayton mansion."[1] The Dayton mansion was the landmark home of Lyman Dayton (1820-65), the great local land developer of Dayton's Bluff, which in Williams' day stood on the present-day corner of Conway Street and Mounds Blvd.[2] But what exactly did Williams mean by "near the Dayton Mansion"? Fifty yards away? One block away? A half mile away? There is no way to know. But the fact that he said "on" Dayton's Bluff implies that Evans' cabin was on the top rather than at the bottom of the bluff. In that case, we can assume that Evans' house and his landing were—like Phelan's house and Phelan's Landing—not right next to each other. As for the location of Evans' Landing, we are left to assume that it was somewhere along the Dayton's Bluff riverfront. According to witnesses it was "near" or "a short distance from" or "30 rods" (165 yards) below a "sandbar."[3]

Earlier we speculated that the sandbar might have been at the mouth of Phalen Creek, which used to flow into the river below the west end of Dayton's Bluff until it was diverted underground into the sewer system in the twentieth century. Sandbars are commonly found at the mouths of creeks, so the speculation that the sandbar in question was in fact located at the mouth of Phalen Creek makes a great deal of sense. But the Mississippi River and its adjoining flood plain have been dramatically altered over the past one hundred and fifty years. The present-day Mississippi River is much deeper and narrower as it flows through St. Paul today than it was in 1839, due to the dredging by the Army Corps of Engineers and land filling of the levee by railroad and highway construction. According to local historian Josiah Cheney, author of the article, *"Early Bridges and Changes of the Land and Water in St. Paul" (1904)*, the Chicago, Milwaukee, and St. Paul Railroad alone filled in "about 3,000 feet," or "about 12 acres" of flood plain, from the mouth of Phalen Creek to the eastern end of downtown, "with an average width of 150 feet and a maximum width of about 240 feet."[4] Nineteenth century paintings and photographs of St. Paul show that below Dayton's Bluff the river widened into a bay that extended north over what is now Warner Road and the adjoining railroad tracks. Bearing this in mind, we can conclude that wherever Evans' Landing was located, it would have been much closer to the base of the bluff than any part of the riverfront is today.

But the question remains: how long did it take Scott and Foy to walk from Evans' house down to their canoe at his landing? According to the 1874 Andreas Atlas Street Map of St. Paul, it was about three or four blocks from the west end of Dayton's Bluff at Conway Street to the riverfront.[5] Thus, we might reasonably speculate that Evans' house was roughly four blocks from his landing. Incidentally, that would be only one block further than the known distance between Phelan's cabin and Phelan's Landing. If we use that educated guess of four blocks then we can make a conservative estimate that it took Scott and Foy at least five minutes to walk down to their canoe after leaving Evans' house sometime around eight o'clock Friday morning. Although we are now trying to maximize all time estimates for Scott and Foy, because of the extremely speculative nature of the time and distance guesses we just made, this is not the place to push the maximizing envelope.

After they reached Evans' Landing, Scott and Foy then canoed only a "short distance" upriver, which Scott estimated at "30 rods" (165 yards), before they stopped at a sandbar to wait for three men in a canoe (Clewett, Mencke, and Pierre Gervais), who were paddling from the other side of the river. Neither Scott nor Foy gave an estimate of how long it took them to canoe from Evans' Landing to the sandbar. Scott did state that "it could not be over half an hour from the time we left Evans' until we reached the sandbar." Earlier we raised the possibility that, given the context of his remarks, Scott might have meant to say, "until we 'left' the sandbar," rather than "until we 'reached' the sandbar."[6] Whatever he meant, Scott's phrase "it could not be over half an hour," could mean any amount of time under thirty minutes. In any case, two men in a "bark canoe" could certainly paddle 165 yards upriver in a few minutes. Is it then reasonable to estimate that Scott and Foy reached the sandbar no more than five minutes after they departed from Evans' Landing and close to ten minutes after they left Evans' house?

Foy estimated that they waited ten minutes at the sandbar for the other canoe to reach them from the opposite side of the river. James Clewett, who was in that other canoe, estimated their crossing time at "ten or fifteen minutes." Henry Mencke, who was also in that canoe, stated that they "saw them on shore at Evans' Landing within 20 minutes previous to our landing at the sandbar."[7] Since ten minutes, a figure used by both Foy and Clewett, is "within 20 minutes," it would seem that Foy's estimate of a ten-minute wait for the other canoe is quite reasonable, especially since Mencke's twenty minutes actually began when Scott and Foy were not at the sandbar but 165 yards downriver at Evans' Landing. Maximizing Scott and Foy's travel time within reason, we could more generously estimate that their wait for the other canoe was fifteen minutes, which was Clewett's maximum estimate. If we accept a fifteen-minute wait at the sandbar, we now have Scott and Foy at roughly twenty-five minutes past the time of their departure from Evans' house.

The next issue is the time Scott and Foy spent at the sandbar when the other canoe arrived. Exactly how many minutes Scott and Foy spent exchanging greetings and "a bottle of liquor" with the other men is subject to interpretation. Foy gave the shortest estimate: "remained long enough to get a bottle of liquor, say about ten minutes."[8] James Clewett gave the longest estimates: "Remained at the sandbar 15 or 20 minutes."[9] Henry Mencke's estimate was between Foy's and Clewett's calculations: "Did not remain on the sandbar to exceed 15 minutes."[10] However, Mencke also added that, "Scott and Foy left the bar, say five minutes before us."[11] If we subtract those five minutes from his original fifteen-minute estimate then we are left with generally the same ten-minute figure that Foy gave for the time he and Scott spent acquiring "a bottle of liquor" from Mencke, who was well known as a whiskey trader. All in all, the most reasonable estimate for this rendezvous at the sandbar would be between ten and fifteen minutes. Since we are trying to maximize Scott and Foy's travel time, we will use the higher (but still reasonable) estimate of fifteen minutes as the total time Scott and Foy spent with Mencke, Clewett, and Pierre Gervais at the sandbar, making their travel time since leaving Evans' house roughly forty minutes so far.

The next issue is the time it took Scott and Foy to canoe from the sandbar to Phelan's Landing. Foy never specified how long it took them to canoe from the sandbar to Phelan's Landing, but he did state that the total time they spent traveling from Evans' house to Phelan's Landing was "not more than half an hour."[12] Foy's estimate of at least twenty minutes on the sandbar (ten minutes waiting and ten minutes acquiring a bottle of liquor) leaves only ten minutes in his "not more than a half an hour" total time estimate for him and Scott to canoe from the sandbar to Phelan's Landing. But Foy never mentioned the time it took them to travel from Evans' house to the sandbar. We estimated that first leg of their journey took about ten minutes. With that estimate, can we conclude that Foy was thus estimating less than ten minutes for their at least a mile and a half canoe trip upriver from the sandbar to Phelan's Landing? That would certainly be a logical deduction. Foy's partner, Stephen Scott, estimated that "we were not more than a half hour coming from the bar to Phelan's Landing."[13] Though ten minutes technically qualifies as "not more than a half hour," thirty minutes would also technically qualify as "not more than a half hour." Scott's wording seems to imply a time span closer to thirty minutes than to ten minutes. Otherwise, he might have said "not more than 15 or 20 minutes."

But another key factor to consider in Scott's estimates is the start and end times he gave for that morning. He stated that they left Evans' house "at probably 8 o'clock in the morning" and then concluded his testimony with the revelation, "Suppose it was nine o'clock when we left Phelan's house."[14] Thus, by Scott's own estimated clock time, after departing from Evans' house all their activities that morning (walking, canoeing, visiting, etc.) consumed one hour. But Foy added a caveat: after docking at Phelan's Landing and walking ("about one fourth a mile," according to Scott) to Phelan's house, Foy said they "remained about 15 minutes at the house."[15] If Scott and Foy spent at least fifteen minutes at Phelan's house, not counting the unreported time it took them to walk from his landing up to the cabin, then we must deduct at least fifteen minutes from the hour of clock time Scott gave for the period between their departure from Evans' house and their departure from Phelan's house to determine how long it actually took them to go from Evans' house to Phelan's Landing. Working backwards, we might reasonably deduce that Scott's real estimate was no more than forty-five minutes for the men to reach Phelan's Landing after their departure from Evans' house.

So far we have allocated a generous forty minutes for the period spanning the time that Scott and Foy left Evans' house to the time they left the sandbar; that would leave them with a mere five minutes (from the forty-five minute total) to canoe from the sandbar to Phelan's Landing, clearly not enough time to paddle at least a mile and a half upriver. But since Scott only estimated the clock times, using the words "probably" and "suppose," we have some leeway to add time to Scott's clock. The critical point is that Foy and Scott are much closer in their time estimates than we might have first thought.

The two other witnesses in the other canoe, Clewett and Mencke, presented another perspective on the voyage from the sandbar to Phelan's Landing. Clewett stated that it took their canoe "about three quarters of an hour" to make that trip but noted important differences between the two canoes traveling the same distance.

*Scott and Foy having a bark canoe and nothing in it, went much faster than we did in our canoe being loaded. Suppose they must have gained one third of the distance between the sandbar and Phelan's Landing, which took us about three quarters of an hour.*[16]

In other words, Scott and Foy's lightweight "bark canoe" made the trip from the sandbar to Phelan's Landing in about one-third less time than Clewett, Mencke, and Gervais' "loaded" log canoe, or thirty minutes instead of forty-five. Clewett's thirty-minute estimate (one third less than 45 minutes) for Scott and Foy's trip from the sandbar to Phelan's Landing is considerably more time than the less than ten-minute estimate we deduced from Foy's testimony.

But Mencke's reckoning of time and distance was a little different from Clewett's. Like Clewett he agreed that their heavy canoe "took...about three-fourths of an hour" to travel "from the bar to Phalen's Landing." But his estimate of the speed of Scott and Foy's bark canoe differed from Clewett's: he "suppose[d] Scott and Foy traveled that distance in half the time," in other words, half of forty-five minutes, or roughly twenty to twenty-five minutes.[17]

Summarizing the estimates we have for Scott and Foy's voyage from the sandbar to Phelan's Landing, we have under ten minutes at the low end estimated from Foy's statement and thirty minutes at the high end estimated from Clewett's statement. And almost exactly in the middle is the twenty or so minutes estimated from Mencke's statement. Thus, the most generous, yet still reasonable estimate we can give for this leg of the trip is thirty minutes, approximately the same time Scott estimated, without making any logical deductions from his clock times.

Adding those thirty minutes to the previously calculated sum of forty minutes, we arrive at a total of seventy minutes maximum for Scott and Foy's complete trip from Evans' house to Phelan's Landing. That means that Phelan has a seventy-minute window of time (ten minutes more than previously estimated) to carry out the tasks he had to do, including transporting Hays across the river, on that eventful Friday morning. If Phelan was innocent and generally truthful in his testimony, we should be able to fit his tasks into a seventy-minute window.

## Constructing Phelan's Minimum Timeline

Reviewing those tasks again, now we'll minimize the time estimates, with an eye to Phelan's side of the time equation, starting again at Evans' house early Friday morning. Evans stated that Phelan left his house "probably a few minutes after" Scott and Foy did. (Scott gave the time of their departure "at probably 8 o'clock in the morning.")[18] "Probably a few minutes after" is imprecise but two minutes would seem to be the most minimum estimate for the time that elapsed between the departures of Scott and Foy and then Phelan. Phelan himself provided the only time estimate we have for his mile and a half walk in the swampy woods from Evans' house to his cabin. During cross-examination, Phelan gave the following statement:

*The morning I left Evans came nearly straight home—do not consider I lost any time with the little deviation from the direct route made in search of the calf. A man may walk from Evans' to my house in about half an hour.*[19]

Let us accept Phelan's own—perhaps self-serving—estimate of about a thirty-minute walk ("with little deviation") back to his home, so that now his minimum time consumption since leaving Evan's house is thirty-two minutes (or 8:32 on Scott's clock).

Once Phelan arrived at home a series of events supposedly transpired, some of which are impossible to accurately measure in time. One glaring uncertainty is the issue of Sergeant Hays' actions that morning—assuming he was still alive. Unfortunately, the only account we have is Edward Phelan's, and some of that account comes secondhand from his "hard of hearing" and not very eloquent neighbor, Genevieve Gervais.[20] We might recall Mrs. Gervais' important testimony about the conversation she had with Phelan on the afternoon of Friday, September 6, 1839—the same eventful day that Phelan walked home from Evans' house and supposedly canoed Sergeant Hays across the river. She said that Phelan came to their house "and in the course of conversation" told her the following story:

*That Hays had crossed the Mississippi that day to go to the Little Crow Village in search of a calf, that a person had passed down the Mississippi that morning, whose name I do not recollect, although the name had been mentioned at the time, however, who had been working on the St. Croix for Mr. Baker. This person, learning from Hays his intention of going to the Indian Village, offered him a seat in the canoe, which Hays declined, saying he thought he would have a better chance of finding his calf or the remains of it, by going down by land on the opposite bank of the Mississippi—by that means he might find the Indians in the act of feasting on the meat of the calf. When this man left the house Hays accompanied him as far as the hill, after which he returned, breakfasted, dressed himself, and then Phelan had went with him across the river.*[21]

If we believe Mrs. Gervais' testimony, Phelan described some of Sergeant Hays' actions that morning before Phelan supposedly "went with him across the river," as well as some of the events that occurred at their residence, also before Hays supposedly left "to go to the Little Crow Village." An intriguing revelation is the visit of the unnamed employee of "Mr. Baker"—i.e., fur trader Benjamin F. Baker, whose trading post was upriver from Fort Snelling at the mouth of Coldwater Creek in present-day Minneapolis—who, on his way downriver, stopped at Phelan and Hays' house and offered Hays "a seat in his canoe" down to Little Crow's village. Condensing Mrs. Gervais' account of Phelan's story to the bare essentials and making a few elementary deductions, we can establish that Sergeant Hays engaged in a minimum of six actions that morning:

1. He entertained a visitor, which at the very least involved a conversation with him inside their house.
2. He "accompanied" the visitor "when this man left the house…as far as the hill."
3. "He returned" to the house and ate breakfast.
4. He "dressed himself."
5. He and Phelan exited the house and walked down "the hill" to the boat landing.

6. He and Phelan boarded a canoe and paddled "across the river."

Before we try to calculate time estimates for each of these actions, we must first consider Phelan's rebuttal of Mrs. Gervais' statement, as well as his own direct account of Sergeant Hays' actions that morning. Justice Joseph R. Brown included Phelan's rebuttal at the end of Mrs. Gervais' 280-word testimony about Phelan's two visits to her home on Friday, September 6 and Sunday, September 8. Brown only para-phrased Phelan's reply to Mrs. Gervais' statement.

> *The prisoner here denied the whole of her evidence, saying he never told her anything of the kind, but that as she was hard of hearing, that she must have mistaken his words. However, since the examination, I find he has made the same assertions to Sophia Perry.*[22]

## An Aside: What Did Sophia Perry Know?

Brown's last remark—"since the examination, I find he has made the same assertions to Sophia Perry"[23]—is an intriguing counter-charge against Phelan's rebuttal. However, it is not perfectly clear whether it meant that Sophia Perry—who was the oldest daughter of Abraham and Mary Perry—claimed that she also heard Phelan tell her the very same story about the actions of Hays that morning, or whether Sophia Perry was merely verifying a limited part of Mrs. Gervais' testimony. The last part of Mrs. Gervais' testimony described Phelan's alleged refusal to see Justice Brown on Sunday, September 8, about his missing partner Hays, when Brown—who had just arrived from Grey Cloud Island, downriver from Little Crow's village—was conveniently next door at the Perry home. Brown's phrase in his entry in the casebook, "since the examination I find," clearly conveys that he interviewed Sophia Perry sometime after the November 1, 1839 hearing. Why didn't he depose her as a witness at that time and include her testimony in his evidence? It is regrettable and frustrat-ing that we cannot know what Sophia Perry told Brown about any conversations she had with Phelan concerning the disappearance of Sergeant Hays and especially about Hays' actions on Friday morning, September 6. Earlier we raised the possibility that the bachelor Phelan might have had an interest in the twenty-five-year-old Sophia Perry (who was born in Switzerland in 1814 and eventually married a French Canadian named Pierre Crevier), and that this is why he didn't want to visit Justice Brown at the Perry home in his "bad" clothes.[24] Maybe he thought that appearing in bad clothes would make a bad impression on the Swiss Miss Sophia. If that was even partly true, then it's quite conceivable that Phelan found several occasions to visit the Perry home and talk with Sophia.*

This raises the question: Sometime after his partner disappeared did Phelan have a conversation with Sophia Perry about the last day he saw John Hays alive? Brown's comment about Phelan's "assertions" to Sophia is a strong indication that he did. But common sense would also indicate it. Wouldn't Phelan eventually tell all his neighbors about the disappearance of his well-liked housemate? And wouldn't all of those neighbors—including the Gervaises and the Perrys—inevitably inquire about the last time Phelan saw him? Whether Phelan was guilty of murdering Sergeant Hays or not, it stands to reason that he would have told Sophia Perry essentially the same story he told Mrs. Gervais. If he was innocent, he would have no reason to change his story; telling the truth would naturally produce a consistent story. If he was guilty and a clever liar, he would stick with one consistent, unchanging story, even if it was a complete fabrication.

But given the gaps in the record, we have no way of knowing how closely Sophia Perry's story would have supported Mrs. Gervais' testimony.

---

* Sophia's younger sister, Rose, was the wife of one of the key witnesses, James Clewett, who was also one of Joseph R. Brown's business partners. Only five months before Hays' disappearance, Rose Perry and James Clewett were married at the Kaposia Indian mission, in what was later proclaimed as the first white marriage in St. Paul. In 1841, Sophia's other younger sister, Adele Perry, married French Canadian Vetal Guerin, who we will later see engaged in a near-violent claim dispute with Phelan over Hays' old land claim. See endnote 24.

## Phelan's Word Against Mrs. Gervais'

Absent that knowledge, we are left with only Mrs. Gervais' account and Phelan's complete denial of it. The problem is that Phelan did not take issue with just parts of Mrs. Gervais' recollections. According to Brown, he "denied the whole of her evidence," apparently implying that she misconstrued what he told her and blaming that on her poor hearing. For the record, Brown gave Mrs. Gervais a chance to respond to Phelan's denial. She replied: "I am confident this is the purport of his words. He knew I was hard of hearing, and spoke loud in consequence."[25]

By her own admission Mrs. Gervais was hard of hearing, so it is easy to believe that she may have misunderstood some of Phelan's words. On the other hand, it is difficult to believe that the "confident" woman misunderstood everything the "loud" speaking Phelan told her. This raises the question: how much of Mrs. Gervais' account of Sergeant Hays' actions that critical Friday morning (specifically those six essential acts we highlighted) should be included in the list of all the tasks and time commitments Phelan had that morning?

Phelan's original testimony of the events of that critical Friday morning was given before Henry Sibley, "a few days after the body [of Hays] had been found."[26]

*Hays disappeared about the 6th or 7th of September, day of the week Friday. He had lost a calf, which he supposed the Indians had taken, and he hoped by visiting Little Crow's Indian Village to find the meat of it. About 9 or 10 o'clock of the above named day I put Hays across the river in a canoe, and he requested me to look out for him towards evening, which request I complied with but he did not make his appearance.*[27]

When Phelan first appeared before Justice Joseph R. Brown, on November 1, 1839, Brown recorded that "the prisoner said he had no further explanation to give of the disappearance of Hays than that contained in his affidavit before H. H. Sibley Esq."[28] However, after Phelan apparently learned something of the testimonies of Stephen Scott, John Foy, William Evans, and others, he revised his original 975-word affidavit by adding the following 182-word statement:

> *The night previous to the disappearance of Hays, I went to Evans' to look for a calf, slept there and returned in the morning. Put deceased across the river about 7 o'clock. Am not aware he conversed with any person on the morning I put him across the river. Think he never contemplated going anywhere else but to "Little Crow Village." When he was found his head and shoulders were out of the water. Hauled him partly on the beach and covered the corpse over with grass and sand. Went down with Mackinaw Boat in the company of Dr. Emerson and Lt. McPhail to where I hauled deceased on shore. The morning I left Evans' I came nearly straight home—do not consider I lost any time with the little deviation from the direct route made in search of the calf. A man may walk from Evans' to my house in about half an hour. When I got home deceased had breakfast ready. Remained sometime after breakfast before going across the river.*[29]

For our present purposes the relevant parts of Phelan's amended testimony are four significant statements:

1. He "put deceased across the river about 7 o'clock," two to three hours earlier than his original estimate of "about 9 or 10 o'clock."
2. He was "not aware" that Hays "conversed with any person on the morning [he] put him across the river."
3. When he "got home deceased had breakfast ready."
4. Hays "remained some time after breakfast before going across the river."

Let us examine each of these statements and see if it is possible to reconcile them with Mrs. Gervais' testimony. First, Phelan's change in time from "about 9 or 10 o'clock" to "about 7:00" may be a conspicuously suspicious and convenient alteration, but is inconsequential relative to Mrs. Gervais' testimony because she made no mention of time. (We will revisit the issue of Phelan's altered time estimates later.) Second, Phelan's statement that he was "not aware" that Sergeant Hays had "conversed with any person" on the morning in question implies that he was specifically denying Mrs. Gervais' account of the unnamed employee of B. F. Baker who had visited Sergeant Hays that morning. Interestingly, his expression "not aware of" was not a very assertive denial of Mrs. Gervais' story of a Friday morning visitor. Third, Phelan's statement that Sergeant Hays already "had breakfast ready" suggests, at least according to Phelan, that when he returned home from Evans' house, he did not have to spend time waiting for Hays to make his breakfast before he could canoe him across the river. Phelan simply had to wait for Hays to eat. Phelan's statement that Sergeant Hays "had breakfast ready" could also be interpreted as an attempt to conveniently reduce the time he spent at his cabin before Scott and Foy saw him alone in his canoe on the river. But whether or not Phelan was telling the whole truth, he was admitting here that he was at home when Sergeant Hays had breakfast, which was one of the details that Mrs. Gervais asserted. That means that despite his adamant denial "of the whole of her evidence," he did in fact agree with some of it. Fourth, Phelan's statement that they "remained sometime after breakfast" agrees with Mrs. Gervais' assertion that Sergeant Hays "breakfasted" and "dressed himself" before Phelan took him across the river. Though Phelan said nothing about Sergeant Hays dressing himself, he also did not deny it when he had the opportunity. He could have easily said that Sergeant Hays was already dressed and "had breakfast ready" when he arrived home that morning. The fact that he didn't may be interpreted as an indirect corroboration of Mrs. Gervais' reference to Sergeant Hays "dressing himself." Moreover, Phelan himself reportedly told Scott that Hays put on his "best clothes" before he left for Kaposia.

Our analysis shows that some of Mrs. Gervais' account can be reconciled with Phelan's own statements. The greatest difference between the two accounts is the issue of the unnamed Friday morning visitor. There is good reason to doubt that there ever was such a visitor. First, Mrs. Gervais simply may have misunderstood what Phelan told her. Maybe he had been referring in part to an event of a previous day and she mixed up parts of two stories. Maybe the combination of poor hearing and a faulty memory of a conversation held fifty-five days earlier distorted Mrs. Gervais' recollections. Second, Mrs. Gervais may have had her information correct but the whole story was fabricated by Phelan to hide the truth of what happened to Sergeant Hays. Perhaps he added the fiction of the Friday morning visitor to make his account of Sergeant Hays' last morning more convincing. Ironically, if Phelan did fabricate the story in order to plant a plausible scenario for Sergeant Hays' disappearance—and maybe subtly point to another possible suspect—that lie only incriminated him further by adding another time-consuming complication to his busy morning. Of course, at the time of his conversation with Mrs. Gervais (Friday afternoon, only hours after the alleged event) Phelan would not have known that a future investigation would find witnesses who would all box him into a very narrow Friday morning timeline. He may have thought that after Scott and Foy returned to the St. Croix River, he would not see or hear of them again. Third, if Hays did have a visitor that morning who left in his canoe for a trip downriver, then why didn't Scott, Foy, Clewett, or Mencke, who were canoeing upriver from Evans' Landing early that morning, see him? None of those men testified that they saw any other canoeist besides Phelan during their early morning voyage upriver to Phelan's Landing.

Given all these points, the most plausible conclusion, consistent with all the evidence, is that there was no early morning visitor to Phelan and Hays' home on Friday, September 6, 1839. That conclusion is also helpful for the present purpose of assuming Phelan's innocence and finding reasonable ways to reduce the time he spent on Friday morning September 6, in between his walk from Evan's house and his canoe trip. Of course, if Phelan was innocent, then the theory that he invented the morning visitor to help hide his crime would be invalidated. But to assume Phelan's innocence does not mean we have to accept his denial of "the whole" of Mrs. Gervais' account. Even an innocent man can make misstatements and overreact to being misquoted.

## Calculating the Minimum Time Hays Added to Phelan's Morning

Returning to the six presumed actions of Sergeant Hays that morning, first we can expunge the first two:

1. Hays entertained a visitor, which at the very least involved a conversation inside the cabin.
2. Hays "accompanied" the visitor "when this man left the house ... as far as the hill."

Subtracting these two actions obviously benefits Phelan since the two together could have consumed at least ten minutes. But Phelan's own admission that he and Sergeant Hays remained at home "some time after breakfast," adds a fifth item to Hays' list of time-consuming actions, amending it as follows:

1. Hays "breakfasted" while Phelan was at home.
2. Hays "dressed himself" while Phelan was at home.
3. Hays and Phelan spent "some time" together at home "after breakfast."
4. Hays and Phelan walked out of their cabin and hiked "about one fourth a mile" down "the hill" to the boat landing.
5. Hays and Phelan boarded a "log" canoe and paddled "across the river," from the "upper end of the island."

Let us see if we can calculate reasonable minimum time estimates for each of these actions. First, how much time did it take Sergeant

Hays to eat breakfast? No one knows, but we can at least make an educated guess after some thoughtful considerations. We should start by acknowledging that the pace of life was much slower in the 1830s than it is today. In the fast-paced, high tech, urbanized America of the twenty-first century, it may not be unusual for someone to wolf down their breakfast in a few minutes before they race off to work. Many don't even eat breakfast because they can't find either the time or desire to prepare it, even though "preparing" it might only require grabbing some fruit or heating something for thirty seconds in the microwave. However, in the much slower paced, agriculturally-oriented America of the early nineteenth century, racing through breakfast would be unusual. Farmers especially understood the importance of a hardy meal before a hard day's work in the field. They also valued the ritualistic times of relaxation that tradition had set aside in the day—breakfast, lunch, and dinner. Of course, they also had fewer distractions than their modern counterparts. To state the obvious, they had no radios, televisions, telephones, cell phones, computers, or CD players to distract them from the tradition of sitting at a table and enjoying the simple pleasures of eating a meal and—if they weren't reclusive—chatting with the other people who shared their table. Anecdotal evidence about American farm life in the nineteenth and twentieth centuries (and this author's own experience of spending time with farmers in the 1960s) would suggest that the traditional American farmer of the past routinely spent at least a half hour at the breakfast table.[30] But the life of a farmer inherently included the unexpected—a broken fence, a loose calf, a sick cow, predators spooking the livestock, threatening storm clouds, etc.—and no doubt breakfast was sometimes as hurried an affair as ours can be today.

All things considered, perhaps a good guess for Sergeant Hays' Friday morning breakfast was something a little under a half hour. But given that there is no way of knowing how long it took Hays to eat breakfast that morning (assuming he was alive to eat it), we'll give Phelan the benefit of the doubt and estimate that Sergeant Hays "breakfasted" in ten or fifteen minutes—even though 10 minutes (our minimum) would be much more typical of a modern American's breakfast time.

Second, how long did it take Sergeant Hays to dress himself? Again, no one knows, but there is some direct evidence on which to base our guess. J. Fletcher Williams described Sergeant Hays as "something of a martinet in discipline, precise and exact in dress, bearing and action…he had a dignified and, respectable bearing."[31] Clearly, Williams described a "dignified" man who was not careless in his dress—the polar opposite of a slob. Williams' use of the word "martinet" is especially noteworthy. According to *Webster's Dictionary*, a martinet is "one who stresses a rigid adherence to the details of form and method."[32] If Sergeant Hays truly was "something of a martinet," then he probably wasn't a fast dresser, or for that matter a fast eater. Indeed, Williams specifically stated that he was "precise and exact in his dress." And what exactly was his dress? Thanks to Phelan's original testimony, we know that at the time of his disappearance Sergeant Hays was dressed in clothes that included "a blue coat and oxford grey pantaloons." And thanks to Ben Gervais' statement, we know that Phelan told him that Sergeant Hays was last seen wearing "square toed" boots. Stephen Scott also added the interesting detail that, according to Phelan, "Hays had put on his best clothes" that Friday.[33]

How long then would it take for a "dignified" man, who was "precise and exact in dress" and "something of a martinet," to fully dress himself in a shirt, pants, coat, (his "best clothes"), socks and boots? A slob in a hurry could surely do it in a couple of minutes. But how long would someone who was meticulous in his dress take to do the routine task? One unknown was how far dressed Sergeant Hays was when Phelan arrived home. We might infer from Mrs. Gervais' account that he was either in his nightclothes or underwear when Phelan arrived, otherwise why would he later have to "dress himself"? Still, assuming Sergeant Hays was alive that morning, it is certainly possible that he was at least partly dressed when Phelan arrived home. All things considered, five minutes might be a reasonable round figure minimum estimate for the meticulous Sergeant Hays to dress himself.

Third, how much time did Hays and Phelan spend at home after breakfast? Phelan specifically testified that they "remained sometime after breakfast before going across the river," the vague and challenging term here is the key word, "sometime." Phelan could have said "a little while after" or, to use William Evans' words, "a few minutes after," but he did not. Is it fair to infer then that Phelan's expression "sometime" means more than "a few minutes"? But even if we assume that, we are still stuck with the problem of pondering an undetermined amount of time.

Perhaps the best approach to this problem is to consider the tasks Sergeant Hays was most likely to do after breakfast. One detail from Phelan's testimony can help us get started. In his original statement Phelan said that after he "put Hays across the river…he requested me to look out for him towards evening."[34] The statement reveals that Sergeant Hays planned on an all-day trek to the Indian village, a round trip of roughly ten miles. A meticulous martinet like Sergeant Hays would have made careful preparations for such a trek—especially considering that the west side of the river was completely uninhabited between Mendota and the Kaposia village. At a minimum Sergeant Hays would have had to pack some food, and though he could always drink from the river, he might have preferred to fill his canteen with the cold spring water that flowed by their cabin. It is also easy to imagine that before leaving for the day, the dignified sergeant would have wanted to wash in the creek, as well as relieve himself in the comfort of their own privy. And maybe there were household chores to finish before he left. At a minimum the meticulous Hays would have washed his breakfast dishes either in the creek, or from a bucket of water he brought from the creek. He might also have made one last cursory look for the missing calf—which after all was his sole reason for making the long journey. Certainly Sergeant Hays could have easily spent a half hour or more after breakfast doing those tasks. However, some of those tasks—washing, preparing a lunch, using the privy—could have been done before breakfast and before Phelan returned home. We should also consider that Sergeant Hays might have been anxious to get an early start on his long trip. With these possibilities in mind, a reasonable estimate of "sometime after breakfast" could be closer to ten or twenty minutes. But to give Phelan the most minimal estimate, we'll allot a mere five minutes for the "sometime after breakfast" period.

Fourth, how long did it take Hays and Phelan to exit their home and walk "about one-fourth a mile" "down the hill" to the boat landing? A variety of evidence reveals that their cabin stood in the vicinity of today's Eagle and Exchange Streets and it was probably nestled directly under the present-day Kellogg Boulevard terrace. Williams described it as a "hovel under the hill." Clearly, the "hill" Williams was referring to was the cliff directly above present-day Exchange Street where Kellogg Boulevard now runs. But that particular hill should not be confused with the hill that Mrs. Gervais mentioned in her testimony. It is clear from the context of her statement that she was referring to the entire hill that rose up from the boat landing— what we might call today the Eagle Street (or Chestnut Street) hill. Phalen's Landing was located at the river's edge approximately at the foot of present-day Chestnut Street. In June 2008, this author timed his steady walk from the southeast corner of Eagle and Exchange Streets, down the hill to the newly renovated Upper Landing. (Luckily, the traffic light was green when he reached Shepard Road so he was able to cross without breaking stride.) The time was six minutes flat, and so a five-minute minimum estimate for Hays and Phelan's walk from their cabin to the boat landing seems reasonable.

Fifth, how long would it take Phelan and Hays to board a "log canoe" at their landing, paddle upriver about four blocks, past the "head of a large island" (now called Harriet Island), then "cross the Mississippi" at that point and finally drop Hays off on the other shore? Fortunately, three of the witnesses gave rough time estimates for a river crossing from Phelan's Landing. Fur trader James Clewett—

who knew the river well, and for some months even prior to his marriage to Rose Perry had resided at the Perry farm, only a short distance upriver from Phelan's Landing—gave the following estimate: "I think it would require ten minutes for a man in a canoe to cross the Mississippi at Phelan's Landing."[35] His companion, Henry Mencke, the whiskey trader who was also an experienced river traveler, concurred with Clewett, except that his estimate was for a round trip: "Suppose a person in a canoe might cross and re-cross the Mississippi opposite Phelan's Landing in 20 minutes."[36]

Stephen Scott, who had a much closer upriver view of Phelan canoeing the river on the Friday morning in question, had a different calculation, mainly because he had a different perspective of where Phelan would have crossed the river that morning. The shortest crossing point from Phelan's Landing to the opposite shore would be downriver, in between the lower (or east) end of present-day Harriet Island and the upper (or west) end of another smaller island now known as Navy or Raspberry Island. Clewett and Mencke's estimates were presumably based on crossing the Mississippi downriver between the islands, and not upriver around the head of the longer Harriet Island. But Scott had observed Phelan canoeing "some distance above Phelan's Landing" and this is one reason why he and Foy were convinced that Phelan could not have crossed the river that morning.

> Do not think it is possible that canoe could have crossed the river. We first saw the canoe some distance above Phelan's Landing; had it come from the opposite shore when we first saw it, it must have come around the head of the large island, which would have required half an hour to do so and we certainly would have seen it.[37]

In essence, Scott was saying that it would take a canoe "half an hour" just to cross the river "from the opposite shore" if the crossing route was "around the head of the large island." Based on where he saw Phelan on the river that morning, that was the only crossing point that Phelan could have used. Though John Foy did not give a time estimate for a river crossing, he did agree with canoe mate Scott about where Phelan was seen on the river. More significantly, he provided additional critical details about Phelan's canoe route that morning.

> *While we were about one and a half miles from Phelan's Landing, we saw a log canoe ascending the Mississippi. Above the landing some distance the canoe went out from shore, near half way between that and the island, turned and came down the Mississippi to the landing place.*[38]

This verifies Scott's assertion that Phelan was canoeing upriver "some distance" from his landing, and it adds the important detail that Phelan was first seen "ascending the river" along the east shore before he was later seen descending the river back down toward his landing. Taken together, Scott and Foy's accounts provide compelling evidence about the route that Phelan would have used if he in fact canoed Sergeant Hays across the river (albeit Scott and Foy swore that there was no river crossing that morning). Again, Scott estimated it would take half an hour to cross the Mississippi upriver around the west end of a long island.

## Timing: How Long Did It Take Phelan to Cross the River, Allegedly with Hays?

What would be the most reasonable minimum time estimate for Phelan and Hays' supposed voyage across the river? Though Clewett and Mencke both agreed on a ten-minute river crossing one-way, via the downriver route between present-day Harriet and Raspberry Islands, Scott was the only witness who gave an estimate for the upriver route: around the head of Harriet Island and then across to the west shore—the route we have strong reason to believe was the only possible route Phelan could have used that morning. Although it might be reasonable to give more weight to Scott's opinion, would it be fair to Phelan to rely only on the guess of one witness whose estimate is twenty minutes longer than the estimates of two other credible witnesses? Perhaps a fair solution to this problem can be found by the use of a small compromise and a large amount of common sense. Since two credible witnesses agreed that it would take about ten minutes to cross downriver from Phelan's Landing—let us just accept that figure as a standard river crossing time. But since two other equally credible witnesses insisted that the alleged river crossing would have taken longer because it followed the longer upriver route —then let us also factor in an estimated time for a "log canoe" to travel from Phelan's Landing to the upper end of that long island (i.e., Harriet Island). In other words, we will add to the standard crossing time of ten minutes whatever amount of time we conservatively figure a log canoe would need to travel from Phelan's Landing to the upper end of the long island. If we accept the compromise then the next challenge will be to calculate the distance between Phelan's Landing and the western end of the "large island," which is no longer an island and may not be as large as it once was.

The 1886 G. M. Hopkins Atlas of St. Paul provides both a detailed map of the old Harriet Island locality and a legend for measuring distance in feet. According to the Hopkins map, the distance between the Upper Landing (Phelan's Landing) and the west end (or head) of Harriet Island was about two thousand feet (and the river was about 1,320 feet wide).[39] To put those measurements into more comprehensible terms, two thousand feet would be about 666 yards, or roughly six football fields, and 1,320 feet is about 440 yards. How long would it take for a heavy canoe (a log one, not a fast bark one) to travel the distance of six football fields? What would be a reasonable rate of speed for a log canoe paddling upriver against the current? Since we don't know the dimensions of Phelan's log canoe (and have no clue about the wind conditions that day), we can only make a reasonable guess that a strong man could paddle a heavy canoe upstream at a rate of about one yard (or three feet) per second, about the pace of a very brisk walk. If we accept one yard per second as a reasonable rate, then a canoe traveling 666 yards would take just over eleven minutes. Rounding down, we can reduce that time to ten minutes, the time Clewett and Mencke estimated it would take a canoe to cross the river, which the Hopkins map shows to be only about 440 yards wide. Accepting that ten minute estimate, Phelan and Hays' supposed river crossing would have taken about twenty minutes: ten minutes to paddle upriver to the head of the island and ten more minutes to complete the crossing. As reasonable as that estimate is, it may be high for a minimum time, given that it literally doubles the time Clewett and Mencke gave for a river crossing. At the risk of being overly generous to Phelan, what if we reduce the estimate for the 666-yard upstream voyage to just five minutes, giving us a total of fifteen minutes for a complete upriver crossing of the Mississippi? Fifteen minutes would be exactly half of Scott's estimate and only five minutes more than Clewett and Mencke's.

Returning to the five tasks John Hays would have engaged in on Friday morning September 6, and calculating their shortest possible times, we can estimate the following: ten minutes to eat breakfast, five minutes to dress, five minutes of miscellaneous tasks after breakfast, five minutes to walk down to the landing, and fifteen minutes to canoe with Phelan across the river, a total of forty minutes.

Next, we can estimate the time of Phelan's supposed return voyage back across the river and up to the critical point where Scott and Foy saw him walking up the hill from his landing. Given the fifteen-minute estimate for Phelan's crossing to the west shore, we can assume the same fifteen minute time for the return trip. Although the final leg of that crossing—the 666 yards from the head of the island to his landing—would be all downstream and presumably faster, the direct crossing of the river without Hays would take longer with only one paddler.

Lastly, we can estimate the time Phelan took to beach his canoe at his landing and begin the walk up the hill to his cabin. Both Scott and Foy observed Phelan beaching his canoe and heading up his hill prior to docking their own canoe at Phelan's Landing. Scott's testimony included the following observation:

*Previous to landing we saw a canoe coming down the river; it landed at Phelan's Landing while we were forty or fifty yards therefrom. Am well-acquainted with Phelan, and am sure he got out of the canoe…Phelan on landing started immediately for home.*[40]

Scott's canoe mate, Foy, gave a similar account, except that he estimated they were farther away when Phelan landed his canoe.

*[H]e went ashore when we were about 30 rods below. Am positive the prisoner got out of his canoe…We landed alongside of Phelan's canoe about 8 o'clock in the morning—he had left the landing before we did.*[41]

Scott and Foy's estimates conflict about the distance between themselves and Phalen at the time he landed his canoe. Scott estimated a distance of "forty or fifty yards." Foy estimated "about 30 rods," or about 165 yards, a four-times-greater distance than Scott's forty yard estimate. If we use our previous one yard per second canoe travel rate, then the yardage discrepancy would translate into a time difference of between forty or fifty seconds for Scott and two minutes and forty-five seconds for Foy. If we consider the two estimates in terms of time, Scott's forty or fifty seconds seems too low. Though that might be enough time for Phelan to hop out of his canoe and beach it on shore, it would not be enough time for him to also walk far enough up the hill to avoid the need to converse with Scott and Foy when they arrived at the landing. Neither Scott nor Foy mentioned any communication between themselves and Phelan at the landing, and if they had had any conversation with Phelan they surely would have mentioned it. It's difficult to imagine that Phelan would ignore Scott and Foy (especially since he had breakfasted with them earlier) as they landed their canoe next to his just moments after he had beached it. On the other hand, Foy's two minute and forty-five second estimate gives Phelan some time to begin his walk up the hill, and thus have his back toward the river when Scott and Foy arrived at the landing; Foy clearly stated that Phelan "had left the landing" before they did. Averaging the two conflicting time estimates, we can make a reasonable guess that Phelan reached his landing about two minutes before Scott and Foy did. Reducing the estimate to a bare minimum, we will allot one minute between the two landings.

## Finishing Phelan's Timeline: Adding Up All the Minimum Estimates

Now we can finally calculate the minimum time Phelan needed to do what he claimed he did on the morning of September 6. Compiling the minimum time estimates, from the moment Phelan left Evan's house on Friday morning to the moment Scott and Foy saw him walking up the hill from his landing, we can add as follows: two minutes to exit Evan's house following breakfast; thirty minutes to walk from Evan's house to his own cabin; twenty minutes waiting at home for Sergeant Hays to eat breakfast, get dressed, and prepare for his journey; five minutes to walk with Sergeant Hays down to the landing; fifteen minutes to board a canoe and cross the river; fifteen minutes to canoe alone back to his landing; and one minute to beach his canoe at his landing and head up the hill. It adds up to a total of eighty-eight minutes. Translated into clock time, that means it would have been about 9:30 on Scott's clock when Phelan would have begun walking home from his landing. But Scott said they "left" Phelan's house at about nine o'clock after spending, according to Foy, "about fifteen minutes" at Phelan's house.

In case anyone forgot, the total *maximum* time estimate we liberally calculated for Scott and Foy's trip from Evans's house, where they left Phelan, to Phelan's Landing, where they surprisingly saw Phelan beaching his canoe, was approximately seventy minutes. Clearly, the discrepancy of eighteen minutes between the seventy minute estimate (maximum) for Scott and Foy, and the eighty-eight minute estimate (minimum) for Phelan critically damages the case for Phelan's innocence. Naturally, the case for his innocence depends on being able to show that it was possible for Phelan to do what he said he did in the time he claimed he did it: transport Sergeant Hays across the river after leaving Evan's house and before Scott and Foy saw him land his canoe. We have estimated that his maximum window of time for that period was seventy minutes. And we have estimated that the minimum time he would have actually needed to do what he said he did was at least eighty-eight minutes. If Phelan was innocent and generally telling the truth, then the latter number should be less than the former number. The fact that it is not (and indeed, there is an eighteen-minute overrun on Phelan's window of time) is a serious problem for him. Phelan's fundamental problem is his story: he swore he transported Sergeant Hays across the river after he returned home from Evan's house Friday morning. If he hadn't told that story and instead simply returned home and proclaimed Sergeant Hays missing, then most of the evidence against him could be reasonably explained away. The murder could have easily been passed off as the act of some Indians who killed Sergeant Hays while Phelan was away. His problem of a time discrepancy would vanish if there were no morning river crossing, and he would not be locked into a narrow timeline or specific explanation of what Sergeant Hays did the morning he disappeared. Under the alternate story that he was away from home and had no idea of what happened to Hays, Phelan would have no compelling reason to offer any explanation for Sergeant Hays' disappearance. Had Phelan told that simple story, then future historians would have been left with more evidence supporting the theory that Dakota Indians (or one Indian named Dowau) killed Sergeant Hays, rather than evidence supporting the theory that Phelan did. However, the fact that Phelan stuck with the story he did—that he personally transported Sergeant Hays across the river that morning—places the case for his innocence into a very untenable position.

Though Phelan's time frame problem is almost enough to hang him, we still need to finish the task of seeing if we can reconcile the evidence with the supposition that Phelan was innocent. One seemingly incriminating piece of evidence against Phelan is the testimony about his actions on Thursday evening, September 5, the night he stumbled into Evans' house with muddy clothes and carrying a canoe paddle.

Phelan's account of what happened that evening as retold by Scott, Foy, and Evans is certainly plausible. He was looking for a calf, it got dark (and in the wilderness it can really get dark), he stumbled in the darkness, fell into a creek, got mud on his clothes and lost his hat. Luckily, he found his way to the home of his friend William Evans. The paddle he was carrying may have served multiple purposes: a canoe paddle, a walking stick, and a staff for steering stray cattle. Although in a broader context this episode could be interpreted as evidence against Phelan, by itself it could simply be interpreted as the innocuous actions of a farmer lost in the dark.

One possible point in Phelan's defense is the argument of motive. If he had killed Sergeant Hays that night with his canoe paddle, why would he have allowed potential witnesses to see him so soon after the crime, before he had a chance to change his clothes and discard the murder weapon? Indeed, why would he have even entered Evans' house with the murder weapon in hand? Wouldn't that show Phelan's consciousness of innocence? One final point about the Thursday night episode: there was no hard proof that Phelan's canoe paddle was the murder weapon. Dr. Emerson only said that "the wounds of the deceased could have been so inflicted by a canoe paddle," and he only made that statement after Justice Brown specifically directed his attention to the consideration of the canoe paddle.[42] The key words are "could have been". The murder weapon "could have been" a canoe paddle. Then again, it "could have been" something else; perhaps a Dakota war club?

## Scott and Foy's Testimony: Three Strikes Against Phelan

Clearly, the most devastating evidence against Phelan comes collectively from the sworn statements of Stephen Scott and John Foy. Scott and Foy made three powerful incriminations. First, they both testified that they saw Phelan canoeing the river alone on Friday morning, not long after they had seen him at Evans' house. More importantly, they firmly swore that not only did they *not* see him cross the river that morning, it would have been impossible for him to do so. Second, Scott swore that on Friday morning he saw "a considerable body of blood," which "appeared fresh," and "drops of blood" on the surrounding "herbage" on the "trail," some "10 rods" (or seventy-five yards) from Phelan's Landing. He added that "the herbage had been trampled very much for some distance round…it appeared as though some heavy body had been laying" there.[43] Third, Scott swore that when he informed Phelan of the shocking discovery of blood on his property—Scott said that he "was under the impression at the time that one of the cattle had been wounded by the Indians"—Phelan only "answered it must have been some of Jervais'[sic] cattle, as none of theirs had been wounded."[44]

First, analysis of Scott and Foy's observations of Phelan on the river makes a convincing case that Phelan, in spite of what he said, never crossed the river that morning. Phelan's river crossing claim simply cannot be reconciled with the evidence presented by Scott and Foy. Either Phelan was lying, or Scott and Foy were lying, and our minimum and maximum time estimates have already carefully established the possibility that Scott and Foy made unintentional mistakes in their estimates.

The second incrimination, Scott's discovery of "fresh" blood on Phelan's property, specifically on a "trampled down" trail leading to the river, is obviously extremely damaging evidence against Phelan. In today's parlance it's a smoking gun. Who wouldn't suspect that the "fresh" blood came from Sergeant Hays? Phelan's only logical line of defense would be that the blood was not from Sergeant Hays but from some other source. A plausible alternative would be that it came from some animal. Phelan himself suggested that the blood "must have been" from some of Ben Gervais' cattle. But as we have earlier shown, both Ben Gervais and his son Alphonse firmly denied that any of their cattle had lost any blood. A better possibility would be that the blood came from some wild animal—perhaps a deer devoured by a pack of grey wolves. The idea that wolves roamed the river bottoms was even mentioned by another witness, Bartholomew Baldwin. Twenty-four days after Scott's discovery of blood on September 6, Baldwin may have come upon the same "trampled down" trail that Scott found, but instead of blood he saw signs of wolves there. Here again is Baldwin's testimony:

> On the east bank of the Mississippi some distance above where the body was found...I observed a trail, the bushes and herbage being much beaten down. Also saw grey hairs sticking to the herbage, think they may have been wolf hairs—there being many tracks of wolves along the trail. Do not think they were hairs of the deceased, as his hair had been cut a short time before his disappearance, whereas the hairs seen by me were long.[45]

Baldwin's emphasis on "many tracks of wolves along the trail" as well as "long grey hairs sticking to the herbage," gives credence to the theory that the blood on the trail may have come from a nearby wolf kill. Fort Snelling records and other contemporary sources confirm that the region was inundated with wolves at that time.[46] However, with the guidance of Justice Brown's questioning, Scott specifically addressed the question of whether he noticed any visible signs of wolves or other animals on the trail that morning, saying: "I do not recollect to have seen any tracks in the vicinity of the blood...I do not recollect to have seen any signs of cattle in the vicinity."[47] That Scott did not see any "tracks in the vicinity of the blood"—even though, as he later said, the river "bottom was wet at the time"[48]— clearly undermines the blood-letting by wolves theory, or for that matter, the bloodletting by any wild animal theory, be it a cougar, a raccoon, a coyote, or the Big Foot monster. It is not clear whether Scott's term "tracks" would have only meant animal tracks and not footprints, boot prints, or moccasin prints. Unfortunately, Justice Brown did not direct him to clarify that detail. But his comment that he was "under the impression at the time that one of the cattle had been wounded by the Indians" was telling.[49] What evidence in the river bottoms, or anywhere else, led him to suspect that "one of the cattle had been wounded by the Indians"? Did he see Indian footprints? Why would he suspect that the blood was that of cattle, when he later said that he did "not recollect to have seen any signs of cattle in the vicinity"? There is no way to know, and Scott himself was trying to "recollect" sights and sounds that he had seen and heard fifty-five days—nearly two months—earlier. In any case, if we consider Scott's testimony, which undermines the wolf theory, alongside Ben and Alphonse Gervais' denial that any of their cattle were wounded, alongside Phelan's own denial that any of his cattle were wounded, then the only remaining possibility is that the blood in Phelan's bottomland came from the only creature known for certain to have shed a lot of blood around that time: Sergeant Hays.

Once again, we are reminded that Phelan's account of Sergeant Hays' morning river crossing is highly problematic. Had Phelan not related the river crossing account, blood on the trail along his riverfront could be viewed as reasonable evidence that Indians attacked Sergeant Hays the night before—when Phelan was away at Evans' house. But that interpretation can never be reconciled with Phelan's claim that only minutes before Scott found the blood on Phelan's property, Phelan had left Sergeant Hays safely on the other side of the river. Obviously, no Indian could have killed Hays Thursday night on Phelan's property if, as Phelan's account would have it, he was still alive that Friday morning. On the other hand, if Phelan argued that Hays was killed by Indians on the other side of the river on his way to Kaposia, and there were no wounded cattle in the area, how could he account for the blood on his property?

Phelan has only one line of defense left: that Stephen Scott was not a truthful witness, that he never saw any blood on that trail, that he simply fabricated that detail to incriminate Phelan. In fact, Scott was the only witness who testified that he saw blood on Phelan's property. Foy did not follow the same bloody trail to Phelan's shanty that Scott did. If Scott could be proven to be lying, then the incriminating "body of blood" evidence that he alone testified about would disappear. But did Scott commit perjury?

If he did, what was his motive? Maybe he had some personal animosity against the big, "bad," "boastful" Irishman. We do know that Scott had been a soldier at Fort Snelling and knew William Evans, John Hays, and Edward Phelan. Perhaps Hays was a friend and Scott was convinced that Phelan had murdered his friend and, worried that the "immoral, cruel, revengeful and unscrupulous" Phelan would get away with the crime, fabricated evidence to ensure that a guilty man would not escape justice.[50]

But there is no evidence—aside from the fact that Scott had been a soldier who knew Phelan—to support the theory. Although Scott's canoe mate Foy did not see the blood on the trail, Foy agreed with virtually all of Scott's testimony, including the fact that when they arrived at Phelan's Landing he "went directly" to Phelan's house and "left Scott at the Landing."[51] And that detail is consistent with Scott's statement that he took a different trail to Phelan's house than Foy did. Furthermore, just because Scott was the only witness to see the blood on the trail does not mean that we have to be suspicious of him. Outside of Foy, and the murder suspect himself, no one else was known to be near the trail at the time Scott discovered the blood. But it's at least possible that one other person may have walked that same trail shortly after Scott had left it. Ben Gervais testified that his "cattle frequently went into the bottom below Phelan's house, as [his] son always went for them."[52] And that son, Alphonse Gervais, elaborated on his several trips to Phelan's bottomland.

> [Our] cattle frequently ran in the bottom below Phelan's house— they go there for the bottom grass … Have driven my father's cattle from there several times during the summer. Passed through the bottom frequently never saw blood there. Know of no cattle having been killed or wounded by the Indians during the summer. Have been in the bottom since the disappearance of Hays and found cattle there.[53]

There are three germane points we can draw from Alphonse Gervais' testimony:

1. He drove their cattle from Phelan's bottomland "several times during the summer."
2. He "passed through the bottom frequently [and] never saw blood there."
3. He had "been in the bottom since the disappearance of Hays and found cattle there."

In the first point, it is noteworthy that he specified that he drove the cattle "during the summer." Although in the United States summer technically (or astronomically) begins on June 20 and ends on September 20, it is, of course, very common for North Americans to consider early September as the beginning of the fall. But there is no way to know what Alphonse Gervais meant by the term "summer," and whether "summer" included the early September day when Scott discovered the blood on Phelan's bottomland.

The second point—he "passed through the bottom frequently [and] never saw blood there"—directly addresses the issue at hand: Did anyone else besides Scott (or Phelan) see blood on the trail along Phelan's bottomland? No one that we know of, since Alphonse Gervais was the only person on record, besides Phelan himself, who we know frequented that bottomland. His father, Ben Gervais, said he "always" sent his son to retrieve their cattle from Phelan's bottomland. Moreover, Ben Gervais also mentioned, in another part of his testimony, that when he and Phelan later searched for Sergeant Hays on September 9, they "passed by the hill road and did not go through the bottom."[54]

In the third point, Alphonse states that "he had been in the bottom since the disappearance of Hays and found cattle there." Based on that statement and everything he had said before—mainly, he "never" saw blood—it is reasonable to assume that even after "the disappearance of Hays" and after Scott's discovery of the blood, Alphonse Gervais was at "the bottom" and still did not see any blood there. Exactly how long after Hays' disappearance he returned to "the bottom" (one day, one week, a month?) he did not specify.

How significant is it that Alphonse Gervais did not see blood at Phelan's bottomland after Scott said he saw it there? It all depends on where exactly down "in the bottom" did he not see any blood? It is not clear precisely what tract of land Ben and Alphonse Gervais were referring to when they said "the bottom below Phelan's house." Generally speaking it had to be the lowland between the river and first major rise of elevation that formed "the hill to Phelan's house." But that lowland or levee was (and still is) a large area that extended irregularly along the river for miles. Their phrase "the bottom below Phelan's house" does seem to narrow the locality to the particular levee land located directly below Phelan's house—or directly below what is now the corner of Eagle and Exchange Streets. However, we need to consider the fact that "Phelan's house" was at the time the only identifiable landmark in the entire area between the Gervais and Perry cabins, just east of Fountain Cave, and the shanty saloon of Phelan's closest neighbor, Pierre "Pig's Eye" Parrant, who since May 1839 had been living about seven blocks downriver from Phelan's Landing, in a "hovel...about where the foot of Robert Street now is."[55] Thus, when Ben and Alphonse Gervais referenced "Phelan's house" it may not have been because that house precisely marked "the bottom" area they were describing, but simply because it was the only reference point available that came close to marking the area they were describing. Today we can give precise locations of places (e.g., along Shepard Road between Chestnut and Washington Streets) but back in 1839 when the site of St. Paul was virtually a road-less wilderness, with only a few cabins widely scattered along the riverbank, people had to be much more general in their descriptions of place locations. Brown, for instance, gave the location of Phelan and Hays' cabin as "near the cave"—even though Fountain Cave was almost two miles away from the cabin. Therefore, we should not just assume that "the bottom below Phelan's house" was limited to a narrow strip of levee land directly below Phelan' house. Rather, it was quite possible that when Ben and Alphonse Gervais referred to "the bottom below Phelan's house," they really meant a fairly large stretch of bottomland that extended several hundred yards east and west of "Phelan's house." The bottom line (excuse the pun) is that we do not really know the size of "the bottom." The fact that Alphonse Gervais "never saw blood there" could simply mean that he never happened upon the spot where the blood was. Scott's description of where the site was is now almost humorous.

> When I started I took a trail that led apparently through the bottom where the road passes in the winter, which is shorter than the summer road. I followed the trail some ten rods [55 yards], when I came to where the road abruptly terminated, and the herbage had been trampled down very much for some distance round.[56]

Not surprisingly, there is no known map of early St. Paul that shows where those primitive winter and summer roads were located. Unfortunately, neither Ben nor Alphonse Gervais mentioned any road other than one made by their cattle. Still more unfortunately, Ben Gervais' very brief description of that cow path was even more vague and confusing than Scott's description: "There is a road from my house going that way which the cattle made."[57]

Did the Gervais' cow path intersect with Scott's fifty-five yard "trail...through the bottom"? Or was the Gervais cow path the very "abruptly" terminating trail where Scott found the "body of blood"? Unfortunately, there is no way of knowing now, but if the cow path and the "trail...through the bottom" were one and the same, then it would have been seemingly impossible for Alphonse Gervais to have missed the spot where Scott testified he saw blood on Friday morning, September 6. Yet even if Alphonse followed that same "trail" days after Scott's discovery, the blood could have dried and discolored, or could have been washed away by rain or by the cleansing actions of the murderer.

To add more confusion to the blood issue, we must recall what the same Alphonse Gervais told J. Fletcher Williams more than three decades later. According to Williams, the adult Alphonse remembered that in 1839 he not only "saw blood on Phelan's clothes," and others found "bloody clothes" under Phelan's cabin, but that Gervais' own dog led investigators to a bloody trail leading to the river. In Williams' words, the dog "smelled the blood, and plainly traced the route by which the body was dragged to the river from thence."[58]

In Chapter Five we assessed the credibility of Alphonse Gervais' sensational revised account but concluded that in fairness to Phelan, we should just put it aside and concentrate on the evidence from sworn testimony. Even so, it would be interesting to assess Alphonse Gervais' later story against his original testimony.

To return to the crucial question of whether Scott lied about his discovery of blood on September 6, there is no clear and credible evidence to fairly challenge his veracity, and we do not know enough about who Stephen Scott was to make any fair judgment about his character. Like so many obscure figures in recorded history, he was a mystery man, known by only a name and an occupation. We can only presume that the former soldier tried to tell the truth when he testified under oath before Justice Joseph R. Brown about the events of September 5 and 6, 1839. Swearing a solemn oath before God to tell the whole truth was and is a very serious ethical, moral, and legal matter. And it was not something nineteenth century Americans took lightly. As a general rule, unless there is clear evidence to the contrary, those who testified under oath should be given the benefit of the doubt as to the veracity of their statements. In fairness to the dead who cannot defend themselves, if anyone living wants to accuse Stephen Scott, or any of the other witnesses who testified under oath on November 1, 1839 of perjury, then the burden of proof is on the accuser. In the case of Scott, there is no credible evidence that he broke his oath and deliberately gave false testimony. But, if we give

Scott the benefit of the doubt and accept his claim that he discovered fresh blood on Phelan's property on the date of Hays' disappearance, then the case for Phelan's innocence has been rendered a devastating blow.

Finally, the third incrimination: Scott testified that when he told Phelan he had discovered blood on his property, Phelan only "answered it must have been some of Jervais'[sic] cattle, as none of [his and Hays'] had been wounded." Phelan's response to Scott is almost as damaging to his case as is the discovery of blood on his land. If Scott recalled Phelan's words and reactions accurately, it is difficult to explain away Phelan's blatantly suspicious response to Scott's startling discovery. To review: Phelan had supposedly gone to a great deal of trouble to find a lost calf the night before. And later that evening, when he stumbled into Evans' house, he told Evans, Scott, and Foy the reason why he was there: he was looking for a lost calf. Early the next morning at breakfast, he no doubt mentioned the calf again to those three men. And later that morning when Scott and Foy arrived at his house, he specifically told Scott that "he had just put Hays across the river to look for a calf."[59] Yet, after all that preoccupation with the lost calf, when Phelan learned from Scott that there was a "body of blood" on his land—which Scott suspected was evidence that "one of their cattle had been wounded by the Indians"—what did Phelan do? Instead of rushing down to the bottom to see the evidence for himself, he immediately dismissed it as blood from his neighbor's cattle because, he said, none of his and Hays' cattle had been wounded.

Phelan's reaction to the bombshell news of blood on his land was not just odd, it was incredible. Is there any plausible explanation for Phelan's suspiciously odd reaction to Scott's startling discovery that is consistent with the behavior of an innocent man? Perhaps we could speculate that Phelan was tired from all the hiking and canoeing and didn't care to trudge back down the hill and back up again. Perhaps his own cattle never grazed in the bottomland, so he was confident that none had been wounded there.

There is at least one small problem with that hypothetical scenario: some of the details could just as easily be turned against Phelan. No doubt Phelan was truly tired after all the undisputed walking and canoeing he did that morning, but his fatigue might not just explain how an innocent man could act suspiciously, it might also explain how a guilty man could act suspiciously. If Phelan was both guilty and tired, then his fatigue might also explain why he carelessly responded to Scott in such an openly suspicious way. One would expect a clever liar and murderer to mask his guilt by outwardly acting like someone who was completely innocent. Yet, even clever liars and murderers can forgetfully drop their guard and the pretense of acting like an innocent person. In other words, if Phelan really was an exhausted murderer, who alone knew that the blood Scott found in the bottom was not from some fictional lost calf, but only from the man he had murdered, then the temptation would have been great to not bother hiking down the hill to look at it.

There is one obvious rebuttal against Scott's rendition of the conversation he had with Phelan about the blood found in the river bottom. How can we be sure that Scott's memory of a conversation held fifty-five days before his testimony was fully accurate? He may have not only misstated Phelan's words but left out important parts of their conversation—parts that may have shown Phelan in a more favorable light. This is not to accuse Scott of perjury, it is merely, like the charge against Mrs. Gervais, a reasonable challenge to the accuracy of a witness's honest recollections. The brevity of Scott's summary of that critical conversation does open up the possibility that Scott left out some important parts, though those parts might not necessarily be favorable to Phelan. Once again, the problem of not having enough evidence in which to evaluate issues re-emerges. It is Phelan's misfortune that there is no evidence existing to refute Scott's version of what Phelan said to him. But it is even more unfortunate that Justice Brown did not give Phelan a chance to state his version of that important conversation he had with Scott. We might recall that Justice Brown did give Phelan the chance to directly respond to what Mrs. Gervais claimed he told her. Why, in his cross examination of Phelan, Brown did not direct Phelan to specifically address the important conversation Scott had with him on the morning of September 6 is yet another unanswerable question Joseph R. Brown left us with.

Since Phelan's entire testimony included no mention of Scott's discovery of fresh blood on his land or the conversation he had with Scott about it, we are left with only Scott's version of what Phelan told him. Although in fairness to Phelan we might hesitate to just accept Scott's one-sided recollections of Phelan's words, Scott's version of what unfolded at "Phelan's house" that morning was quite consistent with John Foy's summary of those same events. Again, Foy's statement:

> *We landed alongside of Phelan's canoe about 8 o'clock in the morning…Went directly from the landing to the house, found Phelan there. Left Scott at the landing. Was not acquainted with deceased. Had seen no other person about the premises but Phelan and Scott, who came some time after me. Went with Scott and Phalen to where a root house was building; while there prisoner stated that he and his comrade (Hays) had some dispute as to where the clay [was] thrown up in digging should be put, Phelan wishing to have it thrown down the hill, while Hays insisted on throwing it up the hill. Remained about fifteen minutes at the house. When we returned to the landing we saw a canoe with some Indians near the landing.*[60]

Foy may not be the most articulate witness but he clearly made an effort to recall all that he saw and heard from the time he and Scott "landed along Phelan's canoe about 8 o'clock in the morning" until the time (about fifteen minutes later) they "returned to the landing [and] saw a canoe with some Indians near the landing." Notably, nowhere in his summary of events did he mention anything about Phelan going down to the bottom to look at the blood that Scott found. He never even mentioned the blood, but as noted earlier, he indirectly supported Scott's account by specifying that he initially "left Scott at the landing" while he "went directly" to Phelan's house and that Scott did not join him there until "sometime after." The reason, arguably, that Scott was late joining him was that he got delayed at the bottom looking at the "body of blood." Foy also mentioned that they "remained about 15 minutes at the house," which was certainly enough time for Scott and Phelan to discuss the matter of the blood at the bottom. The critical point is this: Foy's account shows that regardless of how Phelan responded to the news of Scott's discovery of blood on his land, he ultimately did not act on that news. Instead of going down to the bloody bottom, Phelan showed Scott and Foy the "root house" he and Hays were building.

The fact that Foy did not comment at all about Scott's discovery of blood that morning (in retrospect the most significant event of the day) does seem peculiar. Though we know that Foy was at Phelan's house at the time Scott discovered the blood, we don't know where he was when Scott informed Phelan that he found it. Perhaps he was out of earshot, maybe he was already over by the "root house." Yet even if that was the case, wouldn't Scott eventually tell his companion about the ominous discovery he made on his way to Phelan's house? Although it might not have seemed all that ominous at the time (no one was aware yet that Hays might be missing), Scott still considered it important enough to inform Phelan about it. If Scott mentioned it to Foy, why didn't Foy mention it in his testimony? Maybe because he never personally saw the blood, he didn't feel the need to comment on it. Given the glaring significance of the blood evidence, it is puzzling that Justice Brown apparently did not question Foy about it. Foy's answers to that line of questioning would have greatly helped uncover what really happened that Friday morning.

## Returning to the Theory That the Dakota Killed Hays

Foy's final comment that he observed "a canoe with some Indians near the landing" could have been intriguing evidence to support the theory that Indians were responsible for Hay's death. But because Phelan insisted that he "put Hays across the river" that morning (only about half an hour before Foy saw the Indians near the landing), the Indians in the canoe are not viable suspects in Hay's murder—assuming the fresh blood near Phelan's Landing was Hay's blood. To repeat a crucial point: if Phelan was telling the truth about transporting Hays across the river just before Scott and Foy arrived at his landing on that Friday morning, then it would have been physically impossible for any Indian, or anyone else, to kill Hays on the side of the river that he wasn't on and during the time (Thursday night to Friday morning) when Phelan swore he was still alive. But then again, if he was still alive, what was his blood doing near Phelan's Landing? On the other hand, if Phelan was lying about transporting Hays across the river on Friday morning, and the blood on his land suggests he was, then that lie alone would expose him as Hay's killer: What possible reason would he have to concoct such an elaborate story other than to hide the fact that he had committed murder? In either case, the theory that Indians were responsible for Sergeant Hay's death falls apart.

Phelan's insistence that he transported Sergeant Hays across the river on that Friday morning also seriously undermines an otherwise compelling theory of how and why a Dakota could and would have killed Hays. Remember Phelan's story about the violent confrontation Sergeant Hays had before his disappearance with an unruly, gun firing, young Dakota, who tried to shoot a "looking glass" inside their cabin? According to Phelan, Hays forcibly took the gun away from the intruder and "told the Indian if he came back he would club him." Hays did return the gun, but the Dakota reloaded the weapon and "threatened to tell" Chief Big Thunder about the incident.[61] Whether or not Phelan made up all or part of the incident does not detract from the fact that it was a plausible story. Under those circumstances, an angry young Dakota might have returned to Phelan and Hays' cabin weeks later to "club" the man who had earlier threatened to "club him." If Phelan had returned to his cabin on the Friday morning he walked home from Evans' house and simply declared that Sergeant Hays was missing, then the body of fresh blood that Scott discovered would have been less incriminating against Phelan and more consistent with the possibility that Sergeant Hays was the victim of an Indian attack—perhaps at the hands of the Indian who harassed him earlier, who arguably could have been the same Dakota (the son of Big Thunder named Do-wau) that Thompson claimed later confessed to Sergeant Hays' murder.

Phelan's use of the word "club" is interesting. Phelan claimed that Sergeant Hays "told the Indian if he came back he would club him." Since Sergeant Hays died not by gunshot wounds but by being clubbed to death, Phelan's word choice has more relevance than it might have had otherwise. It was rather convenient for Phelan to inject the word "club" into a story about an Indian wreaking havoc with a gun. The context is also interesting: Phelan told the story of Sergeant Hays' threat to "club" an Indian during his testimony before Henry Sibley "a few days after" Hays' body was found and after Phelan himself had actually witnessed Dr. Emerson's official examination of the body and no doubt heard his conclusion about the cause of death. If Phelan had killed Sergeant Hays and was determined to hide his guilt, then telling the investigator a fabricated story about Hays' recent threat of violence involving a club would have been rather clever. But whether Phelan completely fabricated or selectively embellished the story, he undermined its objective by stubbornly sticking to the implausible and self-incriminating account that he personally canoed Sergeant Hays across the river on the day he disappeared.

Another significant passage in the testimony was Ben Gervais' revelation about Phelan's missing calf—the one supposedly stolen by the Indians.:

> [Phelan] also came to my home on the following Sunday, but I did not understand what him and my wife talked about, except one observation that his calf had returned after the departure of Hays.[62]

If Ben Gervais' statement was correct then the prodigal lost calf—supposedly the cause of so much trouble for Phelan and Hays—had returned home, within two days after Sergeant Hays allegedly crossed the river to look for it. Again, if the calf returned home safely, then presumably the Indians hadn't stolen it. If the Indians were not responsible for the missing calf, then two important deductions would follow: First, the blood Scott found on Phelan's land definitely did not come from the calf. Second, the speculation is negated that Sergeant Hays was killed when he encountered the Indians who had stolen the calf and provoked them into a deadly confrontation. The only possible caveat to those deductions (aside from the possibility that Gervais was mistaken about the return of the calf) is the remote possibility that Indians stole the calf but it later escaped. However, that scenario is extremely unlikely. Culturally, the Dakota were hunters, not herdsmen. Cattle and sheep were of course not native to America. The historical record of Dakota thefts of livestock from the 1820s to the 1830s shows no instance of any Dakota keeping any stolen cattle at their villages.[63] In other words, the Dakota did not steal cattle to raise them but only to eat them; the practice was to slaughter them quickly and depart with the meat before the owner arrived. The idea that any Dakota would have kept a stolen calf alive for several hours (remember Phelan claimed that the calf first disappeared on Thursday and it was still missing on Friday morning) is simply not realistic. If we accept Ben Gervais' testimony that the calf returned, and follow that to the logical conclusion that Sergeant Hays was not killed by Indians in a confrontation over a stolen calf, then the theory that some Dakota killed Sergeant Hays has sustained another serious blow.

Returning to the question of a murder motive, when we first considered the possibility that local Dakota killed Sergeant Hays, the murder motive most consistent with Phelan's testimony was what we might call "the sudden confrontation over the stolen calf theory." That simple scenario is easy to imagine and fit perfectly with Phelan's persistent claim of a missing calf and Sergeant Hays' determination to find it. But if we logically reject the most obvious reason for a Dakota to kill Hays, what motive is left? Obviously, a not-so-obvious motive.

However, just because we believe that no Dakota would have

killed Hays in a confrontation over a stolen calf does not mean categorically that no Dakota would have killed him for other reasons, including ones that are now impossible to know. Thompson and Clewett's brief accounts of the dying Dakota's (Do-wau) alleged confession to Sergeant Hays' murder made no mention of his reason for killing Hays.

Because of the absence of Dakota testimony in the historical record, it is just not possible to analyze the mystery of Sergeant Hays' murder from evidence obtained directly from them. However, we do not need Dakota sources to unravel the murder mystery. The case ultimately comes down to the credibility of Edward Phelan's account of his actions on September 5 and 6, 1839. If by a preponderance of the evidence Phelan's testimony can be proven to be false, then theories of Dakota killers become irrelevant and the real murderer is exposed by his own false statements.

## Taking Stock of All the Evidence

Thus far we have painstakingly tried to test all the evidence to see if it could be logically integrated into the theory that someone other than Phelan—presumably some Dakota—had killed Sergeant Hays. The operating assumption of that theory is the premise that if Phelan was not guilty of killing Sergeant Hays, then his account of what he did on the date Sergeant Hays disappeared would have been generally true, since a sane, innocent man would have had no discernable reason to concoct elaborate lies about such an important matter. Now that we have finished trying to fit the evidence into the theory of Phelan's innocence, we can assess the results.

It is patently clear that the theory has insurmountable problems. Phelan's account of the events of September 6 does not square with the evidence. If his story is true, then several witnesses were either all lying or greatly mistaken about the events they testified about. In order to believe Phelan's account, we have to disbelieve no fewer than six witnesses, all of whom had no known reason to lie. Even if Phelan had a reputation for honesty—which he certainly didn't—it would be unreasonable to accept his version of events over the other witnesses, since he was the only witness with a powerful and provable motive to lie: he was the only one charged with the murder, which meant he was facing a death sentence. Furthermore, no single witness could corroborate Phelan's claim that Sergeant Hays was still alive on the morning of September 6, when Phelan returned home from Evans' house and allegedly transported him across the river. In fact, four eyewitnesses who saw Phelan on the river that morning swore that he didn't cross the river at the time he said he had. Foy specifically testified that he only saw Phelan canoe halfway to the island, alone, and then return back to his landing. Most significantly, we have demonstrated that Phelan did not have enough time to do what he swore he did on the morning of September 6: walk home from Evans' house, wait for Sergeant Hays to finish breakfast (and also dress in his "best clothes"), and then transport him across the river, and return back home before the arrival of Scott and Foy. It is also worth noting that Phelan was the only witness to change a part of his testimony. He originally stated to Henry Sibley that he took Sergeant Hays across the river at "about 9 or 10 o'clock" Friday morning. A month later when he testified before Joseph R. Brown—and no doubt learned that Brown had witnesses who were with him that morning—he changed the time to "about 7 o'clock." The two- to three-hour time difference is significant, and it's suspiciously convenient for Phelan to push back his Friday morning river crossing to seven o'clock in light of Scott and Foy's testimony that they saw him alone at home before nine o'clock.

We have also demonstrated that the various theories about the source of the blood found on Phelan's property on September 6 were not as credible as the theory that the blood came from Sergeant Hays. In addition, no evidence was found of either Sergeant Hays' footprints, Indian footprints, or blood on the west side of the river (where Phelan testified he transported Hays on the morning of September 6) during two separate searches conducted three and five days after Sergeant Hays' disappearance. Add it all up, and the case for Phelan's innocence appears fatally flawed.

In contrast to the fatally flawed case for Phelan's innocence, the case for his guilt will prove compelling. Unlike any theory of his innocence, the case for his guilt will have no difficulty integrating all the evidence together with one notable exception: the evidence suggesting that an Indian (Do-wau) confessed to the murder. Indeed, absent that evidence, there is almost nothing in the historical record that is consistent with Phelan's innocence. Though the Do-wau confession story has some credibility, it can be reconciled with evidence provided by Henry Sibley concerning several Fort Snelling deserters that were killed by Dakota. Sibley's evidence could support the theory that Do-wau did not actually confess to killing Hays, only a former soldier who other Dakota mistook for Hays. Furthermore, the evidence provided by Samuel Pond concerning how the Dakota killed their enemy is not consistent with how Hays was actually killed, as testified to by Dr. Emerson and Lieutenant. McPhail. The Indian confession story may be the best evidence Phelan's defense has—but it isn't enough to match the case against him.

# CHAPTER EIGHT

## The Case Against Phelan
## Does Not Favor Premeditated Murder

The case against Edward Phelan is quite compelling. Characterized by his contemporaries as "immoral, cruel [and] revengeful," he certainly appeared to be more than capable of murdering someone. He not only had the motive, means, and opportunity to kill Hays, his demonstrative lies about the last time he saw him are self-incriminating. But any argument that Phelan killed Hays, if it is to be convincing, must satisfactorily answer the when, where, why, and how of the murder.

Both the evidence and common sense suggest that Hays was murdered on Thursday evening, September 5, 1839, the night Phelan stumbled into Evans' house, muddy and carrying a canoe paddle, at "about nine o'clock."

Where exactly Phelan killed Hays is uncertain, but again both the evidence (the "body of blood" on the "trail…through the bottom") and common sense indicate that Phelan's bottomland was the likely murder scene. Since Sergeant Hays' body was found twenty-five days later, partly in the river, over a mile downstream from Phelan's place (near Carver's Cave), we might presume that on the night of the murder Phelan dragged the body through "the herbage" and then dumped it somewhere in the river. Although he probably made an effort to weigh it down and sink it, time and the elements must have caused it to resurface later and float downriver until it eventually washed ashore at the place where it was found on September 30.

Or maybe that wasn't the place it first washed ashore. Bartholomew Baldwin's statement about the military investigation of the dead body on September 30 adds a wrinkle to that question.

> As we were coming down in the boat (being one of the crew on that day) to bury the body, an Indian on board [Wabsheeda, or Dancer—who Major Taliaferro called "a good Indian"] told me that his son had seen the corpse of deceased some distance above where we found it.[1]

"Some distance above" where the body was found—"near Carver's Cave," or the riverfront below present Dayton's Bluff—would place that site on or near Phelan's bottomland. Baldwin added a few interesting details about "the place pointed out by the Indian." In his account of the "grey hairs" he found "stuck on the herbage" (which he passed off as "wolf hairs"), Baldwin said the location was in "the bottom," along "a trail," and that the bushes and "herbage [were] beaten down."[2] Earlier we surmised that this "beaten down" trail "through the bottom" was likely the same "trail…through the bottom" where Scott found the "body of blood." Adding all the evidence together, we can surmise that Sergeant Hays' body first washed ashore on Phelan's property, close to where Scott found the pool of blood weeks earlier.

The next obvious question is how did Sergeant Hays' body ultimately end up further downriver, near present-day Dayton's Bluff? Phelan had testified that he was informed about the discovery of the body on the evening of September 29, two days after the news was reported at Fort Snelling, by a settler who lived downriver named John Campbell. But it's possible Phelan knew of it days earlier. During cross-examination, Phelan's further testimony reveals some interesting details about the body. Before the military investigators arrived at the scene, "about sunrise" on Monday, September 30, Phelan, completely alone, "found the body"—with its "head and shoulders…out of the water"—and then with no one around to witness it, "hauled him partly on the beach and covered the corpse over with grass and sand."[3]

Both the significance and the absurd irony of the situation are hard to miss. Here we have Phelan, the prime murder suspect, three weeks and four days after the murder, tampering with the body before the medical examiner and other authorities arrive at the scene. Phelan even admitted that he moved the body to shore and covered it with sand and grass. Are we really to believe that was all he did? When Lt. D. H. McPhail, the military official accompanying Fort Snelling's medical examiner, arrived at the scene, perhaps an hour or so after Phelan left it, he found "the deceased laying upon his back, feet in the water and covered with grass and sand"— and notably, "perfectly naked."[4]

Stephen Scott testified that Phelan told him that Hays "had put on his best clothes" before he left for his trip to Kaposia. Phelan himself, in a partly illegible portion of his testimony, apparently said that Hays was last seen wearing a "blue coat and oxford grey pantaloons." We also know from Ben Gervais' testimony that Phelan divulged to him that Hays was wearing "square-toed" boots on the day he disappeared.[5]

The immediate question is what happened to Sergeant Hays' clothes and boots? Is it possible that Phelan removed them from Sergeant Hays' body? Though a twentieth century veteran medical investigator maintains that the river current itself is strong enough to rip the clothes off a corpse, is it unreasonable to suspect that Phelan removed Sergeant Hays' clothes from his body?[6] Hays' clothing may have made identifying his body easier, but Phelan himself testified that Hays' body was identifiable by his distinctive long nose, so he probably didn't remove Hays' clothing in hopes of concealing his identity. Perhaps Phelan took those "best clothes" and "square-toed" boots shortly after the murder because they had high monetary value. In the Upper Mississippi frontier of 1839, manufactured goods like boots and coats were in scarce supply and had a high value as a bartering item. A Mendota fur trader in 1826 paid $2.50 for "a pair of coarse shoes," a considerable sum in the days when a Fort Snelling soldier's pay was only six dollars a month.[7] According to Joseph R. Brown's biographers, Nancy and Robert Goodman, "a frock coat and a crepe tie cost Joe Brown $31 in 1831."[8] No doubt, any backwoodsman coldhearted enough to murder, would consider it a foolish waste of money to allow those valuable clothes and boots to rot with the corpse.

On the other hand, maybe Phelan removed Sergeant Hays' clothing for another reason: to make it appear that the victim was killed by Indians, who also considered fancy clothing very valuable commodities. The Dakota and other American Indian tribes, who had long traded with Europeans and their American descendants, had clearly developed a taste for European goods, especially woolens and linens. Though they continued to prefer their native moccasins to the stiff foreign shoes and boots, the Dakota highly prized European jackets, shirts, blankets, and any colorful cloth—partly because they had no way to produce their own woolens and linens (they had no sheep and raised no cotton) and partly because the foreign woolens and linens were a clear improvement over their traditional deer or buffalo skin garments. According to one fur trade scholar, "cloth was better for clothing than skins because it was light weight, easier to sew, colorful and washable."[9] The Dakota custom was to trade for unfinished cloth and blankets and then refashion them into the style of their own traditional garments. According to Samuel Pond, a missionary to the Dakota in the nineteenth century, the value one Dakota woman placed on a single woolen blanket in 1834 exceeded fifty dollars, almost ten times the monthly pay of a Fort Snelling private.[10] No question, Sergeant Hays' clothing would have had high value to the Dakota. Perhaps Phelan had thought about that and reasoned, correctly or not, that removing Sergeant Hays' clothing might cast more suspicion on the Indians.

Whatever Phelan's reasons might have been, the theory that he removed Sergeant Hays' clothes fits perfectly with the dramatic account that Alphonse Gervais shared with J. Fletcher Williams decades later.

*Alphonse Gervais stated that he saw blood on Phelan's clothes, and that, when Phelan's cabin was searched, bloody clothes were found beneath the floor. He states, moreover, that he found the place, near the cabin, where the act was committed, being led thither by a very sagacious dog he owned, who smelled the blood, and plainly traced the route by which the body was dragged to the river from thence.*[11]

Earlier we set aside Alphonse Gervais' adult recollections because they were not given under oath and were not directly corroborated by anyone else, but in this next stage of inquiry, any evidence connecting Phelan to the murder cannot be ignored.

Williams' rendition of Alphonse's account leaves the impression that the "bloody clothes" searchers found "beneath the floor" of Phelan's cabin were Phelan's own bloody clothes. But, if Alphonse Gervais' three-decade memory was generally correct and some "bloody clothes" were in fact found underneath Phelan's floorboards, it's also possible that they were also the clothes of Sergeant Hays.

However, in all our discussion of what happened to Sergeant Hays' valuable clothes, one underlying fact has been overlooked. All of the accounts of what Hays was wearing (his "best clothes") originated with Phelan. If Phelan murdered Sergeant Hays' and invented the fiction of Hays' Friday morning trip across the river, he may also have fabricated the story about the "best clothes" Hays put on that morning. If Phelan killed Sergeant Hays on Thursday night, September 5, it's not likely that Hays was wearing his "best clothes" at the time. In fact, the most likely scenario, consistent with all the evidence, is that he was not wearing anything fancy on the night of the murder. Indeed, he may not have been wearing much at all. It's possible that Phelan killed Sergeant Hays during some confrontation that erupted late in the day. If a violent argument broke out after dark, when Sergeant Hays was getting ready for bed and was only partly dressed, or wearing only night clothes, then Phelan's job of removing Hays' clothes after the murder would not have been as gruesome and difficult a chore as pulling off all the clothes of a fully dressed corpse.

Returning to the question of Phelan's handling of Hays' corpse on the morning of September 30, we can make a few logical deductions. If we assume that Hays was not dressed in his best clothes at the time of the murder, and that Phelan deliberately lied about what he was wearing, then Phelan had a good motive to undress the body: Phelan had told Scott on September 6 that Sergeant Hays was wearing his "best clothes" that morning. Thus, if Hays' body was found dressed in only plain clothes, Phelan would potentially be exposed as a liar and the discrepancy in clothing used as incriminating evidence against him.

But did Phelan remove Sergeant Hays' clothes from his body on the morning of September 30, or had he already removed them all on the night of the murder? Or did someone else, who was not the murderer (perhaps a Dakota), take Hays' clothes for himself? Or did the river current itself naturally churn the clothes off? According to one Senior Investigator with the Ramsey County Medical Examiner's office, the current of the Mississippi River is powerful enough to churn the clothes off any corpse submerged in its waters for several days.[12]

Any theory that Phelan would have taken Sergeant Hays' clothes off his body on the morning of September 30 must take into account that Hays would have been dead for over three weeks. By three weeks' time the body would have been in a very foul smelling stage of decomposition. The fact that the body had been in the water would have slowed the decomposition a little, and cold water would have slowed decomposition even more. But none of that would have stopped the inevitable odor producing decay that the body would have undergone by September 30.[13]

No doubt, someone would have to be highly motivated to willingly go through the ordeal of pulling the clothes off a rotting corpse. Outside of medical examiners and other professionals who are paid to do that unpleasant work (or loved ones who are devoted to the deceased or people with the rare perversion of necrophilia), no sane person with a functioning nose would willingly engage in such a gruesome and nauseating chore. The question is, would Phelan have been motivated enough to overcome the stench of the corpse and remove all its clothing? Obviously, if the removal of Sergeant Hays' clothes was a desired objective, doing the job shortly after his death would have been infinitely less repugnant than doing it later. But Phelan may not have thought about that at the time of the murder. Perhaps Phelan never expected that the corpse would ever wash ashore.

Yet even if we presume that Phelan did not remove Sergeant Hays' clothes on the morning of September 30—in other words, the corpse was already naked—he still would have had a good reason to tamper with the body on the day he first saw it in the river. We have already concluded that Hays' body likely first washed ashore on or close to Phelan's property. Given that probability, Phelan would have had the motive, means, and opportunity to float the body further down river (simply by using his canoe and his infamous canoe paddle) and deposit it farther away from his land. Consider how glaringly incriminating it would have been for Phelan if the military investigators found Sergeant Hays' body on his land. Such a prospect would surely have strongly motivated him to find the stomach to move the decaying corpse off his property. All things considered, it seems likely that Phelan was responsible for removing Hays' body to the spot on the riverbank (below present-day Dayton's Bluff and near Carver's Cave—the Dakota's sacred "dwelling house of the spirit") where the military investigators found it on September 30, covered with the sand and grass that Phelan admitted he placed on it. As noted earlier, if Phelan intended to pass off the murder on the Indians, then he couldn't have found a better, more convenient site to place the body than near the great sacred landmark of the Dakota, "Wakon-Teebee."

The how and why of the killing is the most intriguing part of the John Hays' murder case—mainly because much of it is an unsolvable mystery. Only the murderer knew the true why and the exact how of the killing. If Phelan was the murderer—and a preponderance of evidence points to that—there is no record that he ever confessed to anyone about it, and his secrets went with him to the grave. But we can still sleuth out some good clues about how and why Sergeant Hays was killed. The state of the victim's body—a severely battered and broken face, "mutilated in a shocking manner" caused by several hard blows "with some mighty weapon," but no reported visible signs of bruising on the rest of the naked body*—suggests a crime of passion.[14] Something could have fueled a rage in Phelan that moved him to pick up a heavy object—a canoe paddle, a shovel, a thick stick, or a rock—and furiously attack Sergeant Hays in a vicious and brutal way. We can only guess what would have triggered such a rage in Phelan. One could easily imagine any number of singular incidents, or longer escalating tensions that might have ignited a murderous fury in a man who may well have had the character flaw of a violent temper. No doubt friction must have built up between the two housemates with such opposite personalities, who had to spend many months and thousands of hours alone together on their isolated farm, attempting to make decisions and compromises together, and in the crammed living quarters of their little shanty. Maybe the meticulous, martinet Sergeant Hays got on the nerves of the rough-edged Private Phelan one too many times. Or maybe more likely, both men increasingly got on each other's nerves and in one final hostile confrontation, Phelan's hot temper, perhaps fueled by alcohol, exploded into a furious and deadly rage.

Furthermore, there are reasons that it seems less likely that Phelan premeditated the murder of Hays. Although the money motive was first suggested by Major Taliaferro, echoed by J. Fletcher Williams and probed by Joseph R. Brown, there are some challenging problems with that theory. First, it is an undisputed fact that Sergeant Hays' money was in the possession of Lieutenant McPhail at Fort Snelling. If Phelan killed Sergeant Hays for that money, how did he expect to get it? Why would anyone believe that in the event of Sergeant Hays' death, Lieutenant McPhail would give the money to Phelan?

Second, the fact that Sergeant Hays was killed (or over killed) in an extremely brutal frontal assault again suggests that the killer would

---

* In striking contrast to the elaborate details presented in a modern coroner's report, Emerson's report was brief and vague.

*Londonderry, Ireland. Circa 1890. Library of Congress Collections.*

Somewhere in the County of Londonderry, perhaps in the old city of Londonderry, Edward Phelan was born sometime in 1816. When he left Ireland is unknown.

*The Five Points, New York City. Painting by George Catlin, 1827.*

Catlin painted the notorious Irish slum eight years before Phelan mustered into the army in New York City. Circumstantial evidence suggests that Phelan may have been a resident of the Five Points prior to his enlistment and perhaps was a member of the infamous "Gangs of New York."

*Fort Snelling. Painting by John Wild, 1844. Courtesy of the Minnesota Historical Society.*

Built between 1820 and 1824, Fort Snelling was the first American garrison in Minnesota and the genesis of the Twin Cities. Ten important characters in the Phelan murder mystery served there in some capacity: Edward Phelan, John Hays, William Evans, Stephen Scott, Bartholomew Baldwin, Joseph R. Brown, Dr. John Emerson, Daniel McPhail, James Thompson and Lawrence Taliaferro. Fur trader Henry Sibley, the first investigator of the Hays murder, lived across the river from the fort in the stone house (built in 1835) at the center of the fur trading village of Mendota.

*The Henry Sibley House, Mendota, Minnesota's oldest private residence and now a Minnesota Historical Society museum. Photograph by Gary Brueggemann.*

*Little Crow Village on the Mississippi. Watercolor by Seth Eastman, 1847-1848. Courtesy of the Minnesota Historical Society.*

Located in present-day South St. Paul, just north of the intersection of Concord Street and Butler Avenue and directly across the river from Pig's Eye Lake, Little Crow's Village, or "Kaposia," was the home of about 300 Mdewakanton Dakota from 1837 until they removed to a reservation in 1853. The Mdewakanton were one of the seven tribes of the great Dakota (Sioux) nation. The tribe originally inhabited the woodlands ninety miles north of Kaposia, around the large lake they called "Mde wakan" or Spirit Lake (now Lake Mille Lacs). Hence, they were called "Mdewakanton," people from Spirit Lake. All seven tribes of the Dakota were driven from the north woods in the eighteenth century by the Ojibwe (Chippewa). Three of the tribes, including the famous Tetons (Lakota), became buffalo hunting nomads and migrated in the nineteenth century to the prairieland west of Minnesota, "the Dakotas." The Mdewakanton were the last Dakota tribe to abandon the north woods and the only Dakota to move into the forests of the Mississippi River Valley. They subsequently subdivided into six historic bands that created six landmark villages, stretching from Winona on the Mississippi River, 110 miles south of St. Paul, to Shakopee on the Minnesota River, twenty miles west of Minneapolis. The Kaposia band was led by a succession of chiefs that carried the name Little Crow. At the time of the Hays' murder, the chief of Kaposia was Big Thunder, son of the first known Little Crow and father of the famous Little Crow who led the 1862 Dakota Uprising.

*Fountain Cave, "the birthplace of St. Paul." Photograph by William H. Illingsworth, 1875. Courtesy of the Minnesota Historical Society.*

A deep natural sandstone cavern of narrow mysterious passages and circular rooms, marked by a cold spring flowing from its entrance, Fountain Cave was located exactly where the Archer Daniels Midland grain elevator now stands, a block west of Shepard Road and Randolph Avenue. After its discovery by Major Stephen Long in 1817, the cave quickly became a popular landmark. On August 2, 1820, explorer Henry Schoolcraft noted that "the cave has been visited by most persons who have passed up the Mississippi, if we may judge from the number of names upon the walls." Eighteen years later, Pierre "Pig's Eye" Parrant brought more notoriety to Fountain Cave when he opened a popular saloon there in June 1838. Early chroniclers of Minnesota history called that saloon the beginning of St. Paul.

Incredibly, before Fountain Cave's entrance was destroyed by the construction of both the grain elevators and Shepard Road in 1955, no one ever reported finding the endpoint of the mysterious cave. In 1891 explorer Willard Glaser penetrated deep into the cave and reported that "at 1,000 feet from the opening of the rock no terminus has yet been discovered." On October 14, 1955, the *St. Paul Dispatch* headlined the last report on the cave before its only entrance was buried under tons of soil and concrete. "The mystery of Fountain Cave's length remains. Some say it extends as far as West 7th and Ramsey [Street]. No one has had the courage to find the end of the tunnel."

*Carver's Cave, 1875. Photo courtesy of the Minnesota Historical Society.*

In November 1766 Captain Jonathan Carver (1710-1780), the first English explorer in Minnesota, discovered "a remarkable cave of amazing depth" inside a "rocky mountain" that eighty-three years later was named Dayton's Bluff. According to Carver, the cave's entrance was only five feet high but "the archway within" was nearly "fifteen feet high and about thirty feet broad." Deeper inside the cave was a lake of "transparent" water and on the moss-covered sandstone walls Carver found "many...very ancient" Indian drawings. Carver learned from Dakota Indians who showed him the cave that they called the sacred site "Wakon-teebe," that is "the Dwelling of the Great Spirit." After Carver published a popular book about his "Travels Through the Interior Parts of North America" in 1778, the cave became widely known as "Carver's Cave." Sixty-one years after Carver's book was published, the body of Sgt. John Hays was found along the river "near" Carver's Cave by some Dakota boys. On September 30, 1839 a "dispatchment of soldiers" from Fort Snelling buried John Hays somewhere near the cave, probably on the grounds now covered by Warner Road and the railroad tracks. The Carver's Cave entrance is no longer accessible but a historic plaque on Mounds Boulevard marks the spot on Dayton's Bluff where it is located.

*Phelan and Hays' cabin site today. Photograph by Gary Brueggemann.*

*Phelan's Landing/Upper Landing today. Photograph by Gary Brueggemann.*

*Present-day overview of the St. Paul riverfront. Photograph by Gary Brueggemann.*

The grain elevator, the tallest and closest building along the river, marks the general location of Phelan's Landing.

*Present-day overview of the Fountain Cave vicinity. Photograph by Gary Brueggemann.*

The grain elevator marks the site of Fountain Cave. The site of the Ben Gervais homestead was behind the smokestack on Ross Island.

*Present-day view of St. Paul's riverfront from Dayton's Bluff. Photograph by Gary Brueggemann.*

Somewhere between the river and the bluff, perhaps underneath the railroad tracks, is the lost grave of John Hays.

*Present-day view of Dayton's Bluff. Photograph by Gary Brueggemann.*

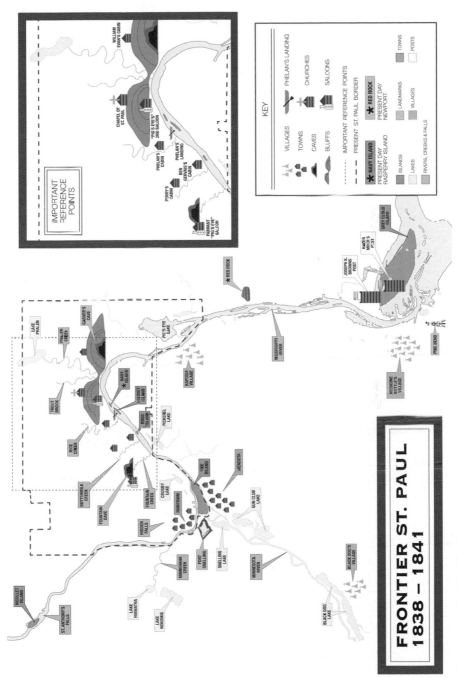

Frontier St. Paul. Map by Mary Brueggemann.

*Benjamin Gervais (1792-1875) and his wife Genevieve Larence Gervais (1804-1885), circa 1870. Photo courtesy of the Minnesota Historical Society.*

The Gervaises were key witnesses in the John Hays murder inquiry. Born in Riviere du Loup (now Louisville), Quebec, during the Presidency of George Washington, Benjamin Gervais moved west to the outpost of Pembina on the Red River in 1809 and at the age of seventeen became a voyageur for the Hudson Bay Fur Company. His voyaging took him as far west as the Canadian Rockies. Ben retired from voyaging in 1812 and joined the new Red River Colony (in present day Winnipeg), affiliated with Hudson Bay Fur Company. Despite the hardships and dangers there—Indians on the payroll of a rival fur company massacred twenty-one settlers in 1816—Ben remained at the colony for twenty-four years. There he met Genevieve Larence, also a native of the St. Lawrence River region, but her birthplace was Berthierville in the Province of Quebec. On September 29, 1823 Ben Gervais, age thirty-one, and Genevieve Larence, age twenty, were married at St. Boniface Cathedral (which still stands today in Winnipeg) by the first bishop of Manitoba, Joseph Provencher. The couple became Red River farmers and had five children there: Alphonse (born 1829), Severe (born 1829), Isaiah (born 1831), Jean Baptiste (born 1834) and Benjamin Jr. (born 1835). After enduring locusts, droughts, frosts, blizzards and floods, the Gervais family abandoned the colony in 1837 and traveled in oxcarts for forty-six days to Fort Snelling. They settled just north of the fort, in present-day Minneapolis, on land that was part of the military reservation.

On July 13, 1838, Fort Snelling Commander Major Joseph Plympton ordered all settlers off the military reservation and so the Gervaises crossed the river and moved to the Fountain Cave vicinity. They built their cabin in a little glen, just downriver from the mouth of Fountain Creek, near the island that was later called Ross Island. It was in that tamarack cabin that Genevieve gave birth to their seventh child, Basil ("the first white child born in St. Paul"), and where two days later, Phelan gave his first account of Hays search for the lost calf.

On May 6, 1840, the Gervaises endured their second forced removal from their home—this time not just by order of Fort Snelling Commandant Major Plympton, but by order of the President of the United States, Martin Van Buren. A year earlier Van Buren had approved the enlargement of the Fort Snelling military reservation to include much of present-day St. Paul and the entire Fountain Cave vicinity. The Gervaises relocated to the top of the present Kellogg Boulevard bluff and built a new cabin near the north end of the present-day Robert Street Bridge. In the fall of 1841, the Gervaises donated a parcel of their land for the community's first church, the Catholic log chapel of St. Paul, which became the village's namesake. Three years later, the Gervaises founded a new settlement, nine miles north of the chapel at a place they called "Little Canada." There the Gervaises helped to start another Catholic church, St. John the Evangelist, founded in the Gervais' log home in 1851.

Five years earlier in 1846, Ben Gervais had the first commercial grist mill in Minnesota constructed on "Gervais Creek," a short distance from "Gervais Lake." Both Ben and Genevieve Gervais are buried in St. John's Catholic Cemetery in Little Canada. Ben's grave reads: "Benjamin Gervais—the first settler of St. Paul."

*Basil Gervais (1839-1926). Photo courtesy of the Minnesota Historical Society.*

The seventh child of Benjamin and Genevieve Gervais and "the first white child born in St. Paul," Basil was the younger brother of Alphonse Gervais (1825-1904), who gave testimony at the John Hays murder inquiry and may have testified at Phelan's trial or hearing at Prairie du Chien. Basil was born probably a day before Hays was murdered.

*Henry Hastings Sibley (1811-1894). Portrait by Thomas Cantwell Healy, 1860. Courtesy of the Minnesota Historical Society.*

Minnesota's first justice of the peace, first representative to Congress, first state governor and the commander of the state militia during the Dakota Uprising of 1862, Sibley came to Minnesota's first town, Mendota, in 1834 as the regional head of the American Fur Company. The son of the Honorable Solomon Sibley (1769-1849)—the first mayor of Detroit, the first Congressman from Detroit and chief justice of Michigan's Supreme Court from 1827 to 1837—Henry Sibley was an impressive blend of brains, brawn, elegance and earthiness. Standing over six feet tall, physically fit, strong and athletic, Sibley was equally adept at wrestling, boxing, hunting and debating the fine points of the law. He was as comfortable interacting with the Indians and rough French Canadian voyageurs as he was interacting with lawyers, judges and members of Congress. Sibley was the first lawman to interrogate Edward Phelan about the murder of John Hays. His investigation of the crime in October 1839 convinced him that Phelan was guilty of the murder and the local Indians were innocent.

*Joseph Renshaw Brown (1805-1870). Engraving, 1860. Courtesy of the Minnesota Historical Society.*

The enterprising, multitalented, incredibly versatile Joseph R. Brown was at one time or another a soldier, musician, fur trader, farmer, judge, road builder, town builder, county organizer, territory and state organizer, legislator, framer of the state constitution, newspaper editor, Indian agent and inventor. He was also the first justice of the peace to serve the settlement that became St. Paul. Though he was a seasoned frontiersman who interacted with some of the roughest characters in the old Northwest, Brown's language was never coarse. According to Thomas Newson, "Mr. Brown had the habit of saying 'By George.' He never swore; he never drank; he never played cards; he did smoke cigars occasionally." On November 1, 1839 Brown, the runaway son of a Methodist Minister, became the second lawman to interrogate Edward Phelan about the murder of John Hays. Like Sibley, he concluded that Phelan was guilty of the crime. It was Brown's order that sent Phelan, in the custody of "special constable" John McCormick, to Prairie du Chien, where he could be detained in the county's only jail ("the dungeon") and tried before the only court in the county.

 The only records that survive from the murder case are Brown's rough transcripts preserved in his justice of the peace casebook. Joseph Brown died suddenly in New York City on November 9, 1870, while trying to secure a patent for a steam-powered tractor he invented. His body was transported back to Henderson, Minnesota, a town he founded in "Brown" County. There, the largest funeral in Minnesota history (before the twentieth century) was held and he was eulogized as one of the greatest founding fathers of Minnesota, the place he first named in1846.

*J. Fletcher Williams (1834-1895). Photo courtesy of the Minnesota Historical Society.*

A native of Cincinnati and graduate of Ohio Wesleyan University, John Fletcher Williams served as both secretary and librarian of the Minnesota Historical Society from 1867 to 1893 and was an expert on the early history of St. Paul. A former local newspaper reporter with "a love for historical genealogical and antiquarian research," Williams authored the first published history of St. Paul in 1876 after spending over ten years interviewing every available early settler of the city. His research of the Hays' murder led him to the conclusion that Edward Phelan was "the murderer of Hays."

*Thomas McLean Newson (1827-1893), 1885. Photo courtesy of the Minnesota Historical Society.*

A native of New York City, Newson came to St. Paul in 1853 and two years later founded and edited the *Saint Paul Daily Times.* An avid abolitionist and "one of the founders of the State Republican Party," Newson interviewed the former slave and St. Paul's first African American settler, James Thompson, in 1884 for a profile in his book *Pen Pictures,* a collection of biographical sketches of St. Paul's pioneers published in 1886. In that interview James Thompson (1800-1884) told Newson two interesting stories that relate to Edward Phelan: one was an account of a fight he had with Phelan over a pig in 1839; the other was the sensational revelation that a Dakota named "Do-Wau, the Singer" confessed to killing John Hays just before he died following the battle of Kaposia. Long hailed as "Minnesota's oldest newspaper editor," the Civil War veteran Thomas Newson died in Spain in 1893 while serving as President Benjamin Harrison's ambassador there.

*August Larpenteur (1823-1919). The earliest photo (undated) of the fur trader who became the longest surviving pioneer of St. Paul. Courtesy of the Ramsey County Historical Society.*

A native of St. Louis and the grandson of a French immigrant who had been one of Napoleon's National guardsmen, August Larpenteur came to St. Paul in 1843, three years after Edward Phelan returned from jail and settled on Phelan Creek. From his work as a fur trader, Larpenteur learned from the local Dakota "that Hays was not killed by Phelan." His defense of Phelan in his "Recollections" (1898) was the most positive appraisal of Edward Phelan on record. It is possible that Larpenteur first met Phelan in 1848 at the Stillwater Convention, when Larpenteur was one of the St. Paul delegates and Phelan was a delegate representing Prospect Hill (the Phalen Creek Valley). Prior to 1850, the year Phelan left Minnesota, Larpenteur lived on the St. Paul river bluff over a mile away from Phelan's Prospect Hill home in the remote valley of Phalen Creek.

If Larpenteur didn't meet Phelan until the Stillwater Convention then the time and place is relevant. In 1848 Phelan would have been thirty-seven years old and the formal setting of their meeting—the historic Stillwater Convention—might have conduced Phelan to be on his best behavior. In 1860 Larpenteur built a stately rural home known as "the Anchorage" at 341 North Dale. There, the pioneer who came to the crude village of St. Paul by steamboat and then routinely traveled by horse and canoe, lived long enough to see trains, streetcars, automobiles and airplanes, as well as witness the transformation of his village into a modern city marked by skyscrapers, a majestic cathedral and a magnificent domed capitol building.

*Lawrence Taliaferro (1794-1871), Fort Snelling's first and longest-serving Indian agent (1819-1839). Portrait, circa 1830 (artist unknown). Courtesy of the Minnesota Historical Society.*

A native of Virginia and a veteran of the War of 1812, the impeccably honest but allegedly arrogant Major Lawrence Taliaferro was appointed Minnesota's first agent of Indian Affairs by President James Monroe, his "patron friend," on March 27, 1819, one year before soldiers began building the garrison that became Fort Snelling. Few Indian agents in America were as devoted to serving the Indians and placing their needs above the interests of the fur traders as was Taliaferro. A diligent record keeper and journal writer, Taliaferro's papers (donated to the Minnesota Historical Society) are a treasure trove of information about the Minnesota region during the 1820s and 1830s. One of his diary entries in 1836 recorded the marriage of his slave Harriet Robinson to Dred Scott, the slave of Fort Snelling's surgeon, John Emerson, who later did the medical examination on John Hays' body. Though slavery was prohibited in the Fort Snelling region by both the Northwest Ordinance of 1787 and the Missouri Compromise of 1820, a few southern officers at Fort Snelling ignored that prohibition and kept enslaved servants there. Taliaferro, who was normally a stickler for the law, especially when it pertained to the rights of Indians, blatantly broke the slavery prohibition by keeping a few of his Virginia slaves at Fort Snelling. Interestingly, Dr. Emerson's slave, Dred Scott, went on to national fame when after Emerson's death, he sued for his freedom on the grounds that he has been illegally enslaved in "free territory." His case ultimately reached the U.S. Supreme Court in 1857, a time when the country was dangerously divided over the issue of slavery. Stunningly, the court not only ruled against Scott, it declared all the federal prohibitions against slavery in the territories unconstitutional. The infamous Dred Scott Decision helped trigger the Civil War and was one of the main issues of Abraham Lincoln's presidential campaign.

Two other entries in Taliaferro's diary were very pertinent to the Edward Phelan case. One penned on September 15, 1839, was the first record of John Hays' disappearance, which also included Taliaferro's suspicion that "Phelan knows something. Hays lived with him and had money." The second entry, written on September 27, 1839, was the first report of the discovery of Hays' body, "near Carver's old cave," which was elaborated into a letter to Commander Major Joseph Plympton. The letter led to Dr. Emerson's examination of Hays' body on Sept. 30.

*Vetal Guerin (1812–1870). Photograph (1870) courtesy of the Minnesota Historical Society. Phelan's adversary in the dispute over the rights to Sgt. Hays' land.*

A native of Saint Remi, Canada, Guerin arrived in Mendota in 1832 at age eighteen as a French-speaking voyageur employed by the American Fur Company after canoeing over one thousand miles from Montreal. Described by Thomas Newson as a "slender man, with sharp features, a mobile face, cool and slow in movements, quiet in his manner and unostentatious in his dress," Guerin staked a claim to Sgt. Hays' vacant property in "the fall of 1839" when Phelan was imprisoned at Prairie du Chien. On top of the prominent white sandstone bluff, at the present-day corner of Kellogg Boulevard and Wabasha Street, he cleared some trees and built a 16 x 20 foot "oak and elm" cabin with a bark roof. When Phelan returned home in the spring of 1840, after being acquitted of Hays' murder, he accused Guerin of claim-jumping his land, the property Phelan had first claimed in partnership with Hays in June 1838. What followed was a year-long claim dispute that ended with Guerin ultimately winning legal title to the land in June 1841. Five months earlier, on January 26, 1841, Guerin married Adele Perry, daughter of Abraham and Mary Perry, at Mendota in a ceremony performed by Father Lucien Galtier. According to Williams, the couple returned to their homestead after the wedding and "a gay and pleasant party was given to the new couple at the house of Ben Gervais during the evening." Guerin's friend, Dennis Cherrier, "fiddled that night until he was exhausted." Nine months after his wedding, in October 1841, Guerin and Ben Gervais donated parcels of their land for the grounds of Father Galtier's Chapel of Saint Paul. According to Williams, Guerin also "gave away…a block for the courthouse, several lots to the church and for other purposes" a few years later. The "plain, humble…honest and candid" Vetal Guerin died poor in his little framed house on the corner of Wabasha and Seventh Streets, on November 11, 1870, at age fifty-eight, after "a long and painful illness." His headstone at St. Paul's Calvary Cemetery was paid for by the St. Paul City Council. Newson remembered him as "a really good man…an unselfish man, kindly disposed, yet decisive in his character and [he] lived a quiet unobtrusive life."

*Rose Perry Clewett and her son Albert Clewett, the first child born on the site of present-day downtown St. Paul. Photograph (1875) courtesy of the Minnesota Historical Society.*

Rose Perry (Perret) Clewett, the second daughter of Swiss immigrants Abraham and Mary Perry and sister of Adele Perry Guerin (Vetal Guerin's wife), was the wife of James Clewett, one of Joseph R. Brown's trading partners and a witness at the Hays' murder inquiry. (No photo of James Clewett is known to exist.) Their marriage at the Kaposia Methodist Mission on April 9, 1839, was hailed as the "first Christian marriage in St. Paul." Born in 1819 in La Sagne, Switzerland, a village along the French border, Rose was the fourth child of watchmaker Abraham Perret (1779-1849) and Mary Ann Bourquin Perret (1790-1859), a woman known for her skills as a midwife. Rose immigrated with her family (including her brother Charles and sisters Sophia and Fanny) to the Red River Colony in November 1821. After enduring six years of incredible hardships at the remote colony, the Perry family joined 235 other demoralized colonists and fled south to the United States in oxcarts.

They reached Fort Snelling forty six days later, in August 1827, and were permitted to temporarily settle on the military grounds north of the fort, on the west bank of the Mississippi in present-day Minneapolis. Eleven years later, Major Joseph Plympton, commander of Fort Snelling, finally evicted all the west bank squatters from the military reservation. It was then that the Perrys moved to a claim downriver near Fountain Cave in June 1838 and became the first family farmers in present-day St. Paul. They made their home a few blocks east of the cave, on a little plateau of open meadow near the top of a rocky, lightly wooded bluff, where a "beautiful stream" called "Buttermilk Creek" meandered to the river, forming a cascade (Buttermilk Falls) above the plateau. There, near Buttermilk Falls, somewhere in what is now the Duke Street, Colborne Street, Palace Avenue block, they built a log house large enough for a family that now included five daughters.

Sometime during the winter of 1839, a twenty-nine-year-old immigrant from England named James Reuben Clewett lodged with the Perry family. Clewett had been employed by the American Fur Company since 1831 and had recently worked with Joseph R. Brown at a trading post on Grey Cloud Island. Exactly how and why he ended up at the Perry home is not known, but that was probably the start of the romance that flowered into James and Rose's April wedding. Shortly after their marriage, James and Rose Clewett made their own home near present-day Fourth Street and Lafayette Road. Rose gave birth to their first child, Albert, there in January, 1840-- twenty-one months before the Chapel of St. Paul was built. The Clewetts called Albert the first white child born in St. Paul because when the village of St. Paul sprang up, Fountain Cave (Basil Gervais' birthplace) was not part of the village.

That spring James Clewett served as Phelan's French translator in his land dispute with Guerin. The Clewetts moved to "Jackson Street hill" in 1843 and then eight years later left town for a new homestead at White Bear Lake, where they raised twelve children.

*The dungeon where Edward Phelan was jailed from October 1839 to the spring of 1840, now in the basement of the Crawford County Courthouse, Prairie du Chien, Wisconsin. Photo courtesy of Kathleen Marie Connor.*

*The earliest photograph of St. Paul, showing the corner of Third Street (now Kellogg Boulevard) and Robert Street. Daguerreotype by Joel Emmons Whitney, 1851 (one year after Phelan left town). Courtesy of the Minnesota Historical Society.*

A block east of this corner was the east end of John Hays' original claim, later owned by Vetal Guerin. This corner of Third and Robert Streets was originally part of the large riverfront claim made by Pierre "Pig's Eye" Parrant in May 1839. Parrant sold the claim a year later to Ben Gervais for ten dollars. In 1844 Gervais sold the lower part of his land to Louis Robert (1811-1874), the namesake of Robert Street, who then built his home and store on the west side of Robert Street, just south of Third Street. The church on the hill to the right was the "First Baptist Church," built in 1849. Hence the hill was called "Baptist Hill." It was later leveled to fill in a ravine. Today it is the grounds of Mears Park.

*The village of St. Paul, 1844. Sketch by Charles William Post, 1889. Courtesy of the Minnesota Historical Society.*

*Chapel of St. Paul. Painting by Alexis Jean Fournier, 1888. Courtesy of the Minnesota Historical Society.*

On land donated by Ben Gervais and Vetal Guerin, "two good, quiet farmers," on the grounds now marked by a monument on the south side of Kellogg Boulevard near Minnesota Street, a Catholic chapel of rough red and white oak logs, was erected in "a few days" during October 1841. The construction work was a community project supervised by Father Lucien Galtier (1812–1866), the young French priest who was the pastor of St. Peter's Church (Minnesota's first Catholic parish) seven miles upriver at Mendota. Isaac Labissoniere (1823-1910), one of the eight men who built the chapel, remembered it as "about twenty five feet long, eighteen feet wide, and ten feet high" with "a single window on each side." On All Saints Day, November 1, 1841 (exactly two years after Joseph R. Brown's inquiry into the death of John Hays) Father Galtier consecrated the crude church as "the Chapel of Saint Paul" and that day the congregation adopted his proposal to change the name of the infant village from "Pig's Eye" to "Saint Paul." Some of the chapel's property, including the cemetery grounds, was originally part of the claim that Edward Phelan made for John Hays.

*Phalen Creek today, in Swede Hollow Park. Photo by Gary Brueggemann.*

*Phelan's cabin site today and the remnants of "Felyn's Falls." The building in the background is the former Hamm's Brewery. Photo by Gary Brueggemann.*

have stood face to face with the victim while delivering the deadly blows. The blood that would have gushed out of Sergeant Hays' battered face would have been tremendous—making it utterly impossible for the attacker to avoid being splattered with blood. Given that reality, why would anyone planning a murder-for-profit choose to kill the victim by way of a messy frontal assault, in which he would have to look the victim in the eye and then proceed to repeatedly batter them? Wouldn't it be infinitely easier, cleaner, and less unsettling for a someone premeditating a murder to simply knock the victim in the back of the head when he wasn't expecting it and then dispatch of him in any number of ways when he was lying face down? Only a vicious sadist who took pleasure in seeing the frightened face of a person about to die and who also enjoyed the sight of blood would deliberately plan a murder like the one that took the life of Sergeant Hays. It's possible that Phelan, who was reputedly "cruel," was also a secret psychopathic sadist, but aside from that possibility, what good reason would he have had to deliberately kill Sergeant Hays in such a morbid manner? Earlier we suggested the possibility that Phelan may have intended to club Sergeant Hays from behind, but that at the last moment the victim turned, escalating the scene. That scenario still holds up, but it may be the only plausible one that works if we assume that Phelan was not a sadist but did premeditate the murder.

Third, Phelan voluntarily walked into a neighbor's house on the presumed night of the murder and allowed himself to be witnessed by three men, while still wearing muddy clothes and carrying a canoe paddle; this does not suggest a planned murder. It could be evidence of a spontaneous killing, but it is hard to conceive of a rational murder plan that would include appearing before witnesses before changing incriminating clothes and discarding a suspicious looking paddle. Earlier we conceded the possibility that Phelan could have planned to kill Sergeant Hays but the plan was interrupted by something unexpected. If that was the case, Phelan wasn't very good at improvising, given the incriminating way he presented himself to the three surprised witnesses who saw him shortly after the murder.

We also previously conceded the possibility that Phelan could have had a monetary motive for murdering Sergeant Hays having to do with the value of Hays' large land claim and cattle, clothing, and other possessions. Phelan did eventually try to take over Sergeant Hays' land when he returned from his detention at the Prairie du Chien jail. And we also have good circumstantial evidence from the 1847 tax assessment records that Phelan may have ultimately acquired Hays' cattle after he returned from Prairie du Chien. The value of Sergeant Hays' land and cattle holdings would have been a tempting motive for murder for any "unscrupulous" cold-blooded criminal. But again, even if we accept that motive as valid, we still can't account for the untidy way Sergeant Hays was killed. Some imaginative minds might conjure up a few scenarios that combine elements of both a rage killing and a premeditated murder-for-profit. Perhaps Phelan was both angry with Sergeant Hays and covetous of his valuable property. Perhaps Phelan had considered that he might be better off with his housemate's property, but without his housemate. Such dark thoughts may never have evolved to the point where he seriously planned to murder Sergeant Hays, but perhaps provoked, and in a flash of fury and quick thinking, Phelan saw how his dark daydream could instantly become a reality—and followed through.

Many different scenarios of how and why Phelan allegedly killed Sergeant Hays can be pieced together from the evidence that survives. The scenario presented in the next chapter is admittedly sheer speculation, but it neatly integrates all the evidence into a credible and comprehensive story.

# CHAPTER NINE

# A Fictional Account of the Murder and Cover-Up Based on the Historical Record

After four months and ten days of living together in their little shanty and working together on their large partnership farm, tensions between Edward Phelan and John Hays—the two Irishmen from two very different regions of Ireland, with two exceedingly different personalities—had naturally developed. Though some neighbors and visitors may not have noticed any outward antagonism between them, in the words of J. Fletcher Williams, "it was known that they did not agree very well."[1] Indeed, when they were alone with each other, which was most of the time, quarreling was routine. Much of their antagonism simply stemmed from their fundamental differences.

By all accounts, John Hays was an amicable man, an "honest, good, courteous and clever old gentleman," who "impressed everybody who met him favorably."[2] True, like many middle-aged men, he was rather set in his ways, a trait no doubt intensified by both his long bachelorhood and long service in the army. Sergeant Hays retained much of the regimen of his life in the military. He was a creature of habit and a lover of routine. He liked to eat at certain times and liked his food served in certain ways. He was particular about how he dressed and his personal hygiene. He religiously shaved every day, bathed as often as he could, and got his hair cut every month. He was accustomed to doing certain tasks, like preparing breakfast, in particular, almost ritualistic ways, which he stubbornly asserted were the best possible methods of doing them. Although he was good at cracking jokes and telling funny stories, there were some things he took very seriously: his honor and integrity, his faith in God, and the absolutes of what is right and what is wrong. Yet he wasn't overtly religious, or overly judgmental; he understood that no one was perfect, and he was certainly no saint. So he got along with a wide variety of people including, at least for a while, a man who clearly did not share his values, Private Edward Phelan.

Unlike Sergeant Hays, Private Phelan did not have a reputation as an "honest, good, courteous...gentleman," and it obviously did not bother him that he didn't. Phelan was a rough man with a rough background. He grew up fending for himself and surviving by the use of his fists and the overdevelopment of his selfish animal instincts. Phelan didn't just lack polish, he lacked character. His core values stemmed from the impulse of following his own self-interest. Whatever Christian faith he was born into, he lost it trying to survive first in the war-scarred, turbulent city of Londonderry, and then on the stinking streets of one of the most violent slums in New York. Phelan was not unlike many of the young hooligans who came from the gang-dominated, criminal-infested slums of New York during the early nineteenth century: he was quick to lie, quick to steal, and quick to fight. The formal discipline of the army (into which he was coerced by a New York judge) tamed his wild nature somewhat, and perhaps the kind mentoring of a Sergeant like John Hays, helped him eventually turn into a seemingly functioning adult by the time his military service, or sentence, ended when he was twenty-seven. Still, Phelan's reputation around Fort Snelling was notoriously bad. No soldier or settler in the recorded history of the frontier fort was ever depicted in a worse light than Phelan. He was conspicuous by only being remembered for his negatives: "Phelan was considered by his superiors as a bad, unscrupulous man." Edward Phelan was "immoral, cruel, revengeful and unscrupulous." Edward Phelan "bore a rather unsavory reputation." Edward Phelan was a "ruffian" who "most civil and well-disposed persons avoided as a dangerous person."[3] Of course, none of those depictions were false. Phelan never fully outgrew the bad behavior of his youth, and he even took a sick pride in the "lawless and criminal life" he had lived in New York. Phelan's imposing size (almost six feet three inches with a "splendid physique"), combined with his rough, aggressive manner, made him one of the most intimidating guys in the Fort Snelling region.

Why gentleman Johnny Hays ever decided to team up with the big thug was a mystery to the soldiers who knew them, but it might have been partly the result of the good sergeant taking a fatherly interest in one of his wayward platoon members. Of course, Hays partnering with Phelan in land claims was a sound business decision since Phelan had the earlier opportunity to claim some of the best land in the Fort Snelling area, and Hays had the money to fund it. From Phelan's standpoint, partnering with Hays was to his advantage. Phelan had been a poor man going into the army, and he was just as poor when he left it. Any sizable land claim would require money and equipment, two things he was sorely lacking. Though no money was required to stake a claim in the opening stage of the land rush to the east side of the local Mississippi, Phelan knew that sooner or later federal land surveyors would arrive on the scene and survey the Land Grant into precisely defined townships, sections, and quarter sections. When that happened (Phelan said he "had heard of surveyors coming to survey the Land Grant" in the summer of 1838), any land claimant who wanted legal title to his frontier property would have to pay the federal land office a minimum of $1.25 per acre for that title. If Phelan hoped to own a quarter section (160 acres) of the land he claimed, he would need at least two hundred dollars, and that was a considerable sum of money for a soldier who was paid only six dollars a month. But just to claim land, clear some trees, and build a cabin would require some necessary immediate investment. At a minimum, Phelan would need a few essential tools: a felling axe for clearing timber, a broad axe for squaring logs, some type of wedging iron, and several yards of rope, as well as a few cooking utensils and other household necessities including candles and flint and steel for lighting fires. Just those few supplies would cost Phelan more than he could afford. Teaming up with the relatively rich veteran sergeant enabled the relatively poor private to finance the building of a cabin, the purchase of some cattle, and the carving out of a farm.

For the first nine months of their partnership Phelan had it mostly his way. Hays was stuck at Fort Snelling finishing out the last year of his enlistment, so Phelan was alone on their land making decisions about virtually everything. He selected each of their land claims; he built the cabin according to his specifications and made it a home according to his preferences. For nine months Phelan was alone in his world and lived according to his own rules. No more army regimentation. He ate when he wanted to and, within the limits of what was available, what he wanted to; he slept when he wanted to and got up when he pleased, and he worked when he decided to work, and relaxed when he decided to relax.

That all changed in April 1839 when Hays' military service ended and he was discharged from Fort Snelling. Now Phelan had to radically adjust to living with another person, one who did not share his values, lifestyle, or habits, and who was much older than him. Now they had to coordinate eating, sleeping, working, and relaxing. Now his older financial partner, who controlled all the money, had a strong say in the way they lived. It didn't take long for Phelan to grow resentful of the deal he had made with Hays. Though there were some benefits to having a housemate (being alone for long periods of time could get depressing), they weren't enough to outweigh the negatives.

To most people John Hays was a very likeable guy, but Phelan was clearly not like most people. Several of the attributes that others found appealing in Hays, Phelan found annoying. The age difference between the two men didn't help. Hays worked at a slower pace; he was deliberate and took exceeding care in everything he did. Phelan, on the other hand, was young, fast, and loose; even at twenty-seven he still had much of the impulsiveness and recklessness of an undisciplined teenager.

But Phelan's resentment of Hays was mostly rooted in his deep awareness that he was completely financially dependent on Hays. It was humiliating for Phelan—the alpha male, the big tough guy who liked to dominate others—to admit that the real power in the partnership belonged to Hays, simply because he had the money and owned all the tools and equipment. Even though Hays was smaller than Phelan, his money, intelligence, age, and sophistication gave him the dominant position in their partnership. And the old martinet sergeant was not afraid to assert his leadership. After all, giving orders to young men was what Hays had done for a living in the military; giving orders to Phelan, the young former private, just came naturally.

But Phelan was never good at taking orders—that's why he had hated the military and why his life in the army truly was a prison sentence for him. Now free from the military discipline, he quickly reverted to his old ways of living just for himself and following no rules but his own whims. A clash between the old, bossy, finicky sergeant—the ultimate conventionalist—and the young, unruly, aggressive private—the ultimate individualist—was inevitable.

Given that Phelan was so much more inclined to settle arguments with his fists than with reasoned diplomacy, it is somewhat surprising that the hot-tempered Irishman managed to restrain himself from assaulting Hays for over sixteen straight weeks. Ironically, it may have been his effort at trying to restrain his violent urges that led to the deadly explosion of rage that finally erupted from him four months and ten days after Hays moved into their shanty. For resentment, jealousy, and anger had been dangerously boiling up in Phelan for several weeks, yet he managed to repress it as much as he could.

A key igniter of Phelan's demonic fury was Hays' turning-point decision to spend fifty dollars to buy an Indian wife. Influenced by his friend Bart Baldwin, the Fort Snelling Indian interpreter who was happily married to a local mixed-blood Dakota woman, Hays became convinced that he too could find happiness by taking a Dakota wife. Baldwin persuaded him of the many advantages. There were hardly any single white women in the remote Fort Snelling frontier, and Baldwin claimed that Dakota women actually made better wives than white women: in Dakota culture, women were responsible not only for the domestic duties of cooking, sewing, and caring for children, but also for the agricultural work of planting and tending the crops of corn, cucumbers, and pumpkins they traditionally grew. In short, Dakota women were ideal wives for farmers. Indeed, they were culturally inculcated to be hard working, loyal, and subordinate wives to their husbands and attentive, nurturing mothers to their children. If Hays could marry a Dakota woman, he would have a loyal, hard-working, unassertive partner, experienced in agriculture, who would help him develop his land into a successful farm and bear children to help with the farm work and carry on his name.

Hays' enthusiasm to buy an Indian girl irritated Phelan. He was jealous that his partner would be able to enjoy the pleasures of a female companion, while he had no realistic hope of marrying anytime soon. He didn't have enough money to buy an Indian girl, and he had utterly failed to woo either of the Perry sisters, the only single women in his corner of the frontier, during his visits to their home. Second, he resented the fact that even though Hays was middle-aged and less attractive then he was, simply because the gray-haired, long-nosed sergeant had the money and connections, he and not Phelan would get the opportunity to have a wife. Third, he also resented Hays for wanting to spend extravagantly—fifty dollars—on something that was of no benefit to Phelan. If Hays wanted to spend fifty dollars to buy more livestock—cattle or pigs or chickens—or additional supplies, or food and liquor, then Phelan would have no complaint. But Phelan resented the indulgence in something that was both expensive and strictly personal. Fourth, if Hays married, he would likely move out of the cabin and take his tools, equipment, and livestock with him, leaving Phelan empty-handed and without the means to make an adequate living. Though it was humiliating to admit it, the truth was that as much as Phelan resented Hays and was annoyed by him, he was not ready to break up the partnership because he depended on Hays for his economic survival.

But Hays wasn't about to let his partner starve. He intended to be fair to Phelan by offering him a good deal on some of his equipment and by being generous in how they divided the livestock and other items that they shared in common. The truth was, with or without a wife, Hays was ready to dissolve their partnership and move out of the shanty. He was tired of living with Phelan, tired of his ill manners, immaturity, and ingratitude. Moreover, he was increasingly apprehensive about Phelan's hot temper, which, when mixed with alcohol, was particularly ugly. After four months of living together, Hays had come to the full realization that he and Phelan not only were hopelessly incompatible but that his housemate was a dangerous man.

## The Trouble Begins

Late Thursday morning, September 5, 1839, young Alphonse Gervais showed up at the shanty door to share the news that his mother had given birth to a baby boy. The two men politely acknowledged the news, and Hays told Alphonse that when his mother was ready for visitors, they would come over and see the baby. Alphonse replied that his family was already preparing to entertain visitors on Friday afternoon. After Alphonse departed, the time seemed right for Hays to divulge the full details of his plan to take an Indian wife, move out of the cabin, and start a new life with a new partner in a new home. Phelan had long been expecting this, but listening to Hays politely but awkwardly articulate his plan made Phelan want to punch him in his long, ugly nose. But he repressed his urge and forced himself to listen to Hays lay out the tedious details of his plan, which was so typical of Hays, the habitual organizer.

Step one: After chores on Friday morning, Hays would canoe to Fort Snelling and meet Bart Baldwin, Franklin Steele, and Lieutenant McPhail to make arrangements for his marriage. Baldwin would serve as his interpreter and counselor when he went to Kaposia the next day (Saturday) to acquire his Dakota wife. Step two: He would return home from the fort later on Friday, and then he and Phelan would canoe downriver to Evans' cabin to inform their friend about his plans. Then they would return home in time to milk the cows and then go and visit the Gervaises. Step three: Early Saturday morning Hays would dress in his best clothes, canoe up to Fort Snelling, pick up Baldwin and then paddle down to Kaposia to negotiate for the purchase of a wife. Step four: If all went well at Kaposia, his new wife would accompany them back to Fort Snelling, where McPhail would have some sort of wedding ceremony planned. Step five: That evening he and his wife would spend their first night together in the back room of Franklin Steele's sutler's store. Step six: On Monday morning he would load supplies from Steele's store into his canoe and one of the fort's Mackinaw boats and then, with as many friends as he could muster, the entire party would row and paddle back down to his claim, where everyone (including Evans, who would have walked to the site, and Phelan, who would have ridden there in Hays' oxcart) would all pitch in and help him build a new cabin.

Phelan immediately pointed out the many ways Hays' plan could fall apart, simply because so many things were so contingent on uncertainties. He also questioned why Hays was so eager to rush into a marriage with someone he hadn't even met and probably would not even be able to talk to unless an interpreter was present.

Hays admitted that the plan was not set in stone and that it certainly was contingent on the cooperation of several people, especially Bart Baldwin, Chief Big Thunder, and of course, the fathers and brothers of Kaposia's available maidens. He acknowledged that this marriage might not happen as quickly as he planned, but he hoped his plan would get things moving so that it would happen sooner rather than later. Hays did not tell Phelan that one reason he was hurrying things along was his urgency to get away from him.

The immediacy of Hays' planned departure forced the two men finally to face the touchy issue of the division of their property. Because their partnership was a loose, informal arrangement, with nothing delineated in writing, dividing their common property was not easy. It was a challenge just to determine exactly what was their common property and what was their personal property. Aside from their separate, marked land claims and their unquestionable personal possessions (like Phelan's hat and knapsack and Hays' trunk and Bible), much of what they shared on the farm—including the livestock, the tools, the oxcart, and the canoe—were never mutually acknowledged to be either their joint property or Hays' personal property. The confusion and complication stemmed from the fact that many of the items were mostly paid for with Hays' money but mostly purchased through the efforts of Phelan. In other words, Phelan was typically the "bargainer" who negotiated the purchase of the items, and Hays was the money man who paid for them.

In the case of the cattle, Phelan selected the cattle and then negotiated with the owner for the lowest possible price. Hays would assess the deal and if he approved it, give Phelan the money to finalize it. Hays did not involve himself in the purchases because at the time he was still in the army and in the confines of Fort Snelling. (Phelan left the Army ten months before Hays did.) The perplexing question was how much in non-monetary terms was Phelan's time and effort worth? One head of cattle? Two head? Three head? Three pigs? An axe and shovel? (Due to the lack of local records, the 1839 value for these items is difficult to calculate. Hays told Baldwin that a cow would cost less than fifty dollars. St. Croix County Tax Assessment Records for 1847, the earliest such records available, show that the average cost of one head of cattle was about twenty dollars and the average cost of one hog was about two dollars and fifty cents.)[4] Other fundamental factors to consider were the value of Hays' land claim and how much compensation Phelan merited for securing it when Hays was still at Fort Snelling. Further complicating that issue were the extensive improvements Hays helped to make on Phelan's claim, either monetarily or by his own labor. The shanty on Phelan's land may have been built by Phelan (with help from Jim Thompson) but the materials that went into it and the tools used to construct it were all paid for by Hays. The fencing on Phelan's land was financed by Hays, and he actually helped build some of it. The root cellar on Phelan's land was dug with shovels paid for by Hays, and he had done half the digging. He also helped clear trees and brush from Phelan's Landing. These tangible improvements were a benefit solely to Phelan because they directly increased the value of his land. One might reasonably argue that substantial improvements like these were sufficient compensation for the services Phelan rendered in claiming Hays' land for him. But Phelan was not a reasonable arguer. In his typical bullyboy fashion, Phelan asserted that he was entitled to half the cattle, at least two of the pigs, and several tools. He further argued that they should equally divide their two vehicles, whereby he would get the canoe, and Hays could take the oxcart. (Never mind that Hays had both acquired and paid for them.) As unreasonable as Phelan was, Hays took pains to be generous and accommodating. Ultimately, however, the sergeant wouldn't stand by and let Phelan bully his way into a settlement that was ridiculously one-sided. Phelan's outrageous demands were both an insult to Hays' intelligence and an offense to his manhood. Hays was kind-hearted, but he wasn't a fool. Neither was he a coward who could be easily intimidated. The sergeant was willing to give Phelan more than he deserved, but he was tired of Phelan's continual attempts to take advantage of his generosity. Phelan's demands approached extortion, and Hays was firmly determined not to give into him. Instead, Hays proposed a fair and reasonable division of their property: Phelan could take his pick of any two cows and one heifer (a young female), plus he could take the bull calf (the only surviving calf that their eight cattle produced) and his pick of any two hogs. Hays also offered an axe, shovel, sickle, small kettle, water bucket, half a dozen candles, eight feet of rope and every eating utensil Phelan had used as his own, including his favorite clay cup.

As for the canoe and oxcart, Phelan would get neither. Although he had the use of both of them for months and treated them as if they were his own, he had no demonstrative claim to either one of them. Hays had paid for and struck the deals for both vehicles. The oxcart he got from the Red River immigrant Peter Quinn, who was the only Irishman that came to Fort Snelling from the Red River Colony (present-day Winnipeg)—the birthplace of the famed "Red River Oxcarts." Hays met Quinn at Fort Snelling when for a time he worked with Bart Baldwin as an Indian interpreter.* He got the canoe, a dugout log canoe, from his friend Franklin Steele, the Fort Snelling sutler. Steele sold it to Hays after he acquired a newer, better birchbark canoe. Hays firmly asserted that the oxcart and canoe belonged to him and could not be considered part of their joint property. If Phelan wanted the canoe he would have to pay for it, and the price would not be cheap. But since Phelan had no money and few possessions he could afford to trade, Hays had no intention of selling his canoe to Phelan. Instead he offered his ex-partner the free use of the canoe on those occasions when he really needed it.

Phelan was furious. Though he tried to make a rational argument for his preposterous, equal-division proposal, making a rational argument was not his forte. His real forte was the use of intimidation. Phelan's boisterousness made Hays uncomfortable but the sergeant had too much experience with Phelan and thugs like him for those bullying tactics to work. Phelan's yelling and cursing eventually subsided and finally, at least for a while, he quit arguing and withdrew into the cabin.

Now he was a sullen, brooding mumbler who only seemed interested in the jug of liquor he was drinking. If getting drunk was Phelan's objective, by the afternoon he had achieved it. But his drunkenness ominously reignited his angry energy, and he went outside and confronted Hays a second time about their property disputes. Phelan now insisted on selecting his cattle immediately. Sensing trouble, Hays humored him by politely agreeing to help him herd and sort the cattle, even though he had just put them to pasture after milking them all by himself. Since the cattle were grazing on the plateau (in present-day Irvine Park) a few hundred yards from their cabin, it would take some time to drive them back into the pen next to the cabin.

---

* Although there is no record of a direct relationship between Hays and Quinn, they were in fact at Fort Snelling at the same time. Aside from the fiction that Quinn sold an oxcart to Hays, all details given about Quinn are true. See Minnesota Historical Society Collection Vol. XIV (1912), p. 621.

When Hays and a stumbling Phelan reached the herd, they discovered that their only surviving calf was missing. Phelan erupted into a cursing tirade, damning both the animal and the Indians he automatically suspected of stealing it. Hays remained calm and tried to assure Phelan that the frisky calf had probably just wandered off. Hays jogged ahead and took a quick 360 degree view of the surrounding landscape. Unfortunately, there was no sign of the calf. Hays wasn't sure which direction to search but headed west with Phelan in tow. But Phelan made it painfully obvious that he was in no mood for a search, keeping up his tirade against the calf and the Indians. Hays' patience was wearing thin but he knew it was not wise to criticize him when he was drunk. Hays soon realized that even though he could use another man's help, he would be better off without the drunken, foul-mouthed Phelan at his side. He suggested that Phelan return to the cabin, sleep off his stupor, and watch for the calf on his way home. For the first time that day, Phelan agreed with Hays. Longing for a nap and tired of walking, Phelan cracked a smile and headed back to the cabin. Pleased to be alone, Hays continued looking for the calf. After walking a considerable distance westward through the meadow, Hays decided to search in another direction. Turning northeast and heading toward the marsh at the top of the bluff (the vicinity of today's West Seventh and Eagle Streets)* he heard a sound in the distance: Was it a bawling calf? His question was answered when he reached the marsh; there was the calf stuck in mud. Hays waded knee-deep into the swamp to reach the calf, something the clean-cut, meticulous sergeant resisted doing, but there was no other choice. The calf was stuck up to its shoulders in muck and mire, and Hays had a devil of a time trying to pull him out. But with a lot of sweat, toil, and fear that the calf was doomed to die in the swamp, Hays finally managed to free the animal. Now the frisky calf was not so frisky. He was covered in mud and exhausted from his ordeal. But Hays was in the same condition, only the mud bothered

---

* According to Williams, that area was originally a swamp.

Hays more than it did the calf. Hays was a fanatic about being clean and neat and so the fact that he was completely covered in mud and stinking of swamp water made him excruciatingly uncomfortable.

Muddy, mucky, and miserable, Hays led the calf down the hill and back to the herd. Then he finished the original job of driving the cattle, calf included, back to the pen. Regardless of the time and the temperature—it was past six o'clock and about sixty degrees—the muddy, grimy, smelly Hays couldn't wait a minute longer to bathe in the creek. Hurrying into the cabin to grab his blanket and nightshirt (no sense in getting fully dressed again and the only clean clothes he had left were his good clothes that he planned to wear to Kaposia), he saw his housemate, sound asleep on the crude cot that served as his bed. He was tempted to wake up the lazy lug and put him to work making supper, but he knew full well that there would be less turmoil if he just let him sleep. Thus, quickly and quietly, Hays grabbed his nightshirt and blanket and slipped out of the cabin, leaving Phelan undisturbed. Down at the creek, he pulled off all of his stinking, mud-crusted clothes, waded in and washed the mud off himself and his clothes. Even though the creek was cold and the air was cool, Hays did not abbreviate his bath—he was determined to be completely clean, no matter how long it took and how cold it might be. Such was the self-discipline and dedication to cleanliness of Sergeant John Hays. When the clean but shivering sergeant finished bathing and had laid out his wet clothes and boots on a nearby rock to dry, he slipped on his nightshirt and wrapped himself in his long woolen blanket. When Hays returned home, his shivering was compounded by strong hunger pangs. It was unusual for the routine-oriented sergeant to wait that long for supper, but the calf episode and the drama of settling up his affairs with Phelan made for a most unusual day. Hays was so cold, hungry, and tired when he returned to the cabin that he no longer concerned himself with disturbing the sleeping Phelan. There was no way to make supper quietly; if Phelan woke up growling, it wouldn't be the first time.

## Phelan's Rising Rage

Phelan woke up ornery but became a little less so when Hays told him that he had found the calf and it was safely penned. But as Hays began to tell the story of the rescue, it was *his* voice that grew louder and more animated. Now it was Hays' turn to vent some of his pent up frustration over the day's many aggravations. But the yawning and stretching Phelan had no desire to hear Hays' complaints. Now his only urgent desire was to go outside and relieve himself of some of the cheap, watered-down whiskey he had drunk. Thus, rudely or not, in the middle of Hays' rant, Phelan walked outside and relieved himself in the weeds by the cattle pen. When he was finished, he started studying the cattle and suddenly his ugly anger returned. Unfortunately for Hays, Phelan hadn't forgotten all the reasons why he was upset with his partner. Although his sleep had dissipated some of his drunkenness, a hangover thirst for more drink made him even more ornery when he remembered that he had drunk the last of his whiskey. On top of that was the sight of the mud-caked calf—that troublesome baby bull that was supposed to be one of the cattle offered to him. Seeing the calf made him think what a lousy deal it was for him to get that little varmint instead of another animal. Yelling out to Hays like it was an emergency, Phelan demanded that his roommate come outside to hear his new proposal for dividing the cattle. Hays, who was just beginning to make his long-delayed supper, was in no mood to go out in his nightshirt only to rehash a deal that was already settled. But Phelan's boisterous yelling was impossible to ignore, so with a sigh of disgust and a weary face, Hays left the cabin and joined Phelan at the cattle pen.

This time, Hays did not repress his indignation. He demanded to know what was so urgent that it couldn't wait until after supper. Hays' assertiveness did not impress Phelan, nor stifle his contentiousness. Phelan pointed to the calf and said he didn't want it. Instead, he wanted either another cow, or heifer, or steer.

Hays was stunned by Phelan's audacity. He had already made a generous deal with Phelan, yet the ingrate was still trying to extort more out of him. Hays authoritatively said no deal. The calf had been thrown into the bargain as a kind of bonus; if Phelan didn't want the calf, he didn't have to take it, but Hays adamantly opposed swapping the calf for any older cattle.

Both men stubbornly held to their positions until finally Hays suggested that they settle the matter in the morning by going to William Evans and enlisting him as a neutral arbitrator of the dispute. Evans owned cattle too. He was good at appraising livestock, and was an honest, good friend of both of them; Hays claimed that their Irish neighbor would be a perfect mediator. But a fair arbitrator was the last thing Phelan wanted. He argued that Evans would be partial to Hays simply because he liked the sergeant better than he liked Phelan. Out of patience and still hungry and cold, Hays returned to the cabin. He grabbed some pemmican (Indian style dried meat) from a small wicker basket and then made a fatal mistake: he opened his trunk that doubled as a table and pulled out his last bottle of fine wine. He should have known better than to drink his best wine on a night when Phelan was mad drunk and all out of his own liquor, but it had been a rough day, and if ever there were a time that he deserved a swig of good wine, it was that night. He was, of course, gambling that he could finish his drink before Phelan came back into the cabin; he would only take a few swigs. Unfortunately, he gambled wrong. Phelan suddenly barged into the cabin and like a wolf smelling blood, he immediately eyed the bottle Hays held in his hand. For the second time that day Phelan broke into a smile, a sinister smile. Feigning politeness, he asked Hays for a drink. Hays refused. First, he pointed out that Phelan had had too much to drink already and second, he reminded Phelan that it was expensive French wine that he had been saving for over a year, and he was hoping to make it last as long as possible. All he could afford for this occasion was a few sips for himself.

Phelan replied that the sergeant was being selfish and reminded him of the times he had shared his whiskey with him. Hays retorted that his money had paid for most of Phelan's whiskey and more importantly, there was a huge difference between the cheap, diluted whiskey that Pigs Eye Parrant sold them and the fancy French wine that he held in his hand.

However, Phelan was not listening to Hays' sound reasoning; he was not in a reasoning mood. His animal instincts were now ruling him and the two strongest ones were the desire for wine and disdain for the man who had it. Phelan dropped all pretense of politeness and belligerently ordered Hays to give him some wine. Hays refused, but Phelan had now moved in close enough to grab for the bottle. In less than a moment a violent struggle broke out—it commenced with a fight for Hays' bottle but soon escalated into an all-out bloody brawl. Because of Phelan's advantage in height and arm length, and the fact that he, the aggressor, had gotten in the first punch, it didn't take long for him to brutally pound Hays into submission. However, just when it appeared that Hays had no more fight in him, he suddenly caught Phelan by surprise with a hard kick to the groin. Taking advantage of Phelan's momentary incapacity, and mustering all the strength he had left, Hays burst out of the cabin and ran for his life toward the canoe landing. Bleeding and hurting, he drew strength from the chilling realization that Phelan would now surely kill him if he caught him. Running and thinking, Hays thought his best bet was to reach the canoe and paddle like mad to the safety of Evans' house. But before he even finished that thought, he was shaken by the sound of Phelan's heavy breathing and mad murmuring behind him. Though Hays had gotten a considerable head start in his race to the landing, the younger and longer-striding, faster Phelan was quickly catching up to him. Somehow, someway Hays found a little more foot speed and managed to reach the canoe before Phelan did. Frantically he dragged it halfway into the river and was just about to launch when the fuming Phelan caught up. Hays grabbed a paddle and in a panic, used it to fend off the madman just long enough to make his escape on foot. Once again Hays ran for his life, only now his only hope was to reach Evans' house by land before Phelan caught him.

Running in the twilight along the rough river bottoms was difficult for both men. But both men were desperate. Hays was running for his life, and Phelan was running to satisfy his overwhelming urge to inflict violence on the person he was pursuing, and also prevent him from reaching Evans' house and spreading the news of his rampage. Hays, with his mind racing faster than his feet, knew that within seconds the mad dog Phelan would be upon him, mauling him with all of his considerable strength. If a fight to the death was inevitable, down there in the river bottoms, Hays knew he had only one advantage and maybe just one small chance to exploit it: the canoe paddle he still carried was a potential weapon he could use to knock Phelan down and disable him long enough for Hays to escape to Evans' house. But for that to succeed Hays knew that he would have to stop running and turn around so that he could wield the paddle against the onrushing Phelan. Hays quickly decided that the "turn around and fight" tactic was his best chance for survival, but it proved to be the last tactical decision of his life.

Like the trained soldier he was, Sergeant Hays executed the "HALT," "About FACE," and "Present ARMS" maneuvers flawlessly. But Phelan was on him before he could really ready himself to fully swing the paddle. Yet, by quickly employing some short rapid swings he still managed to land a few blows on his attacker, but Phelan's long arms blocked them from reaching his head, and none of the blows packed much of a wallop. Nevertheless, the sheer sight of Hays desperately trying to club him, inflamed Phelan's already hot temper into an explosive fiery rage. Now Phelan was really ready to kill. Utilizing his large, iron-fisted hands, he soon was able to grab hold of the wide end of the paddle, after one of Hays' lighter swings, and rip it right out of Hays' hands. Before Hays could withdraw in defense, Phelan instantly hit him in the face with the stub of the paddle. Then in a quick, slick maneuver, he switched his grip from the wide end to the narrow handle end of the paddle. Now he was holding the paddle the proper way, and he immediately swung it with full force directly at Hays' already horribly bloodied face. The blow was so powerful that it instantly knocked Hays down hard on his back.

And without wasting a second, Phelan followed up the knockdown blow with a rapid succession of full swings (similar to how a lumberjack would swing an axe), all of them landing directly on Hays ever increasingly battered, bloodied, and broken face. Exactly which blow was the fatal one would never be known but John Hays was likely dead long before Phelan finished his brutal attack.

Was Phelan's murderous rage a case of temporary insanity? Maybe. Had he deliberately killed Hays with malice and forethought? Maybe. How would the law view the killing? Ultimately was his crime closer to manslaughter or premeditated murder? Clearly it was not premeditated in the sense that the killing was planned. But even in spontaneous, compulsive acts there are moments of time when one has the chance to stop and think about what they are doing. Certainly Phelan had some time when he was running after Hays to contemplate what he was about to do. In that moment of contemplation, he might have right then and there decided to kill Hays. If he had done that, then what he inflicted on Hays was not manslaughter but murder.

But whether or not Phelan consciously and deliberately intended to kill Hays, in the end he had no remorse about what he had done. He did not regret that Hays was dead; he was glad to be rid of him and his annoying habits. Now he would have the farm and all its livestock, tools, and equipment, not to mention the canoe, completely to himself. Now he would have the cabin and all of its contents, including Hays' clothes and personal possessions, completely to himself, and he would enjoy it all without the tiresome meddling of his finicky housemate. In Phelan's mind, his partner's death was really his day of liberation, but if he was not quick, clever, and careful with how he cleaned up the aftermath of his crime, his liberation would be short, and his life would end prematurely on the gallows or would be wasted away in prison.

## A Frenzied Cover-Up

Despite his lingering drunkenness, Phelan knew that he had to think clearly and quickly; his very life depended on it. But suddenly he was struck by panic and fear and overwhelmed by a flurry of taxing questions: What should he do with Hays' body? Should he bury it or dump it in the river? How much time would he have to dispose of the body before someone might come along? What if a neighbor or river traveler heard the commotion and came over to investigate? What about the blood on his face, hands, arms, and clothing? Would he have enough time to clean himself up? And the most centrally important question: What should his cover story be? How should he explain Hays' death or disappearance to the neighbors and local authorities? What alibi would convince them that he was not responsible for Hays' death? He needed a good story, and he needed it fast.

Though he wasn't very smart, Phelan was a skilled liar. He took several pieces of the truth, wove them together with several embellished half-truths and flat-out fabrications, then stitched them all neatly together into an elaborate story that might ring true but would be fundamentally false. Such a false story might ring true partly because it partly was true and also because its true parts would be easier for Phelan to remember and thus he would be able to tell much of it in a more comfortable and convincing manner.

The story that Phelan hurriedly created on the night of September 5 was not his best concoction, but it was the best he could do under the frenzied circumstances. He started with some truths he could easily embellish upon: the lost calf, the suspicion that Indians stole it, Hays' search for the calf, and his plan to go to Kaposia dressed in his best clothes. Building his story around those separate little truths was not particularly difficult to do. But under the panic and stress of the situation, Phelan had neither the time nor the clarity of mind to carefully critique every part of it and consider whether the whole story really worked as a credible and convincing explanation of Hays' disappearance. The linchpin of the story was the missing calf and Hays' determination to find the Indians who he believed had stolen it. The story's objective was to pass off Hays' murder onto some imagined calf-stealing Dakota from Kaposia. Phelan knew that the idea of local Dakota stealing cattle was plausible. Only recently his neighbors, the

Perry's, had lost cattle to Dakota rustlers and everyone knew that local Dakota were regular customers at Pig's Eye Parrant's saloon. The story would implicitly set up the logical murder theory that Hays was killed by Dakota calf rustlers when he encountered them on his way to Kaposia. To work, the story would have to include some account of Hays crossing over to the Kaposia (west) side of the river on the day of his disappearance. That part was crucial for two logical reasons: first, if Hays was going to Kaposia to search for the calf and the Dakota who stole it, then obviously he had to be on the Kaposia side of the river. Second, if the story had Hays searching for the calf on the east side of the river then there would be too great a risk that one of the settlers there (Parrant, Evans, or Campbell) would be able to directly contradict the fact that Hays was ever there. If Hays had been searching there, right by their homes, then surely one of those settlers would have seen him. Indeed, the idea of Hays going downriver on the east shore in search of his calf and not stopping at either Parrant's place (one block east of present-day Shepard Road and Jackson Street) or the house of his friend William Evans would be highly implausible. On the other hand, the west side of the river from Mendota to Kaposia was completely uninhabited and anyone walking on that stretch of wilderness would not be easily seen, even by boaters on the river. Thus, if the calf story was to be credible it had to include an account of Hays crossing the river to search for the calf.

After Phelan finished laying out the story in his mind, the answer to his question concerning how he should dispose of the body immediately became clear. It would be foolish to bury the body, not just because it would take too much time, but also because if it was ever found on his east shore land it would point glaringly to his guilt, and not to the guilt of any Indian on the other side of the river. It would, of course, be too risky to bury the body far off his land; that would take too much time, and the chances of someone seeing him, or uncovering the grave later would increase dramatically. On the other hand, if he disposed of the body in the river, even if it was eventually discovered, that fact would not be inconsistent with the theory that some Indians had killed Hays and they were the ones who dumped him into the river, conceivably after stealing his clothes. And there was the possibility that Hays' body would never be found if it was well-buried at the bottom of the river.

But dragging Hays' bloody body to the river was challenging, nerve-wracking work that would involve risk of being seen, even though it was getting darker. Darkness, however, would not necessarily be a blessing for Phelan. Hauling the heavy body from the thick, uncleared boggy bottoms over to the river's edge, then dumping it into the water and improvising something to weigh it down securely into the muddy bottom, would be an easier job to do in daylight. Worse, darkness would make it harder for Phelan to clean himself up and wash all the blood off himself.

When Phelan started to move the body he nervously discovered that Hays was much heavier than he expected. The blood-covered corpse was dead weight that was both difficult to grab hold of and difficult to move. The bloody skin was slippery to hold but the only clothing he could grab onto was the loose-fitting nightshirt. First Phelan tried to drag the body by the nightshirt but eventually it ripped and got so torn that it no longer worked. Then Phelan came up with the idea of rope. The rope would work as a pull line to drag the body through the brush, and more importantly, he could later use it to tie some rocks on the body to sink it to the bottom of the river. Phelan raced to the cabin, grabbed some rope and then nimbly ran back to the body lying in the brush of the boggy river bottoms. Panting heavily, he hogtied the feet and then dragged and pulled the body through the brush and "herbage" down to the edge of the river. Exhausted and sweating profusely, he stopped to rest and gathered his thoughts. He would need to find some suitable rocks to weigh the body down. That wouldn't be a problem with all the limestone abounding along the river banks. But then he needed to figure out the best way to tie the rocks to the body. That would be a tougher problem.

After a few moments of rest, Phelan made a quick search for a big, flat slab of limestone, like the kind he saw so often when he was walking along the river. He soon found two rocks that seemed perfect: they were big, flat, and heavy, but not too heavy to carry. He hauled the limestone over to the body, then paused to think more about how best to fasten the rocks onto the corpse. He decided that he should attach one rock to Hays' chest and tie it around his torso with the rope. Naturally, that would require first untying the rope from around the feet, then getting the rope wrapped around the back and sides of the body, with the rope's end pieces coming together at the chest. As Phelan started maneuvering the body, the nightshirt tore even more. Suddenly an idea hit him and he took the shreds of the torn and ragged nightshirt and tied them together into a makeshift rope.

This second rope he used to tie the other rock around Hays' feet. Now Phelan believed that the body was weighted down enough to sink to the bottom of the river. Satisfied with his work, but still sweating and tense, he laboriously dragged the naked corpse wrapped in rocks into the water and pushed it down to the muddy river bottom. The body sank, but to ensure that it stayed submerged, Phelan found a few more slabs of limestone and dropped them into the water directly over the sunken body. Now Hays' body was completely invisible. Phelan hoped that all his work would be good enough to keep the body hidden until time and the elements washed away Hays' bare bones far down river. What he didn't know or fully appreciate was just how powerful the current of the mighty Mississippi River was.

After hiding the body in the river, Phelan concentrated on cleaning himself up. Since he was already waist-deep in the river, he waded out a little further and completely submerged himself in the cold water. The coldness of the water shocked the last traces of intoxication right out of him. Unlike his late roommate that he killed, Phelan did not have the self-discipline to endure a long and thorough bath. As he ran out of the water freezing cold, he was immediately shaken by something even more chilling than the night air: there were still visible bloodstains on his shirt and pants. Though it was getting darker by the minute, it was still light enough to see that mere river water was not an adequate cleanser of blood. In a panic, Phelan rubbed sand and mud on his pants and shirt. The pants weren't so bad; he had been wading in the river in them, and that alone must have rinsed much of the blood out. The pants were dark grey, and the fact that over time they had been splotched with a variety of other stains may also have helped camouflage the blood. But his shirt was an entirely different matter. It was so saturated with blood that probably no amount of plain washing would ever clean it. But the light was too dim, and Phelan was too cold to spend any more time trying to clean his shirt down there at the river. Now the most pressing need was to get back home and warm himself in the cabin, where he could change his clothes and more comfortably figure out what else he needed to do to cover up his crime.

But before he left the river, Phelan wisely remembered to erase all the telltale body-dragging marks he had made on the beach. Using a handy tree branch as an improvised rake he hurriedly (before full darkness came) smoothed over the sandy shore where he had dragged the body. Satisfied that the most glaring sign of the body dumping was erased, Phelan anxiously headed for home.

After making his way back to the cabin in the dark, a cold, tired, and tense Phelan encountered an almost comic mix of both good and bad fortune. Fortunately, before their fight Hays had managed to start a fire in the hearth. Unfortunately, it had burned out. Fortunately, there were still some hot embers glowing which Phelan used to light a candle, thus saving him the trouble of having to use the flint and steel in the dark. Unfortunately, Phelan did not have any clean shirt to change into, which was not surprising since he only owned three shirts and two pairs of pants. Fortunately, he was able to find one shirt that wasn't too dirty and was a good enough replacement for the unsalvageable bloody shirt. Unfortunately, his only other pair of pants was soiled in cow manure and lay outside next to an almost equally filthy shirt. He should have cleaned those clothes that morning, but as was so typical of Phelan, he had procrastinated doing it. Fortunately, Hays had some clean pants but unfortunately, they were far too small for Phelan, and besides, he knew it would look suspicious if he were seen wearing any of the missing man's clothes. Fortunately, the muddy pants Phelan was wearing did not show noticeable blood stains. Unfortunately, the cold dampness of his pants was uncomfortable, and he was frustrated that he had nothing else to wear. Fortunately, Hays' wool blanket was large enough to wrap around Phelan's whole body and provided some comfort.

Whether or not the mix of good and bad luck that night evened out, Phelan did not consider himself very fortunate. He was still cold, tired, hungry, and stressed from the ordeal of his frenzied crime and cover-up. Sitting alone in the dim candlelight, surrounded by the mess of the earlier brawl, Phelan had a powerful urge to leave the cabin for someplace where he could be with another human being and perhaps even mooch a meal from them. Maybe the ghost of John Hays was haunting the cabin and trying to spook the man who murdered him. Or maybe the big, tough murderer was just plain scared to be alone in that particular dark cabin on that particular dark night. Fear, stress, and fatigue clouded Phelan's mind. He knew he had to get control of his feelings and rationally think things out, something he was not very good at doing. The first question to be decided was whether it would be a good or bad idea to spend the night at the home of one of his only friends, William Evans, ironically the very place that Hays was trying to reach before he was murdered.

On the plus side were several appealing lures: he would have the comfort of being with a friend in more pleasant and less dark (literally and figuratively) surroundings. Knowing Evans as he did, Phelan was sure that the fellow Irishman and comrade from Fort Snelling would offer him some food and a warm place to sleep, as well as some calming conversation. And beyond those attractions there were other important benefits: visiting Evans that night would give Phelan the chance to put to rest his nagging fear that Evans might have heard some disturbing commotion coming from Phelan and Hays' property. Phelan knew that in the still of the night and in the midst of a wilderness, sounds could carry a long way downriver, and he feared that Evans might have heard some of Hays' cries. If he had, then

Phelan reasoned that it would be better for him to find out right away so that he could shrewdly adjust his story to accommodate that fact before he told his story to anyone else. On the other hand, if Phelan learned that Evans never heard any disturbances coming from their place then some of his anxiety would be thankfully lessened. Another good reason for visiting Evans on that night of the murder was the early establishment of an alibi. Phelan thought it might be wise, before that night was over and long before anyone learned that Hays had disappeared, to plant his alibi with Evans. He would tell his friend the story about the lost calf, supposedly stolen by Indians, and Hays' intention to search for it at Kaposia the next day. If Evans, Hays' good friend, bought the story then Phelan believed that everyone else would as well. But if Evans expressed any doubt about any part of the story then Phelan would know right away that the story was flawed and still be able to fix those flaws (without Evans getting too suspicious) before he told the story to anyone else. In other words, telling Evans the missing calf story that night would be an important test trial for Phelan's cover story of why his roommate was gone. Phelan understood that he was staking his life on the hope that everyone would believe his story. Given such high stakes, he knew he couldn't afford any discrepancies; the story had to be perfectly plausible, and Evans would be a good test.

Yet there were also serious negatives to visiting Evans so early after the murder. Was Phelan prepared mentally and physically to tell this story convincingly to anyone? Was the story ready to be told? Clearly there was a danger in telling it too soon, before it had been fully refined. Evans was Phelan's friend but he was Hays' friend too. Phelan knew the risk that Evans might turn against him if he suspected Phelan of doing any serious harm to Hays. Phelan had to face the possibility that Evans could end up doing more to incriminate him than to support his alibi.

While he was weighing his options and calculating his next move, Phelan suddenly remembered the canoe paddle! In his preoccupation with disposing of Hays' body he had completely forgotten to pick up and clean the bloody canoe paddle. Phelan cursed himself for being so stupid but tempered his anger with the acknowledgement that he was lucky that he at least remembered it when he did, because there was still time left to rectify the mistake. Phelan quickly concluded that now it made even more sense to go to Evans' house. His reasoning was based strictly on the consideration of two intersecting factors: the unattractiveness of traveling at night and now the unavoidability of doing it. One difficulty of going to Evans' house that night was the challenge of hiking in the dark. Although the combination of moonlight, the familiarity of the route, and the light of a torch would make the walk to Evans' place manageable, Phelan always avoided hiking alone in the wilderness at night if possible. But since he had to go down to the dark bottomland for the paddle anyway, he figured that he might as well continue on the rest of the way to Evans' house.

But he was concerned about the torch: the light of a big, bright torch might draw unwanted attention to the area of the river bottoms where the murder occurred and where the murder weapon still lay covered in blood. Phelan decided to use a kindling stick he saw smoldering in the fireplace, and he grabbed the cool, unburnt end of that stick and smiled when he saw red embers still glowing on its other end. "Perfect," he thought for the small, subtle light he needed to retrieve the paddle and clean the blood from it.

But before he left the cabin, he paused and carefully thought about any other mistakes or miscalculations he might have made, and whether there was anything at the cabin he should do before he left. Two critically important items soon occurred to him: his hat was missing and his bloody shirt was lying on the cabin floor. Phelan now realized that sometime during or after the murder he must have lost his hat because now it was neither on his head, nor anywhere in the cabin, yet he distinctly remembered wearing it just before the fight started. His anxiety spiked again. Though his identifiable hat had not played a part in the murder, if left near the murder scene it could directly implicate Phelan. It was obvious to Phelan that in addition to retrieving the paddle, he also would have to search for his hat.

As for the bloody shirt, Phelan wasn't sure how he should dispose of it. Initially he wanted to burn it, but the fire was out and the shirt was wet, and the candle wasn't enough to burn a wet garment. He could have built a real fire in his fireplace, but it would take too much time and trouble. Hays had used up all the dry kindling grass and most of the kindling wood in the hearth to start the fire he had made earlier that night, and it would take too long to gather enough kindling to start another fire. Above all, Phelan was not going to spend any extra time in that messy, spooky cabin; he needed to get the paddle and find his hat, and then proceed on to the comfort of Evans' house. So Phelan stashed the bloody shirt under the cabin floor, which he was easily able to do from outside the cabin and then he would burn it another day. Now he felt confident enough to leave the cabin and head to the river bottoms. With his small, dim stick torch in his hand, he walked cautiously back down the path, in the dark, to the bottomland.

Phelan's return to the scene of the crime actually lessened his anxiety, mainly because the murder weapon was so easy to find. Lying near the center of the trampled-down brush, the paddle was impossible to miss, even in the dim light of the stick torch. One large pool of blood was also distinguishable but the little torchlight did not illuminate enough for Phelan to see the full extent of the blood evidence. What Phelan could not see in the darkness was just how widespread the blood splattering was. But he wasn't even going to attempt to clean up the blood and blood-splattered brush in the dark. He decided that early the next morning, in the daylight, he would go back to his cabin, grab his water bucket and, using the water from the nearby creek (later called Rice Creek), wash away all the visible blood from the murder scene. But now the pressing task at hand was to find his hat and clean off the blood from the paddle.

Finding his dark-colored hat proved futile. Despite a careful search of the murder scene area, Phelan could not find his hat. But then suddenly he remembered setting his wet hat on the river bank following his bath in the river. Yes, the more he thought about it, the more convinced he was that the hat was down at the riverbank, lying on the exposed roots of a big tree. Thanks to his refreshed memory, Phelan was now much less worried about his hat. Rather than waste any more time looking for it in the dark, he decided he would retrieve it the next day on his return home from Evans' place. He was comforted by the thought that there would be nothing incriminating or suspicious about his hat lying on the riverbank if someone by chance happened upon it. If anyone found it there they would simply conclude that some passing river traveler had lost it.

Satisfied with his decision about his hat, Phelan proceeded to the task of cleaning the canoe paddle. The creek wasn't far away and Phelan had no difficulty reaching it, even though his little stick torch had burned out. Kneeling on the creek bank, Phelan vigorously washed the paddle by the light of the moon. As best as he could tell, the paddle was washed clean but there remained one incriminating mark that no amount of cleaning could wash away. The wide end of the paddle that had been used to batter Hays' skull had a long crack down the middle. Phelan tried to calm himself with the thought that the crack could be easily explained away. All he had to do was concoct a story about the paddle hitting a rock. He could pretend that he used the paddle both as a walking stick and as a staff to herd the lost calf back home if he found it, but on the way to Evans' house he fell off a log crossing the creek by Evans' Landing (later known as Phalen's Creek) and cracked the paddle on a rock. That fabrication would also conveniently explain his muddy pants and missing hat. The more Phelan thought about this scenario the more impressed he was with it. On several other occasions he had actually used the paddle as a walking stick, especially on his walk between his landing and his cabin. Moreover, the paddle was an excellent walking stick that would prove useful on his walk in the dark to Evans' house. Now everything was coming together for Phelan: he had the paddle, he knew where his hat was, and he had plausible explanations for why he was muddy, hatless and carrying a cracked canoe paddle.

When Phelan continued his journey to Evans' house, he soon appreciated even more how useful the canoe paddle was as a night walking stick. The bottomland had areas of marsh and the paddle worked well in those places as a kind of probing tool to help locate the spots of solid ground. But in the dark, stepping in the mud was sometimes unavoidable. But when he stepped in the mud, for the first time in his life Phelan didn't curse about it. No, on that strange, twisted night, getting a little muddy was not a bad thing. Indeed, getting muddy in a natural and innocent way meant that there was some partial truth to his explanation for his muddy boots and pants. And he was pleased to see in the moonlight that the crack on the paddle was now completely covered in mud.

When Phelan reached the creek that was destined to be named for him, he almost laughed at how easily his fabrication about falling into that creek could become a reality. The logs bridging the creek were not that wide, and his wet, muddy boots were slippery. Tall trees along the creek shaded out the moonlight, making his path pitch black. Not surprisingly but certainly ironically, Phelan slipped and stumbled into the creek. But he nimbly regained his balance and escaped with only some creek water on his already wet boots. It wasn't the dramatic kind of fall that he had concocted for his story, but at least it proved the plausibility of the lie he was going to tell about how he slipped on a log, fell into the creek, lost his hat, cracked his paddle, and ended up all muddy and wet.

Despite the earlier confusion and two horrendous mistakes (forgetting the paddle and losing his hat), his cover-up now seemed to be working out nicely. Phelan even gloated to himself about how clever he was in solving so many problems. But he also knew that he couldn't afford to be overconfident. The murder of Hays was a serious crime that could cost him his life. Phelan understood that there could be no more mistakes, no more carelessness of any kind. When he talked to Evans he had to be very careful about what he said and how he said it. He had to pretend that he was his same old self and act as if nothing extraordinary had happened that night, except for that fiction of the lost calf.

Phelan's anxiety rose as he got closer to the light from Evans' cabin. He now had second thoughts about the paddle. Its incriminating crack was now completely covered in mud, but Phelan wondered if it wouldn't be better not to even mention it to Evans. What would be the point, he pondered, of drawing attention to the crack on his paddle when Evans would probably never even notice it? He decided that he would say nothing about the crack unless it became necessary or advantageous to explain it by his original "breaking it on a rock in the creek" story. But as he thought about the paddle he got a little nervous about exactly what he should do with it. Should he carry it to the doorway so that Evans would immediately see it and he could use it as a prop to tell his story about the lost calf and how he had fallen off a log? Or should he just casually prop it up against the cabin outside and go in without it? Again he faced the question of whether or not he should draw attention to the canoe paddle, which no one else but himself knew was a murder weapon. Was it a mistake to have Evans see the murder weapon that night? Or was it a brilliant subterfuge, a way of demonstrating that he had nothing to hide and there was nothing suspicious about his paddle? But more to the point, under normal circumstances, why would anyone view a simple canoe paddle as a suspicious object? Even though the circumstances were certainly not normal for Phelan, he reminded himself that for Evans it was probably just a typical Thursday evening. There was a fair chance that Evans might not even notice that he carried a canoe paddle. If he did, the chances were good that he would think nothing of it. And Phelan knew well that remembering details was not one of Evans' strong suits. Though Phelan's earlier confidence was waning, he concluded that his original decision to carry the paddle to Evans' place was still sound. If it added more realism to his story, then there was no problem with carrying it right up to Evans' door.

As he walked up to the cabin door, Phelan prepared himself for telling Evans his story with just the right amount of emotional flair to make it believable. But when he knocked on the door he realized that it was impossible for him to repress all of the anxiety that came from one of the most traumatic and eventful nights of his life. When Evans opened the door, Phelan's anxiety exploded into panic: there, inside the cabin, were two other men. One was Evans' and Hays' good friend, Stephen "Scotty" Scott, a former Fort Snelling soldier who Phelan also knew but didn't particularly like. The other guy was a stranger. Phelan was flabbergasted by his bad luck: Of all the nights for Evans to have guests why did it have to be that night? Phelan had counted on telling his story to Evans alone but now he had no choice but to tell it to two more people, one of them a stranger and the other one was someone he knew would be very difficult to fool.

## Evan's Surprise Guests Unravel Phelan's Plans

Phelan knew when he entered the cabin that he must have looked startled and shaken to the three men who gathered to greet him, but he hoped that if he could quickly regain his composure, the men might pass off his startled demeanor as the normal manner of a man who had just fallen into a creek. Phelan could only hope that the men saw it this way, and he did everything he could to play up his fall into the creek. When he finished telling his whole story, including the details about the lost calf, he was relieved by the reactions of the men. They all seemed to believe him; none of them challenged his story or gave any outward sign that they doubted anything he said. But that by itself was not enough to relieve his still overwhelming stress. The imposing presence of those two unexpected guests rattled his nerves and frustrated his expectations of how the evening and the next morning were supposed to unfold. Phelan learned in anguish that Scotty and his friend (some guy from the St. Croix River named Foy) were on their way to "St. Peters" (Mendota), and that Scott intended to visit Hays the next morning on his way upriver with Foy. Knowing that Scott and Hays were good friends, Phelan painfully understood that nothing short of a tornado would prevent Scott from stopping at their cabin the next day. And most depressingly, there was nothing credible or non-incriminating that Phelan could tell him that would change his mind.

But if Scott went through with his plan to visit Hays on Friday morning that would wreak havoc on Phelan's own important plans for that morning. Phelan had planned to finish three essential parts of his cover-up on Friday morning: he was going to wash away the blood from the murder scene, clean up his ransacked cabin, and pick up his hat on the river bank. But now how would he be able to do any of those tasks before that pest Scott and the guy named Foy reached his cabin? Worse, Scott was coming to see Hays, the man Phelan had murdered. How would Hays' killer be able to convince Scott that his friend had gone across the river to look for the calf, when that calf was still in the pen and the canoe was still beached at the landing?

There was no escaping the fact that Phelan faced some serious problems. He desperately needed to get away by himself so that he could figure out a new plan. But Evans' small cabin and the socializing mood of the rest of the group made that impossible. Phelan was in no mood for socializing but he realized that it was vital to appear as his normal self; he knew that his life might depend on how well he could control his nerves and his outward appearance. But some things at Evans' cabin happened exactly as Phelan expected. Evans was the generous host who Phelan assumed he would be; he offered Phelan some leftover supper, which he had already shared with Scott and Foy. Scott shared all of the liquor that was left in his wineskin with the other three men. Phelan was desperate for some alcohol, but he knew he needed to remain clear-headed so that he could modify his plan when he was lying in bed later, or rather, on the floor with the other guests. But to avoid suspicion the normally liquor-loving Phelan had to take at least one swig of Scott's liquor and then, to fit in with the rest of the group, he feigned disappointment when it was gone.

However, when Phelan heard Scott's comment that he needed

to buy more liquor, a hopeful idea flashed into his mind that might delay Scott's trip to see Hays. Perhaps, Phelan thought, he could persuade Scott to stop at Pig's Eye's new saloon on his way upriver. That would buy him some extra time on Friday morning to get some of his cover-up work done. That hopeful thought motivated Phelan to muster all of his persuasive powers and desperately try to convince Scott to stop at Pig's Eye's place. But Phelan faced a distinct challenge: Evans knew that Phelan did not like Pig's Eye and that he was critical of the way Parrant watered down his whiskey. How could Phelan—who openly mocked Pig's Eye's broken English and ridiculed the quality of his whiskey in front of people like Evans— sell Scott on the idea of buying his liquor from Pig's Eye, without appearing ridiculously inconsistent and suspiciously out of character? The challenge required subtlety, coyness, and the disingenuousness of a con man. Phelan subtly tried to strike a balance between mocking Pig's Eye and the deficiencies of his whiskey, while still highlighting the advantages of Pig's Eye' new saloon, namely, its convenient location between Evans' and Phelan's Landings, the low prices, and the claim that he was now diluting his whiskey less than he had when he operated at Fountain Cave. It helped Phelan that Scott knew about Pig's Eye and the Fountain Cave saloon. But what really raised Phelan's hopes was Scott's curiosity about Pig's Eye's new saloon. Scott asked some questions, and Phelan was encouraged that his subtle sales pitch appeared to be working.

When the conversation ended, Phelan was almost sure that he had persuaded Scott to visit Pig's Eye's saloon the next morning. He couldn't be positive that he would, there was always a chance that he might change his mind. Nevertheless, Phelan was optimistic that his talk with Scott had achieved its objective. But he was concerned with how Evans might have interpreted the conversation. Though Evans never said or did anything to challenge what he told Scott, Phelan had a strange feeling that his friend might suspect there was something fishy about Phelan pushing Pig's Eye's whiskey on Scott. Evans could be a difficult man to read and Phelan's nerves were so rattled and his sensitivities so heightened that it was possible he imagined something that wasn't there. In any case, Evans' real or imagined suspicions were the least of Phelan's problems. Before the night was over Phelan had to figure out a new plan that would accommodate a visit from two men looking for the man he murdered.

When the men were ready for bed, Phelan found a spot on the floor that was some distance from the other guests. When the cabin went dark and all conversation ceased, Phelan was finally alone with his thoughts. Now he could slowly plan out his morning and hopefully somehow work out some solutions to the nearly insurmountable challenges that Scott had caused him. As Phelan reflected on how to reformulate his unraveled cover up, he was stymied by several dangerous unknowns. How much time would he have in the morning before Scott and Foy arrived at his landing? How much time would it take him to wash away the blood from the murder scene? How long would it take him to clean up the cabin and herd the calf and the rest of cattle out of the pen and over to the part of the pasture that was out of view from the river, the landing, and the cabin? Answers to these questions were critical, but they were unanswerable because of the many unknowable factors. Phelan faced a maddening dilemma: How could he make plans to do those critical tasks if he didn't know how much time he had to do them? He was particularly haunted by the nightmare possibility that Scott and Foy would arrive just as he was cleaning up the murder scene and catch him red handed washing away blood.

## The Revised Cover-Up

After much anguish, Phelan finally decided to simplify and prioritize the tasks. He could skip picking up his hat that he had left on the riverbank near where he had dumped Hays' body. There was a chance that Scott and Foy might discover it on their way upriver, but Phelan tried to assure himself that the dark hat perched on the roots of a tree would not be visible from the river. Next, as important as it was to clean up the murder scene, Phelan decided it was too dangerous to clean up any blood on Friday morning. There was a risk in not cleaning up the blood in the brush, but he decided there was an even greater risk in doing it on the morning when people were coming to visit. And he wasn't sure how noticeable the blood scene was because he hadn't observed it in the light of day. He hoped by some miracle that it wasn't very visible, perhaps obscured by surrounding high brush. In any case, Phelan decided to avoid any major cleanup work at the murder scene in the morning. But the site was near his route home, so he thought he could afford a few minutes to see how visible the blood was and maybe throw some brush over it.

Cleaning his ransacked cabin was another task Phelan thought he could postpone. As long as it wasn't raining when Scott and Foy came, he figured he could just keep them outside the cabin during their visit, which he would try to make as short as possible. He could easily draw them away from the cabin by showing them the root cellar he and Hays had been building, and if he started digging while they were talking, his guests might get the hint that he had work to do, and they would politely leave for St. Peter's.

But one significant problem remained to be solved. Phelan's original story about why Hays was not at home on Friday was that he had crossed the river and gone to Kaposia to look for the calf that he suspected the Indians stole. But a key detail of the story was missing, and if the right piece wasn't found then the whole story would fall apart. The missing detail was the answer to a basic question: How exactly did Hays cross the river? Phelan had to answer it with care and foresight because that little detail could create a huge stumbling block to his story's credibility. If Phelan told his visitors, Scott and Foy, that Hays had canoed himself across the river then the obvious (and incriminating) question would be: Why was his canoe still at Phelan's Landing? If on the other hand Phelan told Scott and Foy that he canoed Hays across the river and then returned to the landing, then the incriminating question would be: How did Phelan manage to cross and recross the river so quickly? A third optional answer would also be problematic. If Phelan told Scott and Foy that some passing river traveler kindly canoed Hays across the river, then the incriminating question would be: Why didn't Scott and Foy, who were downriver at Evans' Landing early in the morning, see that traveler canoeing down the wide river?

Any answer Phelan chose was problematic, but he finally settled on the second option, that he had canoed Hays across the river. The first answer, that Hays canoed himself across the river, could have worked if Phelan had hidden the canoe where no one would ever see it. But Phelan was not willing to sacrifice his use of the canoe for what would have to be a long, indefinite period of time. Yet there was another problem with that first answer and it was double-edged. If Hays canoed himself across the river and walked down the west shore to Kaposia, then his canoe should have been beached on the west shore—but it wasn't (a fact that could be verified by anyone who searched that shore for Hays). If on the other hand, Hays stayed in his canoe and paddled downriver along the west shore on his way to Kaposia, then why didn't Scott and Foy see him traveling downriver on their voyage upriver? Of course, this was the same problem that the third answer (the kind river traveler transporting Hays) had and it was why Phelan rejected it.

Once Phelan decided that his story had to include the key detail of canoeing Hays across the river Friday morning, he realized that timing would be his greatest challenge. He decided to devote most of his limited time on Friday morning to acting out that key part of his story. In order to make his lie about canoeing Hays across the river believable, Phelan felt he needed to get in his canoe, paddle across the river, and then return to his landing, just as if he had actually done what he claimed he did. If he could cross the river and then return to his landing just before Scott and Foy arrived, then those men would become his alibi witnesses that he had in fact canoed back from the west shore on Friday morning.

But, would Phelan have enough time to canoe all the way across the river and then return to his landing before Scott and Foy arrived? Besides crossing the river, the bare minimum tasks he had to do on Friday morning could be reduced to four chores: his mile and a half trek from Evans' house to the cattle pen next to his cabin, a quick check of the bloody murder scene on his way home, herding the calf and cattle out to pasture, and walking back (about three blocks) down to his landing, where the canoe was beached. Given that all those tasks were absolutely necessary, the only time-reducing control Phelan had for Friday morning was to quicken his pace. And so he was determined to speed up everything he had to do. He would be driven to always move quickly— running, jogging, paddling, at a relentlessly rapid pace. If he could do that, then his reduced time would markedly increase the chances that his new plan would succeed.

What Phelan couldn't control was the time it would take Scott and Foy to paddle up to his landing. He hoped, of course, that they would stop at Pig's Eye's saloon. It was wishful thinking, but Phelan hoped that Scott would find a former Fort Snelling comrade there, and that he and his old acquaintance would spend a half hour or more drinking and reminiscing. If Phelan was a religious man he might have prayed for his wishful vision to become a reality. But religious faith was something he never really had, although even if he was a true believer, how could he have asked God to help him succeed in covering up a murder?

Phelan could have used some divine intervention to help him fall asleep. He was so worried about the pressures of the next morning that he was tormented by insomnia. He was also frustrated when he realized that as much as he wanted to get a head start on Scott and Foy by leaving at the break of dawn, it would look suspicious if he left Evans' house before breakfast. Everyone who knew Phelan (including Evans and Scott) knew that he would never pass up a free breakfast. If Phelan got any sleep on Thursday night it was only during the last hour just before dawn.

When Evans got up and noisily started making breakfast, Phelan was relieved to finally get up and on with the day that might well determine whether or not he would get away with murder. Over breakfast Phelan once again took the opportunity to mention his missing calf and Hays' intention of going to Kaposia to look for it. He also found an opening to remind Scott about Pig's Eye's reasonably priced liquor. Phelan desperately wanted to race home when breakfast was over, but he knew he had to appear calm and relaxed in front of Evans and his guests. It pained him to linger, but he remained seated when Scott and Foy got up to leave. Then Phelan got up and gave Evans an awkward excuse about how he needed to look for the calf again and so he too had to say goodbye. Phelan wasn't sure how smoothly his departure from Evans went, or whether his friend sensed anything strange about his abrupt exit, but at that point he could no longer worry about what kind of impression he left on Evans. Now his only concern was to follow his updated plan as rapidly and effectively as he could.

Fortunately, the trail back to his cabin was different than the path Scott and Foy took to their canoe. Their path went south, directly to the river and his path went west, directly to the ford of the creek that would be later named after Phelan. When he was sure no one could see him, he ran along that westward trail as fast as he could. But soon the combination of being winded and the danger of twisting an ankle on the rugged trail caused him to slow down to a jog. The creek crossing was one place where he had to slow down, otherwise he risked falling into the creek and wasting more time. Even worse, he could injure himself badly in a fall and end up having to crawl home.

After a successful and uneventful run and jog over sandy, rocky and marshy terrain, Phelan finally reached the murder scene. Although it could have been worse—the blood splatters could have been visible from even further away than the roughly fifteen yards distance they actually could be seen—it was still pretty bad. The blood on the ground and in the brush was frighteningly glaring. Even worse, Phelan's boot prints were clearly imprinted on the bloody ground. With a few artful sweeps of his handy canoe paddle Phelan quickly smoothed away all traces of his tracks. Once again Phelan appreciated the value of carrying a canoe paddle on land, and he didn't worry about the blood on it; he could rinse it off in his own creek (Rice Creek), which was less than a minute away, and anyway, he'd be paddling across the river with it soon.

Phelan was winded but thankful when he reached the cattle pen at the top of the hill. He quickly opened the pen, herded the cattle (including the infamous calf) out toward their pastureland, again with the aid of his handy canoe paddle, then ran back down the hill to his landing in record time. Panting and sweating, Phelan pulled the canoe into the water, hopped in and started paddling toward the lower end of the long island that the locals called Devil's Island and future generations would call Harriet Island. But then when he gazed downriver he saw something in the distance that caused his heart to race into panic mode. It looked like a canoe. Though it was too far away to identify who was in it, he couldn't help fearing that it was Scott and Foy. If it was—and he was demoralized by the deduction that it was—then obviously they hadn't spent any time at Pig's Eye's place. (Phelan would have cursed his luck had he known that by sheer chance whiskey trader Henry Mencke met Scott and Foy on the river and in less than twelve minutes sold Scott the liquor he wanted.) Phelan was flustered, he had hoped he would have enough time to make it across the river before he sighted Scott and Foy canoeing upriver. But assuming that the approaching canoe was Scott and Foy's, and Phelan now had no doubt that it was, Phelan figured there were only two outcomes if he continued on his present course across the river—they were both bad. Either Scott and Foy would change their course (from the east to west shore) and then head directly toward Phelan's canoe in a friendly attempt to catch up to him; or they would not interfere with his river crossing and continue on their original course directly to his landing. In either case, the results would be disastrous. If they got close enough to Phelan's canoe to see that Hays was not in the boat with him, his lie that he canoed Hays across the river that morning would be exposed. On the other hand, if they arrived at his landing while he was on the other side of the river, they would have the unrestricted freedom to walk around Phelan's property looking for Hays. There would be nothing to stop them from looking inside the ransacked cabin, or even wandering by the bloody murder scene. One of the worst situations Phelan could envision was the thought of nosey Stephen Scott snooping around his property the morning after he murdered Hays before he cleaned up the evidence of the crime.

Given those two bleak alternatives, Phelan felt that his only option was to reverse course and quickly turn upriver, away from the other canoe and toward the upper end of the island.

He hoped that if he hugged the tree-lined shore and then sped over to the tip of the thickly wooded island, he might stay out of view of the other canoe. If the other canoeists could not clearly see him, he might still be able to pretend to them that he had actually crossed the river. It was a long shot, but it was the only chance he had to save his story that he took Hays across the river. Of course, everything would depend on how early and clearly Scott and Foy observed Phelan canoeing on the river. If they saw him when he first spotted them then he was out of luck. But there was a chance, and he held to it desperately, that Scott and Foy had not noticed him. Perhaps instead of looking far ahead, their eyes were fixed more toward the nearby river bank. If that was the case, then maybe they would keep their eyes on the shore long enough for Phelan to race over to the island. That hopeful thought motivated Phelan to paddle like mad against the current knowing that the faster he went, the greater the distance between them and the closer he would get to the shielding trees of the island.

But canoeing alone up the mighty Mississippi at a steady clip was exhausting work, especially for a man who had just finished a mile-and-a-half run. Phelan knew that Scott and Foy paddling together could easily outpace him and soon get close enough to see that he was traveling alone. But fearful that if he looked back at them he might see them signaling him, he kept his eyes straight ahead and veered toward the island. But halfway to the island, in the open river, the sight of the other canoe was now unavoidable. What he shockingly saw was that Scott and Foy had advanced so far that if he was going to reach the landing before they did, Phelan would have to turn and head back to his landing immediately. Yet, that would mean that he wouldn't reach the island, where he could have hidden for awhile in an attempt to create the illusion that he had actually crossed the river. Now he would have a much harder time selling his story to Scott and Foy that he had canoed across the river. But it would be even worse if Scott and Foy roamed around his property by themselves, so he paddled back to his landing, partly relieved that he no longer had to work against the current, but terribly anxious that his cover story was falling apart.

Now that he was paddling downriver, Phelan knew he would reach his landing before Scott and Foy would. But it was still too close for comfort. Weary and unsure of his next move, Phelan dreaded having to talk with Scott and Foy at that awkward and unexpectedly early time. But if he reached the landing only a few moments before they did then he couldn't possibly avoid talking to them. Thus, his new goal was to reach his landing far enough ahead of Scott and Foy to avoid having to talk to them. He didn't care if they considered him rude, his only concern was salvaging his cover-up of the murder.

As it turned out, Phelan beat Scott and Foy to the landing by about three minutes, just enough time to beach his canoe, dip his canoe paddle in some mud to hide the crack, and walk far enough up the hill to credibly pretend that he didn't hear the voices of the canoeists landing behind him. As Phelan headed home, he tried to walk both briskly and nonchalantly at the same time, hoping that his actions didn't look as suspicious to the men arriving at his landing as he feared they did.

## Scott and Foy's Untimely Visit

When he reached his cabin, Phelan tried to calm down and prepare himself for what he would tell these annoying, untimely guests. He wasn't sure what they saw on the river or what they thought about what they saw there. He decided not to initiate any conversation

about what he had been doing in his canoe or volunteer any information about Hays unless they asked. There was still a chance that
they were oblivious to his suspicious actions that morning. If they
were in fact clueless about what he had done and what he was so
desperately trying to hide, then Phelan had to be careful not to do or
say anything to change their undiscerning perceptions. On the other
hand, if Scott and Foy arrived with suspicion on their faces and a
barrage of accusatory questions about the whereabouts of Hays, then
his worst fear would be realized and he would be doomed.

All too soon, Foy showed up alone on the cleared grounds of his
cabin. Startled that he was alone, Phelan immediately dropped the
pretense of being nonchalant and asked him where Scott was. When
Foy shrugged his shoulders and guessed that he was still down at
the river bottoms, Phelan almost fainted. Down in the bottomland
snooping around was the last place he wanted Scott, who had an
annoying way of nosing into things that weren't his business. Phelan
was so unsettled that it was difficult to mask his feelings. But Foy was
relaxed and unassuming—and a stranger who didn't know how the
big Irishman typically reacted to things. All that helped ease Phelan's anxiety about how he must have looked to him. Still, Phelan
inwardly panicked that Scott might stumble across the bloody murder scene. Executing his plan to keep his visitors away from the cabin,
he directed Foy over to the root cellar and forced himself to act like
he wanted to talk about it. Phelan was relieved to discern that Foy
gave absolutely no indication that he was suspicious of anything that
Phelan had said or done. Though Foy was not a very talkative guy,
Phelan made their conversation even more awkward by being so dis-
tracted by the fear of what Scott might find in the bottomland.

After chatting with Foy for what seemed like an hour but was
really only a few minutes, he heard Scott shout out to him. Phelan no
sooner yelled back that he was "over here by the root house" when
he heard the words he most dreaded to hear: Scott was shouting that
there was "a body of blood in the bottom." The words struck Phelan
like a knife in his chest. His worst nightmare had become real. It

was no longer a case of "what if" Scott had found the bloody murder scene, now it was a case of *fait accompli*. But as terrified as he was, Phelan knew that he had to muster some semblance of composure if he was to have even the slightest chance of finessing his way through this colossal crisis. It took all his willpower to go over to Scott, who was still several yards away, and listen to the rest of what he had to say. To Phelan's great relief, Scott's interpretation of what he saw down in the bottom (including "drops of blood on the herbage") was not the evidence of a murdered man but the signs of a slaughtered calf.

Apparently Scott was thinking of the missing calf that Phelan had told him about, the calf that Phelan accused Indians of stealing. Believing that story, Scott had jumped to the conclusion that the "body of blood" he saw in the river bottom was evidence that the Indians had butchered the calf there. Phelan was forced to make a quick decision: if he agreed with Scott's conclusion that the blood was evidence of the slaughtered calf, then it would be only natural for him to go down to the bottom with Scott and Foy and examine the evidence for himself. But that would be dangerous. Bringing yet another man, Foy, with a different set of eyes to observe the murder scene, not to mention giving Scott a second opportunity to look at it, was just too risky. But how could he avoid the dangers of examining the murder scene without casting suspicion on himself? What excuse could he give Scott for not being interested in his discovery? What could he tell him that would avoid the calamity of these two visitors in his presence examining the murder scene?

The best response that Phelan could come up with under the stress of the moment was the lame but partly true assertion that his neighbor's cattle routinely grazed down in the area of the river bottom, and the blood most likely came from one of his cattle. He also threw out the possibility that maybe the Indians who stole the calf from up on the plateau, also shot an arrow or two at one of his neighbor's cattle grazing in the bottomland, just for fun, and left a wounded and bloody animal down there. Perhaps if Phelan had been a more clever and cagey murderer he could have come up with a better response. Maybe he would have been wiser to simply embrace Scott's slaughtered-calf theory and exploit it in a way that would enhance his cover story. For example, he could have feigned outrage at what the Indians had done to his calf, then told Scott that he was sure the Indians had taken the meat back to Kaposia and that Hays was on his way to Kaposia, probably hot on their trail, and may be able to get some of the meat back.

On the other hand, perhaps Phelan's theory about his neighbor's cattle bleeding in the bottom was actually a more plausible explanation than the theory that his calf had been slaughtered there. If Indians had really butchered a calf, they would surely have left entrails and some part of the carcass on the slaughtering ground, more than just the blood that Scott saw. The fact that there was nothing but blood at the scene was clearly more consistent with the theory that a living, wounded animal had bled there.

In any case, no matter how plausible Phelan's response to Scott's announced blood discovery was, he could tell from Scott's reaction that he wasn't very impressed with it. And now Scott wanted to know where Hays was. Phelan had been anxiously expecting that question. How Scott would react to his answer would tell Phelan a good deal about whether Hays' friend was suspicious of him. It was critical that Phelan answer the question deftly, even though he was extremely mentally and physically fatigued from not just the pressure of the moment, but from all the pressures of the day. Once again Phelan tried his best to project a calm and natural manner when he told Scott in a forced matter-of-fact way that Hays was on his way to Kaposia to find out what happened to their calf. He jokingly mocked Hays by mentioning that his always-meticulously-dressed housemate foolishly wore his "best clothes" to the Indian village. He added the fiction that Hays wore his best clothes there because that would give the Indians another motive to kill him, namely, to steal his valuable clothes. Hays' clothes came to mind because the sergeant had in fact planned on going to Kaposia dressed in his "best clothes," only he was going there not to find a calf but to find a wife. Then

Phelan added the key detail that caused him the most concern: he revealed that he had canoed Hays across the river. All the while he talked, Phelan watched Stephen Scott's facial expressions. The signals were mixed. Scott showed subtle signs of skepticism, but he never challenged any part of Phelan's story, and he didn't ask any questions. Phelan was ecstatic that Scott never questioned him about his phony morning canoe trip across the river, but he still had a distinct feeling that Scott didn't fully believe what he had said. Had Scott plainly seen that he never crossed the river that morning?

Phelan acknowledged the possibility that Scott had serious doubts about his story but was intimidated by him and afraid to confront him. If that was the case, then Scott's lack of frankness was the price a bully like Phelan paid for being an intimidating man. But Phelan's haunting fear was that if Scott was keeping his suspicions to himself, then he might not keep them hidden for long. Once he got safely away from Phelan's intimidating presence, what would stop him from sharing his suspicions with his friends at Fort Snelling? That was a very real danger, but what could Phelan do about it? If Scott suspected that Phelan had done some harm to Hays, there was nothing Phelan could do or say now that would change his mind, and nothing short of killing him that would prevent Scott from telling other people about it later.

Instead of worrying about the things he couldn't control, Phelan tried to concentrate on the things he could control. For whatever reason, Scott had not asked him how he managed to canoe Hays across the river and return home in the little time he had that morning. Phelan was grateful for that and eager to get Scott and Foy on their way upriver to the St. Peters' trading center. Phelan picked up a shovel, started digging out more of the cellar, and complained about how much work he had to do. Scott and Foy quickly took the hint and said their goodbyes, but Phelan had the feeling that they were as anxious to leave as he was for them to depart.

Phelan wisely guided them onto the main path to the landing, thus avoiding the risk that they might take the trail that led to the murder scene, the same one that Scott had fatefully taken earlier. As the three men began walking down the hill they had a clear view of the river, and what they saw made Phelan think that finally some good luck had come his way, for coming upriver were some Dakota in their dug-out canoe. The timing couldn't have been more perfect for Phelan. The Indians gave him an opportune chance to remind Scott and Foy one last time about the Indians who supposedly stole his and Hays' calf. Phelan milked the sight of the Indians for all it was worth. He went on a deliberate rant about all the trouble the Indians had caused the settlers. He explained that not only had they stolen his calf, but recently some local Dakota had killed a few cattle owned by his neighbor, Abraham Perry. (Once again Phelan cleverly mixed fact and fiction, for it was true that a year earlier local Indians had killed some of Perry's cattle.) Phelan concluded his tirade by half-jokingly warning Scott and Foy to watch out for Indian arrows on their way upriver. As the two men walked away from him and toward their canoe, Phelan took some satisfaction in the fact that the last thought he left them with was a dark and sinister image of the Indians. He hoped that perhaps instead of thinking about the various suspicious things he had done, their minds would be on the dangerous, unruly Indians who stole Hays' calf, killed Perry's cattle, and could cause them trouble on their way upriver. He also hoped that he had successfully planted the idea that if anything happened to Hays, the Indians would be the most likely ones to have harmed him.

Phelan took some comfort in those thoughts, but he knew there was still a danger that Scott could cause him trouble if he doubted Phelan's explanation for Hays' absence, and if he decided to share his suspicions with other people besides Foy. Only time would tell what trouble, if any, Scott and Foy would cause him.

## Cleaning Up the Mess

Now that they were gone, Phelan wasn't sure whether he had dodged a bullet and was home free in getting away with murder, or whether he was in grave danger of getting caught and being arrested for murder. Of course, the fear of being caught would never leave him and it was the ultimate source of his motivation for doing whatever was necessary to cover up his crime. In that regard, Phelan still had some important work left to do: clean up the bloody murder scene and clean up his ransacked cabin. To prevent anyone else from seeing the blood in the bottom, he made the clean-up of the site his first priority. Though he was physically drained from the nonstop action of the morning, he found the energy to grab a bucket from his yard, fill it with water from the creek and then empty it on the blood spills. After several repetitions of that process, Phelan judged that all the visible blood had been adequately washed away. But by then he was just too tired to clean his cabin, so he decided to take a little rest under the shade of his favorite old elm before tackling the next chore. Phelan's mind was too busy to sleep but resting did his overworked muscles some good and gave him some quiet time to plan out the rest of his cover-up.

After less than a half hour rest, Phelan entered his shanty and with the benefit of some sunlight shining from the open door and small window, he examined the damage. The place was a mess but Phelan was not in a mood to spend a lot of time cleaning it. Furthermore, he didn't believe that he really needed to clean it up thoroughly just to hide the signs that a fight had taken place there. He was content to do just enough picking up, straightening out, and sweeping away to make the room passable for any surprise visitor who might come inside the cabin. During the clean-up, Phelan contemplated the plan he had made for burning the blood-soaked shirt that he had stashed underneath the cabin floor on the night of the murder. He now had second thoughts about burning it. The truth was he didn't like the idea of destroying his favorite shirt, and he started to wonder if there wasn't some safe way to save his shirt and still remove the blood evidence from it. He understood the two negatives of trying to clean the shirt. First was the danger that someone might see him doing it; second was the problem that it might not be possible to remove all the incriminating blood from the garment. However, the thought that there might be some way to save his prized shirt, maybe by cleaning it, or maybe by dying it a darker color, intrigued him. He finally concluded that he would simply keep the shirt hidden under the floor until he found some safe time and smart way to clean or dye it later.

But his own shirt wasn't the only clothing item he had to consider. Since he had told Scott that Hays wore his best clothes to Kaposia (and that was the story he wanted to stick with) it was essential that he not let any future visitor to his cabin see those clothes there. He therefore grabbed Hays' dress blue coat and fancy grey pants from the wooden peg they were hanging on and carefully stashed them under the floorboards. His plan was to hide them there until a future opportunity arose to safely sell them to an unsuspecting stranger. The clothes were worth a lot of money and would be highly valued by whites and Indians alike. Selling them would be easy (they would easily fit an average sized man); the challenge would be to find the right person to sell them to, someone who did not know Hays and did not live in the region. Phelan was confident that sooner or later he would find such a person and when he did he would receive enough money to buy some nice clothes for himself.

After he finished his cursory housecleaning, some rising hunger pangs pushed him to rush into the next phase of his cover-up scheme, partly because it included the possibility of a free meal. Back when he was resting under the shade tree, he had contemplated the best way and the best time to inform his neighbors about Hays' absence. Though he hadn't worked everything out, he had decided that his next priority must be to visit Ben and Genevieve Gervais and tell them the first part of his cover story. Phelan believed that convincing the Gervaises that Hays had left his farm to look for a calf that he suspected the Indians had stolen was absolutely critical. He knew all too well that of all his neighbors, Mrs. Gervais would be the one most inclined to question his story. Phelan had long sensed that Genevieve did not trust him and it seemed like she was naturally skeptical of everything he said. Yet, in spite of that, or perhaps partly because of it, Phelan couldn't help admiring the feisty Frenchwoman. Though barely five feet tall, she was a tough, hardy lady who wasn't afraid to speak her mind and wasn't afraid to correct anyone if she believed they did wrong. Many a time she had boldly stood up to Phelan and corrected his bad language, or his bad behavior, or his bad attitude. Phelan admired her boldness, mainly because there weren't too many people around who showed the courage to stand up to him, and he respected people with courage. But her boldness and natural skepticism could prove his undoing if she detected that what he said about Hays was untrue. As potentially problematic as Mrs. Gervais was, he needed to talk to her sometime soon simply because she was probably expecting he and Hays to visit her that day. Her son Alphonse had informed them Thursday morning that she had given birth to a baby boy, her seventh child and the "first white child" born in the Fountain Cave settlement. When Hays heard the news he took the liberty of telling the boy that he and Phelan would come over the next day to see the baby. Though Phelan had little interest in seeing a baby, he did not object to it at the time because he bet that the birth might be the occasion of some sort of social gathering and that would mean food, refreshments and an opportunity to see the pretty Perry girls. But now a day later, the situation was dramatically different. Hays was dead and Phelan was desperately trying to hide the fact that he murdered him.

## Phelan's Unavoidable Visits to the Gervaises

Phelan believed that his smartest move would be to canoe to the Gervais' cabin and matter-of-factly tell everyone there why Hays wasn't with him. Maybe, he thought, it would actually be better for him if all the Perrys and Ben's brother Pierre and his wife were there. That way more people would hear his story about Hays and yet, because of the large gathering, none of them would likely give him full attention or really scrutinize his story. Phelan's hunger also got him thinking about all the good food that the Gervaises would have. Genevieve's midwife, Mrs. Mary Perry, was not only the best midwife in the region,[*] she was also one of the area's best cooks.[5] Phelan was certain that midwife Mary, assisted by her daughters and Pierre Gervais' wife, Sophie, would have cooked plenty of food for the occasion.

Not surprisingly, Phelan decided that he should proceed immediately to the Gervais cabin. However, on his way to his landing he took a little diversion and walked down to the place on the river bank where he remembered he had left his hat. And there, on the large protruding roots of a cottonwood tree, he found it, exactly where he left it the night of the murder. To his dismay, the bright sunlight revealed that the hat had some blood stains on it. Fortunately for Phelan, the dark blue color of the hat subdued the redness of the stains (now they looked brownish) and after a little sand washing they were hardly noticeable. Though greatly relieved that his hat would still be useable, he cautiously decided to not wear it until the time he could more thoroughly clean and dry it. Thus, carrying his hat in his hand, Phelan walked over to his landing, threw the hat into the canoe, launched the log boat into the water, hopped in and began paddling up river. After passing the large island (now called Harriet Island), he approached a smaller island (now called Ross Island), where just beyond and nestled against the bluff was the large log house of the Ben Gervais family. When Phelan arrived at the cabin (just a short distance from where he beached his canoe), he was surprised to discover that the only adults inside were Genevieve and Sophia Perry (not to be confused with Pierre Gervais' wife Sophie). Under ordinary circumstances he would have been thrilled to see Sophia Perry in an uncrowded setting since he was really infatuated with her. But now the thought of telling his story to just her and the always skeptical Genevieve Gervais made him a little apprehensive.

Greeting Mrs. Gervais, Phelan was genuinely impressed with her healthy appearance and remarked that he couldn't believe that she had just given birth only two days ago. Though the baby was asleep

---

[*] Edward Neill stated that Mary Perry was "an accomplished *accoucheur* and was a favorite with the officer's wives and by her skill put many an Army surgeon to the blush, although they were not jealous of her attainments." Her cooking prowess is sheer speculation.

in the crib, Genevieve spoke in her normal loud voice (a childhood illness had partly impaired her hearing and caused her to compensate for it by speaking loudly) and cheerfully told Phelan a summary account of the birth of her boy Basil. She gratefully noted all the help that the midwife, Mary Perry, and her whole family had given her and explained that Mary and her other daughter had returned home to finish their own chores just an hour before. After mentioning that her husband Ben and her older sons were out working in the field, she asked Phelan the question he was waiting for: "Where was Mr. Hays?"

Knowing that she was hard of hearing, Phelan used a loud but intentionally unexcited voice to tell his now well-rehearsed story of Hays' search for the stolen calf. However, he smoothly added a new detail to the story. During his trip over to their house he thought about the possibility that someone in their family might have observed Scott and Foy's canoe beached at his landing that morning. He therefore thought it would be clever to incorporate into his story some account of an early morning canoeist who happened to visit them. Once again combining fact and fiction, he decided to make the imaginary visitor a partial blend of Scott and Foy: a traveler coming from B.F. Baker's trading post, who was heading to the St. Croix River, the ultimate destination of Scott and Foy, which was far enough away from the Gervais home that no one in the family would be able to disprove the story. When Phelan told his expanded story to Mrs. Gervais and Sophia Perry, he made sure he told it in his usual sarcastic style. Quite fittingly, he presented the new anecdote about the morning visitor as if its main intent was to ridicule Hays. As Phelan narrated it, Hays had a chance to get a free and easy ride across the river (and even all the way down to Kaposia if he wanted it) but the finicky prude refused the offer because he wanted more time to dress and eat his breakfast. And because of that, poor Phelan got stuck with the job of having to canoe him across the river. When Phelan finished his story he was content with his performance but concerned about how his audience of two received it. Though Sophia's facial expression was difficult to read, he could tell from Genevieve's face that she was not fully satisfied with what she had heard. As expected, Mrs. Gervais had some pointed questions for Phelan: "Did they have any recent problems with the Indians?" "Was it safe for Hays to go to Kaposia alone?"

Phelan finessed his answers by repeating some of the same comments he had made to Scott and Foy about the Indians. As for Hays traveling alone, Phelan cleverly replied that he had offered to accompany him but the sergeant wanted Phelan to stay home and watch over their farm. Phelan wasn't sure his answers completely satisfied her, but he was happy to drop the subject when the baby started crying. As Mrs. Gervais went to attend to the infant, she told Phelan to help himself to the food spread out on the table. He gladly obliged her and stuffed himself with a feast of ham, corn, and fish. After eating and spending a few awkward minutes trying to converse with Sophia, he thanked the women for the food and said he had to get back home to tend to his chores. On his way out the door he gave a special smile to Sophia and then left the house, waving to Ben Gervais, whom he saw in the distance.

On his trip home, Phelan reflected on his talk with Mrs. Gervais. All in all, he thought it went better than he expected it would. Now his only major worry was Scott and Foy. He could only hope that they would not be busybodies and cause trouble for him. His fervent hope was that they would just simply do their business at St. Peters and then return directly back to the St. Croix River where, if Phelan was lucky, they would remain and he would not see or hear from them again.

After Phelan returned home from the Gervais house late Friday afternoon, he took a break from doing any more cover-up actions. The break turned out to be a rather long one. He spent most of Saturday in a drunken stupor, trying to soothe his worries by drinking the rest of Hays' wine and another jug of cheap whiskey he bought from Parrant with coins Hays had left in the cabin. It wasn't until Sunday morning when Phelan finally headed back to the Gervaises to inform them that Hays had failed to return home from his trip to

Kaposia. Telling that piece of fiction to his neighbors was one of the last crucial parts of his cover-up. But Phelan had misgivings about how he would handle the inevitable questions that would be naturally asked of him. Now he was certain that Mrs. Gervais would demand more details about Hays' so-called trip to Kaposia. She would insist on learning the where, when, why and how of the story. Phelan was not looking forward to facing Mrs. Gervais' tough questions, but he knew there was no way to avoid it.

As Phelan mentally prepared himself for the important meeting, he came to realize that his task was less complicated than he had first thought. All he had to do was report that Hays never came back from Kaposia and then act as if he were concerned about him. He only needed to repeat his story that Hays had requested Phelan "to look out for him towards evening" at the landing place across the river (which was fully visible from Phelan's landing), and that Hays never showed up. After reporting that, what else could he be expected to say? His simple story was that he didn't know where Hays was, or why he hadn't returned. He could guess that maybe he had gone further downriver to Hazen Mooers' place, but he didn't know. Phelan believed that if he stuck to that simple story and the strategy of acting as though he knew nothing more about the matter, he would successfully stand up to Mrs. Gervais' questioning.

When Phelan reached the Gervais house, once again Ben and his oldest son Alphonse were outside doing chores, but this time there were no other visitors inside their home. Now Mrs. Gervais had her hands full tending not only the baby but also her four youngest children (Severe, age ten, Isaac, age eight, Jean Baptist, age five, and Benjamin Jr., age four).[6] Phelan hoped that the children might cause enough distractions that the mother would be unable to question him thoroughly about the pretended disappearance of Hays. Putting on a somber face and feigning a sense of urgency, he solemnly told Mrs. Gervais the reason for his visit. As soon as she heard it she gasped and cried out, "Oh, no! He hasn't come back yet?"

And just as Phelan expected, she hit him with rapid-fire questions, including the standard where, why, what and how inquiries. Phelan followed his strategy and kept the limits of what he told her very narrow. Eventually, however, he felt he had to give her something more than merely an "I don't know." In an attempt to calm her fears and also to delay her from possibly initiating a formal investigation, he told her that there was a good chance Hays was down at Hazen Mooers' place on Grey Cloud Island, since on another occasion Hays had expressed an interest in going there. That was another half-truth but Phelan thought it made sense. Kaposia was about one-third of the way to Grey Cloud Island, so it was conceivable that if Hays had gone to Kaposia, he might well have thought to go the rest of the way to see his fur trader friend Hazen Mooers, who also lived just across the river from Medicine Bottle's village, the small Dakota community that had broken off from the Kaposia band and had a reputation for being less friendly to whites. It was not that far-fetched to theorize that Hays could have reasoned that some Indians from that village had stolen the calf. And since Mooers spoke fluent Dakota, who better to help him investigate the matter than Mooers, who traded with Medicine Bottle's band?

A visit to Mooers would explain why Hays was late returning home. If he was down at Mooers' trading post, then naturally he would have just waited there until he could get a canoe ride back home from either Mooers or one of his employees who regularly voyaged upriver to St. Peters to acquire their trade goods.

But adding the Hazen Mooers detail to his story proved to be a blunder. No sooner had Phelan finished telling Mrs. Gervais about this possibility than she excitedly told him that by an amazing coincidence Justice of the Peace Joseph R. Brown, Mooers' Grey Cloud Island neighbor, was at the Perry's house that very moment. "Yes," Genevieve exclaimed, Brown had passed by their place earlier on his way to see Mr. Perry about some matter. Phelan knew Genevieve's claim was true because he had seen another canoe beached on their shoreline when he had landed his canoe there. Naturally, Mrs. Gervais suggested that Phelan go up to the Perry's house to inquire if

Justice Brown had seen Hays or heard anything about him on his way upriver from Grey Cloud Island. The news that a justice of the peace from Grey Cloud Island of all places was just up the hill at the Perry's place naturally unsettled Phelan and made him wonder if he wasn't cursed with bad luck by the ghost of John Hays. He tried his best to hide his panic, but he feared that Mrs. Gervais had detected how the news had flustered him.

Phelan scrambled for an excuse for not going to see Brown and then suddenly after looking at his muddy, grimy pants, one flashed into his mind. He told Mrs. Gervais that he didn't want Sophia Perry to see him again in his dirty clothes, so he would go home first and change clothes before he visited the Perry's. He assured Genevieve that he would catch up with Brown later. Whether or not Mrs. Gervais completely bought the excuse, Phelan impressed himself with how rapidly he was able to improvise a very plausible response. He knew she was aware of his feelings for Sophia; his reluctance to visit her home not looking his best was not that strange. Indeed, anticipating that he might see Sophia again at the Gervais house, Phelan had even made a special effort that morning to shave and clean himself up. The only reason he was still wearing the dirty yet not visibly blood-stained pants was that he still hadn't cleaned his other pants that were caked in cattle manure. He should have washed them on Saturday but he was too drunk, too lazy, and too much of a procrastinator to do it then. Besides, he thought that wearing the same dirty pants he wore the night of the murder would be less incriminating than to be seen suddenly wearing clean pants.

The bad news that Joseph R. Brown was at the Perry's place did have a silver lining for Phelan. It gave him a natural excuse to leave the Gervais house earlier than he had anticipated. Now he could tell Mrs. Gervais that he had to rush home to change his clothes and then hurry back to see Brown at the Perry's house. Of course, Phelan had no intention of returning anytime soon but he could come up with an excuse for that later.

But before he could leave the house, Ben Gervais came inside and, with only a passing nod to Phelan, rushed over to check on the baby and admonish his noisy children. Phelan's departing remarks included a contrived detail that he deliberately wanted to divulge to the Gervaises that day. Realizing that sooner or later Ben or one of his sons would notice that the missing calf was no longer missing, Phelan mentioned (in his best sarcastic voice) that ironically the original cause of Hays' departure, the missing calf, had straggled back safely to their herd late Friday afternoon. Now Phelan would no longer have to worry about keeping the calf hidden from his neighbors. Yet, his revised calf story caused him a new worry: Did Mrs. Gervais and her husband really believe the story? In an attempt to assure both of them that he was truly concerned about his housemate, he promised them that if Hays did not return that afternoon, he would come back the next morning and start a search for him, all the way down to Kaposia if necessary.

The concern on Mrs. Gervais' face was telling, but at that point Phelan knew there was nothing more he could say to ease her worry about "dear Mr. Hays." Phelan left the house haunted by the image of Mrs. Gervais' sad, worried face. There was now no question that she would spread the word of Hays' disappearance and lead the charge to have the men search for him. But Phelan was determined to control events. Any search for Hays must be led by him. He would indeed return to the Gervaises the next morning and lead Ben Gervais alone on a bogus search for the man who was already dead and laying at the bottom of the river.

## The Joseph R. Brown Problem

Phelan returned home mentally exhausted from the strain of Mrs. Gervais' interrogation and the unwelcome news that Joseph R. Brown, the only lawman in between the Mississippi and St. Croix Rivers, was visiting the Perry's. He needed time to unwind and contemplate his next move. Whatever it would be, one thing was certain: despite what he told Mrs. Gervais, under no circumstances would he go and see Justice Brown at the Perry home.

Brown's presence at the Perry place presented Phelan with a stressful conundrum. If he avoided visiting the Perrys and simply relied on Mrs. Gervais to inform them about Hays' disappearance, then eventually both families would interpret his absence as very suspicious behavior. He could well imagine their reaction if he never showed up at the Perry's that day, and he could virtually hear the accusatory questions of his neighbors: "Where is Phelan?" "Why isn't he here?" "Isn't it strange that Hays' partner doesn't take the time to come and tell his neighbors about his disappearance?"

On the other hand, if he did go to the Perry home that day—just to avoid suspicion—and inform the family of Hays' disappearance, then he would run the grave risk of encountering Brown. And Joseph R. Brown was the last person in the territory he wanted to see. Though Phelan only knew him by reputation, Brown's reputation was enough to alarm him of the danger he posed to the killer of Sergeant Hays.

Ironically, much of what Phelan knew about Brown he had learned from Hays. The housemate he had killed used to tell him about "Joe Brown," the man he called "the smartest soldier ever stationed at Fort Snelling," who was also "one of the most interesting and talented fellows" Hays had ever met. Hays claimed that even though Brown had little formal schooling, he had "more brains and horse sense than all those West Point officers put together." According to Hays, Brown planted the first wheat at the fort as a young soldier (which was the first wheat planted in the region), and became the favorite of Colonel Snelling because of his work in developing the fort's farm, which became the largest farm north of St. Louis. He also earned fame by exploring Minnehaha Creek with the Colonel's son, Joseph Snelling, and ultimately discovering its source, Lake Minnetonka. Though Sergeant Brown had retired from the military long before Phelan arrived at Fort Snelling, Sergeant Hays knew him well and kept up with news of his exploits after Brown left the army and became a fur trader. Hays had learned that Brown had mastered the Dakota language and over time had taken at least two Dakota wives. The last Hays had heard, Brown was the father of a dozen children.

But Hays was not the only source of Phelan's knowledge of Brown. James Clewett, the Englishman who had married Rose Perry the past spring and had lived at the Perry home, was one of Brown's fur trading partners. Though Phelan did not like Clewett—partly because he was English (like many Northern Irishmen, Phelan was prejudiced against Englishmen) and partly because he was jealous of his marrying Rose Perry, a woman Phelan had been interested in— he couldn't avoid occasional encounters with him and sometimes engaged in conversations with the man who knew Brown even better than Hays had.

Clewett also trumpeted Brown's cleverness and his extraordinary and diverse talents. It was Clewett who told Phelan that Brown had gone down to the county seat of Prairie du Chien and persuasively convinced the Crawford County Commissioners that the settlements up north between the St. Croix and Mississippi Rivers not only needed a justice of the peace but that he was the best man for the job. Clewett chuckled when he boasted to Phelan that his business partner was now the only official lawman east of the Mississippi and north of Wabasha. And Clewett maintained that Brown was truly the best man for the job because in addition to being tough, courageous, fair, and wise, no one he knew could read men (white or Indian) better—or detect lies faster—than Brown.

Clewett's words haunted Phelan, that clever man with the talent for lie-detecting was just upriver from Phelan's home. The danger Brown posed to Phelan was chillingly obvious. If the former Sergeant Brown was able to question Phelan about the disappearance of his old comrade Sergeant Hays, Phelan's lies would not hold up well to the clever man's interrogation. Phelan feared the frontier judge precisely because not only had Brown known Hays personally, he knew the Dakota Indians intimately. How could Phelan's story about Hays and the calf-stealing Indians withstand the scrutiny of Hays' comrade—"the smartest soldier ever stationed at Fort Snelling"— and the veteran Indian trader who had been closely connected to the Dakota for over ten years?

Thanks once again to his dirty pants Phelan found a solution to his dilemma. The sight of those mud-, blood-, and grime-soiled pants reminded him of what he had told Mrs. Gervais when he explained why he needed to go home: he had told her that he was going home to change clothes, and now he surmised it would be wise to do just that. But given that his only other pants (and his only other useable shirt) were soiled in manure, he would necessarily have to wash and dry them before he could change into presentable clothes. Phelan knew that it would take a few hours to wash and dry his dirty clothes in the open air. So that would be his excuse for his delay in going to the Perry house. Phelan bet that by the time his clothes were dry, Brown would be gone (probably up at Rumtown in his new whiskey shop) and so—dressed in clean clothes and looking his best—he would be able to comfortably visit the Perry family and tell them himself about Hays' disappearance.

Now that he was committed to washing his manure-caked clothes, Phelan thought it would be wise to "kill two birds with one stone" and also finally wash the muddy, bloody, grimy pants he was wearing, the pants that were muddy and grimy enough to hide the blood that was splattered on them on the night of the murder.

Phelan used a thick stick to lift up the stinking, manure-crusted pants and shirt, which were both draped over the top rails of the cattle pen. Then, carefully keeping the pungent pants and shirt at arm's length, he walked over to the creek and dropped them into the water. He decided to let them soak there, hoping the steady flow of the stream would naturally clean them. Whether it would or not, he had no intention of picking them up any time soon.

But the pants he was wearing, the ones he wore the night of the murder, were another matter entirely. Phelan was more than willing to use his own hands to thoroughly clean the pants that held incriminating evidence against him.

He took off his boots, socks, and pants, and wearing nothing but a long shirt and his undergarments, he walked into the creek and began vigorously washing the pants against the rocks. To Phelan's shock and dismay, he discovered that washing the pants made the blood splotches more visible; unfortunately, washing the pants only removed the mud and grime. Apparently it had been the mud and grime that had hidden the blood stains on the grey pants, and now with the camouflaging mud and grime washed away, faded brown blood splatters were plainly visible on both pant legs.

Yelling and cursing at the failure of all his washing and rubbing, and utterly frustrated, Phelan gave up and resigned himself to the hard fact that the blood was not going to come out of the pants. Now he asked himself whether the pants were even salvageable.

Phelan quickly concluded that the most practical solution for now was to just do what he had done earlier with his bloody shirt: stash them under the floor boards of his cabin until he could figure out how to salvage them.

Now he went back to the soiled pants soaking in the creek; they were the only pants he had left. Fortunately, the soaking had washed away most of the manure from both the pants and shirt, and he only needed to rub them a few times on the rocks to get them thoroughly clean.

After he was satisfied with his cleaning of the pants and shirt, Phelan put on his socks and boots and carried all the wet clothes (including his blood-stained pants) back to his cabin. After draping the clean pants and shirt over a fence rail, Phelan hurried over to the side of the cabin and, in a space between two foundation stones, he stashed the blood-stained pants under the floorboards, right next to the bloody shirt he had hidden the night of the murder and a few feet away from Hays' best clothes, which he had carefully wrapped in a blanket and placed there on Friday.

Now that all that work was finished, Phelan took a rest and waited for his clothes to dry. He thought about doing some chores, but on further reflection he decided that now that he was clean from the creek washing he didn't want to get sweaty and dirty again, especially since he was going to wear his freshly cleaned clothes over to the Perry's. Then he thought that perhaps he could do some less strenuous chore, like fishing for his supper, but on second thought he ruled out fishing for two reasons. First, he only had a shirt to wear and he didn't want to go down to the river half naked in full view of any passing boaters. Second, it might not look good if any of his neighbors saw him fishing on the day he was supposed to be concerned about finding his housemate.

As he was thinking through his options, Phelan was startled by the sight of a canoe approaching his landing. It looked like Evans' canoe, and within a few moments it was clear that it was indeed William Evans coming to visit his two friends. Only Evans didn't know that one of those friends had been murdered by the other one.

Phelan had mixed feelings about Evans' surprise visit. On the one hand, his pants weren't dry; it was not a good time for a visitor. Maybe Evans would find it odd that Phelan was washing all his clothes in the middle of the day. On the other hand, the timing of Evans' visit could be fortuitous. Evans' visit would give Phelan yet another excuse for his delay in going to the Perry home. Moreover, he had been thinking about the importance of informing Evans about Hays' failure to return home from the trip to Kaposia. He knew that sooner rather than later he had to tell Evans the rest of the fictional story he had deliberately introduced to him the night of the murder, the lie that after he had left Evans' house he had canoed Hays across the river so that Hays could search for that calf that he presumed had been stolen by the Indians. Now that Evans was coming to see him he would not have to delay conveying that important detail any longer.

It didn't really matter what Phelan thought about the timing of Evans' visit. The hard reality was that Evans was coming to visit, and he would be there in a few minutes. Fortunately for Phelan, Evans' walk up the wooded hill from the landing placed him out of view from the place where Phelan was standing, which thankfully was near the post where his wet clothes were hanging. Seizing the opportunity of being out of Evans' eyesight, Phelan quickly grabbed his wet pants, kicked off his boots, pulled the damp pants up over his legs and then put on his boots again, all in less time than it took Evans to walk into view. By the time Evans reached the shanty Phelan was there and ready to explain that his pants were damp from a slip in the river while landing his canoe.

As it turned out Evans never asked about Phelan's damp pants; he probably didn't notice they were damp. But the damp pants were not Phelan's chief concern. All that mattered now was telling Evans the same story about Hays that he had told Mrs. Gervais.

Phelan knew instinctively that Evans had to be handled differently than Mrs. Gervais. Though less emotional and less assertive than Mrs. Gervais, Evans could be just as skeptical of fishy stories as the feisty Frenchwoman. Moreover, he knew Phelan and Hays better than she did and thus was even better able to detect Phelan's lies. But Phelan, the master liar, was ready for Evans, and he told the story in a very convincing way, shrewdly tailoring it to the peculiarities of Hays' close friend. Particularly compelling was his inclusion of Hays' possible trek to fur trader Hazen Mooers' place. That rang true to Evans because he knew that Mooers was a friend of Hays and would have helped him communicate with the Indians at Medicine Bottle's village. He also knew that Mooers would offer Hays a canoe ride back upriver as soon as it was convenient.

Phelan was relieved and pleased with how well the story went over with his friend. Evan's reactions (both verbal and nonverbal) told Phelan that he believed what Phelan told him. But not wanting to push his luck, Phelan thought it would be wise to keep Evans' visit short. No sense, he reasoned, in risking the chance that Evans might eventually notice something suspicious if he spent a long time with Hays' killer, near the very place where Hays was murdered.

It was easy to manipulate Evans into returning home after only a twenty-minute visit. Phelan induced him to leave with the half-truth that he was on his way to tell the Perrys about Hays and subtly suggested that Evans could keep an eye out for Hays on his way back downriver and from the high vantage point of his bluff-top home. Evans accepted Phelan's suggestion without hesitation and, acting like it was his idea to return home, hurried back down the hill to his canoe.

As Phelan watched Evans disappear into the brush, he was pleased at how well he had handled the unexpected visitor and how nicely everything seemed to be working out. His clothes were washed and drying, Evans was on his way home, updated about Hays and acting like he believed all the lies he had told him, and he now had two understandable excuses for why he hadn't immediately gone to see Brown at the Perry house.

Now Phelan could relax, lie out in the sun, and wait for the damp pants he was wearing to dry. He was in no hurry because he had to give Justice Brown enough time to finish his business at the Perry house and then head upriver to Rumtown. It took an hour for his pants and shirt to fully dry on that increasingly cloudy, comfortably cool September day. By the time Phelan had changed into his clean pants and shirt and was ready to begin his slow walk over to the Perry home, it was late in the afternoon.

When he reached their cabin on the hill thirty minutes later, Phelan was delighted to learn that not only had Brown gone but Mr. Perry was away building fencing—and surprisingly none of the Gervaises had been there yet to tell them that Hays seemed to be missing. Sophia and her mother and sister were the only ones home, and Phelan got his information from Sophia, who was alone outside the cabin on her way to bring the cows in for milking when he arrived. Phelan told her (in as solemn a voice as he could speak) his now well-rehearsed story of Hays' disappearance. He also feigned disappointment that he had missed Brown but stumbled in explaining why he hadn't been able to immediately run to their house to see him after Mrs. Gervais told him that Brown was there. Phelan couldn't guess what Sophia thought about his awkward explanation but one thing was clear: she was sincerely concerned to hear about "Mr. Hays." With a sad look and speaking softly, she assured him that she would pass the news on to her family.

Phelan was more than happy that Sophia would tell her parents about Hays, that would spare him the burden of having to do it himself. He wanted to chat a little longer with the pretty girl, but he didn't want to run the risk that her mother might come out of the cabin, forcing him to tell his story again, and running the risk that Mrs. Perry might challenge him with questions he couldn't answer. Giving the excuse that he needed to get home in case Hays returned, he politely said goodbye to Sophia and walked briskly back to his cabin, somewhat satisfied by all he had accomplished that day.

Phelan's lingering worry was what Mrs. Gervais might do if she really doubted his story about Hays. That stressful contemplation made him even more determined to control events by taking charge of the search for Hays. He resolved that the next morning he would preempt any possible plan that Mrs. Gervais might have for organizing a search party by asking her husband alone to help him look for Hays. Ben Gervais was a man that Phelan thought he could control, not just because he was nine inches shorter than he was but also because he was mild mannered. He also guessed that Mrs. Gervais would be pleased that her good husband would be directly involved in the search for "dear Mr. Hays."

## Phelan Controls the Search for the Man He Killed

The next morning, immediately after chores, Phelan canoed to the Gervais farm and yelled out to Ben to join him in a search for Hays down to Kaposia. Ben dutifully agreed, and after grabbing a few pieces of pemmican from his cabin for their lunch, hustled down to the river and hopped in Phelan's canoe. Phelan shrewdly didn't leave his canoe, to avoid having to deal with any more inquiries from Mrs. Gervais.

Hays' killer cleverly orchestrated the sham search so as to keep Ben Gervais far away from the actual murder scene on his land. He concentrated the search on the west shore and made sure that the only times they got out of the canoe were on that side of the river. The absence of any visible footprints on the beach where Phelan claimed he dropped Hays puzzled Gervais, and he expressed surprise that the landing place showed no sign that anyone had recently walked there. Phelan worried that Ben Gervais, the old voyageur, might be getting suspicious about his story. But unlike his outspoken wife, Ben Gervais was not one to instantly divulge what he was really thinking. If he was skeptical of Phelan's story he kept his doubts to himself.

As they slowly canoed downriver to Kaposia, Phelan did his best to pretend that he was earnestly looking for any sign of his dead housemate. When they finally sighted some footprints on the beach he feigned excitement that they might be Hays' tracks. But a closer view proved the prints to be too old, too off course, and even the wrong shape (Hays wore boots, not shoes) to pass for Hays' tracks. Phelan acted disappointed, but in that instance he wasn't acting. He had sincerely hoped that by chance they might find some footprints somewhere along the beach that could reasonably pass off as evidence that Hays had been there. But the only footprints they saw along the entire shoreline to Kaposia were these old shoe prints that came from the wrong direction.

When the two men reached Kaposia and beached their canoe near the much larger log dugout canoes of the Dakota, Phelan was surprised and relieved to see mostly women and children at the village. Apparently the men were out hunting somewhere. Ignoring the increased chatter of the villagers and the many stares directed at them, Phelan quickly led Gervais past the long, bark-covered Dakota lodges and over to the Methodist mission house, the log cabin that the ex-slave Jim Thompson (the only man known to have beaten Phelan in a fight) had built in 1837 under the supervision of Methodist minister, Alfred Brunson. Now the mission house was the residence of thirty-two-year-old John Holton, his wife Sarah, and their ten-year-old son David. A native of Pennsylvania, Holton was a lay missionary who also served as the village's "Indian farmer," a white man assigned by the Indian agent Lawrence Taliaferro to teach the Indians American farming methods.[7] For the sole benefit of Gervais, Phelan asked the Holton family, who were all outside harvesting their vegetables along with some young Dakota women, if they had seen John Hays. Their answer hardly surprised him: No, "he had not been there ... they had heard or seen nothing of him."[8]

Phelan did not want to press them for more information because he feared they might say something in defense of the Dakota that would undermine the theory that the Indians were involved in Hays' disappearance. He felt awkward talking to people who lived among the Dakota and might challenge him with questions of their own such as: Why would Hays walk all the way down to Kaposia alone? Why didn't he just report the theft to Taliaferro? Fortunately for Phelan, the Holtons were in the middle of their chores and he shrewdly used that as an excuse to leave them to their work and head back home.

Phelan and Gervais' return trip home was uneventful. Nowhere along the river did they find any "trace whatsoever" of Hays' walk to Kaposia.[9] Phelan couldn't tell whether that fact raised any suspicions in Ben Gervais' mind about the story of Hays' trek downriver three days earlier, but the old voyageur never directly challenged the veracity of the story. In any case, Phelan was relieved that his good neighbor did not confront him with any of its inconsistencies.

It was late in the day when they landed the canoe back on Gervais' land. Since both men were eager to return to their respective homes, Ben Gervais just hopped out of the canoe, waved goodbye, and headed to his cabin. Phelan was glad that Mrs. Gervais was nowhere in sight because he was too physically and mentally fatigued to deal with her expected interrogation. He was exceedingly concerned, however, about what Ben would tell his wife about what they saw and did not see on their long search downriver. As he paddled back home alone with his thoughts, he couldn't help imagining the worse: that Ben might tell the already suspicious Genevieve that Phelan must have done something to Hays because there was no evidence that the sergeant had ever walked down to Kaposia. Phelan's anxiety rose as he contemplated that Mrs. Gervais might instigate a wider search for Hays led by some of his friends from Fort Snelling.

By the time Phelan reached his landing his mind was deeply engaged in what he could do to prevent too many more people from getting involved in another search. To preempt an army of Hays' Fort Snelling friends from launching their own search and inquiry,

Phelan decided to go to the fort the next day, seek out Hays' good friend Bart Baldwin, and lead him alone on a second search for his missing partner. Baldwin's involvement in a second search would give it legitimacy to Hays' old comrades at Fort Snelling since everyone knew how close the Indian interpreter was to Hays. Moreover, given the Indian factor underlying Phelan's story about Hays' trek to Kaposia, no search would be credible unless it included someone like Baldwin, who could fluently speak Dakota. From his past associations with Baldwin, Phelan was confident that he could manipulate him enough to keep the search away from the part of the river where Hays' body was buried.

The next morning, Tuesday September 10, after finishing his chores, Phelan implemented his scheme and canoed to Fort Snelling to inform Baldwin about his friend's disappearance and to request his help in a search for Hays. Baldwin was stunned and listened intently to Phelan's story of the lost calf, Hays' insistence on trekking to Kaposia to look for it, and Phelan and Ben Gervais' recent unsuccessful search for him after he failed to return home. Phelan slyly added a relevant anecdote he contrived to cast greater suspicion on the Indians. Embellishing from some real incidents that other settlers had had with the Dakota, he told a yarn about how one day, a few weeks before Hays' disappearance, a rowdy, menacing, young Dakota ("about 18 years old") fired his gun at "a looking glass" inside their cabin. Hays justifiably got angry and wrestled the gun away from the reckless shooter. Though the sergeant eventually returned the gun to the lad, he sternly warned him that "if he came back he would club him." The Indian defiantly responded by threatening to tell Chief Big Thunder about his mistreatment.[10] Phelan suggested that maybe Hays' disappearance was connected to that Indian.

Baldwin did not question the story simply because he was keenly aware of several similar incidents and knew firsthand how reckless and menacing some young Dakota could be when they were drunk. His boss, Major Taliaferro, was trying his best to stop the trade of alcohol with the Indians but traders like Pig's Eye Parrant literally specialized in selling liquor to the Dakota. The proximity of Pig's Eye's saloon to Phelan and Hays' cabin made the whole story quite believable, although Baldwin wondered why his friend hadn't told him about it; if he had, Baldwin could have gotten Major Taliaferro to investigate the incident. He was also plainly perturbed at Hays' foolishness in walking alone to Kaposia only a few weeks after he had a violent encounter with one of the villagers.

Baldwin was anxious to begin a search for Hays immediately, but his duties at the fort that morning demanded that he stay there until the afternoon. Phelan feared that if they started that late they would not have enough daylight to make it to Kaposia, let alone return home before dark. Ultimately both men agreed that Phelan would return to the fort early the next morning, and they would devote the entire day to a thorough search for Hays.

When Phelan returned to Fort Snelling the next morning, Wednesday, September 11, Baldwin was ready and waiting at the boat landing. Phelan was pleased to see that Baldwin carried a full knapsack; he obviously had brought plenty of food for their trip. But Baldwin looked grim and troubled. As he loaded his gear and an army musket into the canoe, he told Phelan that he was fiercely worried about his friend and had a chilling fear that they would find him dead.

Phelan knew, of course, that Hays was dead but he wasn't going to let Baldwin find his body. Like the search he made with Gervais, Phelan would steer the canoe to the west side of the river, opposite the shore of where Hays' body was sunk.

For the benefit of Baldwin, Phelan landed his canoe at the beach where he supposedly left Hays five days earlier commencing his walk to Kaposia. Because he and Gervais had walked over that part of the shoreline two days before, their footprints were plainly visible. Baldwin asked Phelan if they had seen any traces of Hays' footprints there before they had trampled over the ground. Phelan wanted to lie but he knew that Gervais would tell the truth if anyone asked what he saw the day he and Phelan conducted their search, so Phelan told Baldwin the truth, but suggested that Sunday's rain and a rising river tide could have washed Hays' tracks off the beach. Just like Phelan's earlier search, he and Baldwin saw no other footprints along the river except for those same old wrongly-directed shoe prints that he and Gervais had seen on Monday.

After a long and uneventful trip down the Mississippi, made longer by the lack of easy conversation, Phelan and Baldwin finally arrived at Kaposia. Phelan felt uneasy when he saw that this time there were many men at the village. Apparently they had arrived at a time when most of the villagers (men, women, and children) were at home. Though he tried to suppress his anxiety, Phelan was uncomfortable walking among so many Dakota men, especially the young warriors he had falsely accused of stealing his calf and was also trying to blame for allegedly killing Hays.

Phelan was somewhat relieved when he saw how friendly the Dakota were with Baldwin and how clearly at ease he was with them. Phelan was impressed with the instant rapport Baldwin established with the men that surrounded him. Phelan learned later that three of the men were Baldwin's brothers-in-law, but that could not have been the only reason that Baldwin had good, friendly relationships with all the Dakota who gathered around him. It was plain to Phelan that all those Indians genuinely liked the Dakota-speaking white man. Phelan suspected that there must be something in Baldwin's personality that drew the Dakota to him. Phelan was curious to know what Baldwin and the Indians were talking about, especially when they all started laughing. Phelan could only guess that Baldwin had not yet asked them about his missing friend.

When the chuckling ceased, Baldwin pulled out some tobacco from his knapsack and offered it to just four of the men, who all graciously accepted it with slight smiles and nods of approval. Phelan learned later that those four men were Baldwin's three brothers-in-law and a man named "Wabsheeda" (or the Dancer), a favorite of Major Taliaferro and also a good acquaintance of Baldwin. Now the conversation turned serious and seemed limited to just the four solemn-faced men who received the tobacco and the visitor who gave it to them; it was now obvious to Phelan that Baldwin was finally directing the conversation to the subject of Hays.

Phelan grew increasingly uncomfortable knowing that the men were now in some way talking about the story he had made up about Hays. Maybe Evans and Baldwin believed the story but how, Phelan pondered, could he expect those Indians to accept it, especially when it was so accusatory of Kaposia Indians? Phelan feared that these Indians would expose his lies and persuade Baldwin not to believe his story about Hays. Adding to Phelan's stress was the fact that he couldn't understand a word that Baldwin and the Indians were saying. He could only stand there and try to look calm, but that was getting harder and harder to do.

Looking off at the nearby mission house, Phelan suddenly thought of a way to ease his tension and at the same time thwart another potential problem. He was concerned about having to face the lay missionaries, the Holtons, again, and about the possibility that they might discredit his story about Hays. But since he was at Kaposia again, on the pretense of a second search for Hays, at least some chat with the Holtons was unavoidable. Phelan thought it might be to his advantage if he could manage to talk to the Holtons alone, without Baldwin. Phelan knew that Baldwin would thoroughly question the family about Hays, and if he did, such inquiries could easily uncover information that would both exonerate the Indians and incriminate Phelan. To avoid that danger, Phelan needed to control the situation and keep Baldwin away. This might be his best chance to talk to the Holtons alone, while Baldwin was deeply engaged in a serious discussion with his brothers-in-law, an unintelligible conversation that was making Phelan so uncomfortable that even a visit to the Holtons would be a welcome relief.

Motioning to Baldwin, Phelan pointed to the mission house and quietly told him he was going over to speak to the Holtons. Considering the awkward situation he was in and the intense stress he was under, Phelan managed to move away from the five men speaking Dakota and walk toward the mission house rather smoothly. Though

248

he hadn't given Baldwin much chance to object to his departure, Phelan thought—maybe it was wishful thinking—that Baldwin didn't seem to mind that he was going to the Holtons alone.

The mission house was a different scene than he had encountered with Ben Gervais on Monday. John Holton was nowhere in sight; today Mrs. Holton was seated on a stool outside the mission house, reading passages from the Bible to her son and three adolescent Dakota girls, who were all sitting on the ground around her and listening to her animated words. Normally Phelan disliked Bible stories, in part because he didn't know the Bible very well, and because what little he did know of it seemed to condemn most things he did. But today Mrs. Holton's Bible lessons gave Phelan a perfect excuse to keep his visit brief. Even if Phelan had wanted to stay and chat (which he surely didn't), it would be rude of him to interrupt her for anything more than a quick question or two about Hays, especially since she and her husband had told him two days earlier that they had "heard or seen nothing" of the missing man. Phelan didn't ask Mrs. Holton where her husband was; if he was nearby she might go and get him, or tell one of the children to get him, and Phelan had no interest in submitting himself to the Indian farmer's inevitable questions.

But Phelan didn't have to worry about John Holton. When Phelan inquired about Hays, Mrs. Holton volunteered that her husband was across the river at Red Rock helping the new Methodist missionary, Reverend Kavanaugh, build a cabin. (The Reverend Benjamin Kavanaugh and his family had been assigned by Reverend Brunson to establish a new mission school downriver from present-day Pig's Eye Lake, at the future site of Newport, where there was a landmark granite boulder, partly painted red by the Dakota.)* Phelan was delighted that John Holton was too far away to trouble him and also glad that Mrs. Holton didn't bother him with any new questions. Now all he

---

* That same "Red Rock" now stands on the grounds of Newport's First Methodist Church, at Glen Road and 11th Street. The equally historic Kavanaugh mission house also stands on those same grounds, next to the rock and historical plaque.

had to do was wander back to Baldwin and hope that his Dakota friends hadn't told him anything that cast doubt on Phelan's story.

## Enhancing the Theory that Indians Killed Hays

When Phelan returned to Baldwin and the four men, he was astonished to learn that instead of incriminating Phelan, the Dakota had revealed information that was more incriminating to some of their fellow villagers. Baldwin quietly told Phelan what his honest brothers-in-law had divulged to him—that there were several young men who were openly hostile to the whites and who especially resented the missionaries who had boldly built their house right in their village and tried to change the people's religion and their way of life. The brothers-in-law claimed that it was the presence of the missionaries that drove Medicine Bottle and his family and followers to move to Pine Bend, across the river from Hazen Mooers' trading post, and establish their own more traditional village. They also said that two of Chief Big Thunder's own sons were associated with the militants, even though it was Big Thunder himself who had personally permitted the missionaries to live in the village, mainly so his people could learn more productive ways of growing food and making clothing from the whites. Finally and most importantly, they admitted that Chief Big Thunder, who had been the great defender and protector of the missionaries, now regretted welcoming them into his village. He was also now voicing regret about signing the land treaty of 1837, which allowed so many whites to settle in their territory. The sensational upshot was that Chief Big Thunder was presently giving tacit approval to those militants who harassed the missionaries by killing some of their livestock and stealing some of their vegetables. Baldwin wondered in an audible whisper if maybe some of those militants killed Hays.

Phelan was exhilarated by what he heard. What Baldwin divulged fit perfectly into his scheme of blaming Hays' disappearance or death on the Indians. Baldwin's report also shed light on why Mrs. Holton wasn't very inquisitive on the two occasions he talked to her. He had been grateful that she was terse and passed off each of her brief responses as merely the reactions of a busy mother and wife. But now he realized that she was probably reluctant to say much in front of the Dakota girls who, thanks to the Holtons, understood English. Phelan guessed that if the Dakota girls hadn't been there she would have opened up about the problems they had with the villagers. Phelan wished that Mrs. Holton had told him about their Indian problems; it would have spared him the stress he suffered from worrying that the Holtons might undermine his cover story. Undermine his cover story? Instead, the Holtons had information that enhanced his cover story.

During their canoe trip home, Baldwin couldn't stop talking about the inside information he learned from his brothers-in-law. He was eager to share it with Major Taliaferro but he had promised them not to tell the Indian agent what they had said. The brothers-in-law did not want to be responsible for starting a rift between Chief Big Thunder and Major Taliaferro, two men they respected. And they didn't want other members of their village to find out that they had shared some of their community's close secrets with a white man. Baldwin wouldn't break a promise to his friends and in-laws but he was frustrated that he would have to keep mum to Taliaferro about what he had uncovered at Kaposia. Baldwin was not Taliaferro's primary interpreter (the mixed-blood Scott Campbell was) but it would certainly advance his standing with the Indian agent if he could offer him some useful intelligence about Chief Big Thunder. Baldwin's honor to his word prevented him from telling any of his information to Taliaferro directly. But what he could tell Hays' friends at the fort was another matter. Baldwin believed they deserved to know what he had uncovered: that there was a good chance their friend had been killed by some militants from Kaposia.

As Phelan paddled and listened to Baldwin talk, he felt content and confident for the first time in days that he was going to get away with murder. It was obvious that Baldwin's mind was on Chief Big Thunder and the hostile militants. Phelan almost laughed when he thought how wonderfully things were falling into place. Instead of being a threat to uncovering his crime, Baldwin was inadvertently helping him cover it up by leading the charge that the Indians had somehow killed Hays. Baldwin was even speculating that the young gun-firing Dakota in Phelan's fictional story may have been his killer.

Phelan felt completely comfortable with Hays' friend, confident that the man Hays had called "Bart" no longer posed any danger to him. He calculated that there would be little risk and much to gain if they made a brief stop at his cabin. Bringing Baldwin back to his cabin would show him that Phelan had nothing to hide, and it would enable Baldwin to tell others later that he saw nothing suspicious looking at Phelan and Hays' home. The day before Phelan had acquired a jug of Pig's Eye' whiskey, so he suggested they make a quick stop at his place for a little refreshment.

When they beached the canoe at his landing, Phelan made sure that they walked directly to his shanty, safely avoiding the trampled spot where Hays had been killed. Phelan surprised himself by how relaxed he felt when he brought Baldwin into the shanty where the deadly fight with Hays had actually begun. Of course, nothing remained in the shanty that would raise Baldwin's suspicions that anything criminal had occurred there. Phelan purposely allowed Baldwin to freely move about the cabin and grounds, plainly demonstrating that he had nothing to hide. After drinking some whiskey and chatting more about the alleged young Dakota intruder who had tangled with Hays a month earlier, Phelan escorted Baldwin back down to his landing and together they boarded the canoe and commenced paddling upriver. When Phelan dropped his canoe mate off at Fort Snelling, he was convinced that Baldwin had not the slightest suspicion that it was Phelan who had killed his friend. Phelan returned home overwhelmed with relief and hopeful that he could now finally enjoy the benefits of a life without his housemate, but with all his housemate's property.

For two weeks Phelan lived like a hermit and mostly enjoyed it. He needed some time alone, away from people's questions about Hays, and also time for reorganizing his homestead the way he wanted it. Working the farm alone, however, was not that easy. But the work helped him keep his mind off lingering worry that someone somehow might uncover his crime. He understandably took a long break from canoeing and just used the oxcart and his own feet for transportation. He didn't leave his own land for days.

## A Shocking Discovery Forces Another Cover-Up

But because he wasn't using the canoe, he was less likely to notice the terribly incriminating evidence that was emerging from the river near his landing. Phelan would never forget the afternoon of September 26, 1839, when walking down to his landing to finally use his canoe he was shocked to see Hays' gruesome, bloated body lying on the shore, not too far from where he had sunk it in the river twenty-one days earlier. Time and the elements had floated the body up from its watery grave. The relentless power of the river current must have loosened the ropes and freed the body from the weight of the rocks. The sight of the discolored corpse greatly unsettled Phelan, and he panicked as the reality set in that the cover-up of the murder was glaringly uncovered. Once again he was at risk of being caught with devastating evidence on his property. Phelan's anxiety exploded when he realized that Hays' body could have been lying there in open view for hours, or even worse, days. He wasn't sure when he had last been down at the landing, or near enough to it, to have noticed the body on the beach. He feared it might have been as long as two days but he hoped that it was less than twenty-four hours and hoped even harder that the body had only recently resurfaced. His heart raced when he realized that maybe the body had already been seen by a passing river traveler. If that was the case then he was probably doomed, but his survival instincts moved him to concentrate on the things he could control. It was urgent to hide the body immediately so that at least from that moment on, no one on the river would be able to see it.

Phelan desperately wanted to move the body further downriver from his land immediately. However, he realized that such a move in broad daylight would be too dangerous. He hastily decided that he would temporarily cover the corpse with sand and debris and then at sundown he would secretly move it down river.

After frantically covering the decaying corpse with sand and drift-wood, he returned home to figure out how best to move the body off his land later that evening. He knew that no matter how he chose to move the body it would be a challenging, high risk operation. Floating the corpse downriver, alongside his canoe—guiding it by a pole or canoe paddle—might be the easiest method; but he would run the risk of being seen by anyone at Pig's Eye's place who was loi-tering around his landing that evening. On the other hand, moving the body in the oxcart would also entail serious risks and difficulties. For one thing, there would be no avoiding the gruesome job of hav-ing to lift the rotting body onto the cart. For another thing, moving the creaking oxcart through the rough bottomland would be loud and might attract the attention of anyone at Pig's Eye's place. More-over, the sight and sound of an oxcart moving at night was so unusual that it would surely draw the notice of anyone there who was even half-sober. Using the oxcart would involve the additional challenge of finding a passable pathway to the river, which even in the daylight would not be easy. And if he did reach the river he would have to lift the body off the cart and drag it into the river.

All things considered, Phelan decided that the easiest, least noisy, least repulsive way to move the body would be to float it down the river with the aid of the canoe.

When sundown finally came Phelan raced back to his canoe, pad-dled it down the shore a short distance to where the body was bur-ied, jumped out of the canoe, and, using both the paddle and his feet, swept and kicked the sand and driftwood off the body. Now that the corpse was uncovered the real repulsive work was next. Phelan now had to somehow push, drag, or roll the body into the river. The water was only a few yards away, but moving Hays' heavy, stinking body even that short distance was difficult for someone who did not want to touch the repugnant flesh with his hands. Using his trusty paddle both as a wedge and as a pushing tool, Phelan labored hard to roll the body into the river. The yards seemed like miles but slowly and steadily the body moved and rolled right into the water.

Relieved that the body was finally in the water, but still perspiring from all the work it took to get it there, Phelan got back into his canoe and slowly began to push the body down river. Phelan's hoped to push it far enough down the Mississippi that the current would naturally carry it all the way to Kaposia, or beyond. The body floated well in the river but it tended to drift toward shore. Phelan realized that unless he kept steering it away from the shore it would eventually wash up again on the beach; if he wanted to ensure that Hays' body ended up far from his land he would have to steer it downriver a good distance. But that would mean he would have to guide it at least as far as Pig's Eye's Landing, and that was the place he most wanted to avoid because that was where people would likely be outside along the river. Pig's Eye often entertained customers well into the evening, and day or night, some of his customers liked to do their drinking outside. If Pig's Eye still had customers there that evening, Phelan knew it would be impossible for him to canoe past his landing undetected. He could only hope that on this night, like many nights, all of Pig's Eye's customers were gone by sundown.

As Phelan slowly steered Hays' body downriver, he could see in the twilight that there was only one canoe docked at Pig's Eye's Landing, and thankfully it looked like Parrant's own boat. Even more fortunate, there was not a soul at the landing, or anywhere in sight. But the light in the window of Parrant's cabin signaled that Pig's Eye was home and not asleep. Would Pig's Eye see or hear Phelan passing by his landing? He easily would if he looked out his window. Phelan had to weigh the risks of passing Pig's Eye's Landing—and he had to do it fast because his canoe was closing in on the dock.

Phelan's nerves were eating away his boldness. He decided to play it safe and back paddle away from Parrant's Landing. Though he preferred to push the body further downriver, the dangers of being seen with Hays' body were too great; there was still a chance that a late-voyaging river traveler could pass by. Phelan knew that every minute he spent on the river with the body of the man he murdered only increased his chances of being caught red-handed. Phelan decided that the best course of action would be to quickly push the body out toward the middle of the river and then fervently hope that the current would carry it a long way down the Mississippi. Phelan did just that then, still tense from the whole endeavor, paddled rapidly back to his own landing.

When Phelan reached his cabin panting and sweating, he wasn't sure exactly what he had accomplished. He had managed to move the body away from his land. But how far away it would float and where it would end up he did not know and could only hope that it was far enough away not to cast suspicion on him.

## The Final Cover-Up

"At sundown" on Sunday, September 29, Phelan found out where the body ended up. John Campbell, a new settler who lived downriver from William Evans, visited Phelan to inform him that he and some of his Dakota friends had found the body of a white man in the river near Carver's Cave. Though he didn't know Hays very well, Campbell had heard he was missing and suspected the dead man was Hays. Since Hays was Phelan's housemate, Campbell asked Phelan to go downriver and see if he could identify the body. Phelan pretended to be shocked by the news, though he was secretly glad that the body had drifted as far as Carver's Cave, and told him he would certainly go and see it as soon as he could. Thinking that he could use more time to collect his thoughts and plan what he should tell the authorities, he told Campbell that it was too late in the day to make the trip, but he would go "the first thing in the morning."[11] Campbell agreed that it was getting late and he also wanted to return home before dark. Phelan thanked him for coming and, feigning a sad face, assured him once again that he would go and see the body "the first thing in the morning." And in that regard Phelan wasn't lying.

Early the next morning, "about sunrise,"[12] Phelan paddled down-

256

river to see for himself exactly where Hays had washed ashore. On his way there he stopped at the beach where Hays had originally washed up to sweep away with his paddle all the telltale signs that he had rolled him back in the water. That done, he continued on and a half hour later, when he saw Hays' body partly resting on the beach and partly in the river—only "his head and shoulders were out of the water"[13]—he was pleased that it was lying so close to Carver's Cave, the sacred cave of the Dakota.* Maybe, he thought, whoever investigated Hays' death would interpret that as a sign that Dakota had killed Hays. In any case, Hays' body was beached in a better location now than it had been near Phelan's Landing.

As Phelan looked at the grotesquely disfigured, discolored remains of John Hays in the sunlight, he was shocked to see that his canoe paddle had plainly left marks on the body from all the pushing and wedging he had done when he moved it off his land. Phelan feared a medical expert might be able to tell that those marks were recent. A smart medical expert might deduce that the body had been recently moved. Now Phelan had a new problem to worry about, and he wasn't sure how to solve it.

But suddenly he thought of a simple solution. He would repeat, in reverse, what he had done before: move the body out of the water with the paddle, and then cover it up with sand and debris. And he could offer good reasons for doing that. He could explain to anyone who asked that, out of respect for the dead, he thought that he should cover up the naked body—especially since Hays had been a very modest man. After all, it was lying on a part of the beach that was easily visible to anyone passing by on the river. Furthermore, if the

---

* Discovered by English explorer Jonathan Carver in 1766, "Wakon-Teebee" (Dwelling House of the Spirit) was a sacred, ancient landmark of the Dakota long before Carver found it and publicized it in a popular book. For a time the cave was the traditional grand meeting house of all seven tribes of the Dakota nation. However, during the early nineteenth century, fallen limestone and sandstone eventually blocked the entrance of the cave and it remained virtually inaccessible until 1837 (two years before Hays' murder), when its entrance was effectively cleared by explorer Joseph Nicollet. Today the cave is once again inaccessible but a historical plaque near Mounds Boulevard and McLean Avenue marks the bluff it's in.

body was left partly in the water it could drift away from shore and disappear forever in the dark, long, rolling river. Satisfied that these were good reasons, Phelan decided that he would openly admit that he had moved the body to shore with his canoe paddle, which would explain the fresh bruises on the body. (And he enjoyed the irony that it was the very canoe paddle he had used to kill Hays.) Phelan bet that by openly drawing attention to his paddle, he would actually deflect suspicion from it. In other words, acting like he had nothing to hide might well lead people into believing that he really did have nothing to hide.

So he went ahead, using his paddle to push and roll Hays' body almost completely out of the water. Then he used the paddle and his feet to shovel and kick enough sand over the body to fully cover it. For good measure, he threw some grass over the grave to set it apart from the rest of the sandy beach and clearly mark the spot where Hays was buried. He wasn't trying to hide the body—too many people had already seen it—but rather his plan was to openly tell people exactly what he had done that morning, all for good, perfectly understandable reasons.

As he was covering Hays' body, Phelan remembered what he had told Stephen Scott several days ago about Hays having worn his best clothes to Kaposia. Phelan was now encouraged by the idea that Hays' naked body could be interpreted as evidence that the Indians had stolen his fancy clothes, which everyone knew were items that the Indians highly valued. Maybe, Phelan hoped, the people investigating Hays' death would look at all the evidence—the location of the body near the sacred cave, Hays' missing clothes, and his story about Hays' walk to Kaposia in search of a stolen calf, only a month after having a violent encounter with a young Dakota—and logically tie it all together in the misdirection of blaming the Indians for Hays' death. Phelan could fervently hope for that but he knew that his actions in the coming hours would greatly determine whether the imminent murder investigation directed its suspicions toward him or toward the Indians.

The pressure of it all once again unsettled Phelan's nerves. He tried to calm himself by repeating the guiding principle that had helped him through the many decisions he'd had to make since the murder: "Try to think like an innocent man. Try to think like an innocent man."

What would an innocent man do after he found the battered body of his friend on the beach? He would go and report it to the authorities at Fort Snelling. As much as he dreaded doing that, Phelan realized that to maintain his pretense of innocence he must go to the fort and report that the body that Campbell and the Indians found was in fact his lost housemate, John Hays; his face was badly disfigured but his long, distinctive nose was a plain giveaway that it was him.

Realizing that he had no other choice, Phelan canoed up to Fort Snelling to report Hays' death. But about a mile short of the fort, Phelan saw a Mackinaw boat, filled with soldiers, a few civilians and one Dakota, coming downriver. As he got closer he saw that the lead officer on the boat was Hays' old friend, Lt. Daniel McPhail. He also noticed that Bart Baldwin and the Fort Snelling sutler, Franklin Steele—one of Hays' civilian friends—were also on board the crowded oar boat (which was equipped with one mast and a single sail). Phelan quickly told McPhail the whole story of finding Hays' naked body by the cave and then temporarily burying him on the beach in a sand mound marked with grass. McPhail informed Phelan that they had already heard about the dead body "near Carver's Cave" and in fact were on their way to find and examine it. Phelan shrewdly volunteered to lead them to the grave. But since his boat landing was just a short distance downriver, he told McPhail that first he wanted to drop his canoe at his landing before joining them all on the Mackinaw boat. McPhail agreed to that and so Phelan turned his canoe around, led the Army boat to his landing, beached his canoe, and then jumped on the Mackinaw.

## Phelan's Tense Time With the Military Investigators

Though he was nervous in the company of McPhail and so many of Hays' friends, Phelan knew it was advantageous for him to accompany the first official investigators of Hays' remains. Posing as the grieving housemate, Phelan directed McPhail to the grave with as much sorrow as he could fake. When the boat landed on shore, Phelan led the group to the sand mound and within minutes a squad of soldiers uncovered Hays' body and began washing it off with river water.

Dr. John Emerson, the same Army surgeon who was stationed at Fort Snelling when Phelan served there, quickly took charge of the examination of the body. Although the doctor examined the whole body, he clearly concentrated on the glaring head wounds. Surprisingly, Emerson didn't seem too interested in the fresh bruises caused by Phelan's canoe paddle on the lower half of the body. Phelan assumed that the doctor passed them off as the result of Phelan's use of his canoe paddle to move the body out of the water, as he had related to him. But the doctor's disinterest in the recent bruises was hardly a cause for relief. It was chilling for Hays' killer to watch the doctor examine the horrible damage that he had done with his canoe paddle to Hays' face. Though Phelan purposely positioned himself behind the circle of men who were closest to Dr. Emerson (McPhaill, Baldwin, Franklin Steele, and the soldier who was Emerson's primary assistant), he could still see enough to follow the examination of the man he killed.

It didn't take Dr. Emerson long to announce his conclusion. "I have no hesitation in declaring it as my belief that the death of [Mr.] Hays was caused by the aforesaid injuries."[14] The "aforesaid injuries" were the severe blows to Hays' head. Emerson officially reported that Hays' face was "mutilated in a shocking manner—the bones of face were broken in several places as if done with some mighty weapon."[15]

It didn't take a medical expert to state the obvious: every man there who saw Hays' battered and broken face knew that he had been murdered—brutally beaten to death by someone wielding some sort of "mighty weapon." Only Phelan knew what the mighty weapon really was. He tried to repress the look of guilt and anxiety, but Bart Baldwin didn't help him in that regard.

Baldwin's raw reaction to seeing his friend's badly mutilated body was a striking contrast to Phelan's phony face of grief. Baldwin struggled to control his emotions: he yelled, wept, cursed, and genuinely grieved, exactly as one might expect a friend to react on seeing the body of a brutally murdered friend. In an effort to comfort Baldwin and Hays' other close friends, Dr. Emerson offered that the victim had probably died quickly and could have even been killed instantly after the first blow. He also told Baldwin, McPhail, and the others who gathered around him that, as his examination of the body was complete, he saw no reason that they couldn't conduct the final burial of the deceased right there on the beach. (The doctor didn't have to tell anyone there that Hays' stinking, decomposing body needed to be put in the ground as soon as possible.) Lieutenant McPhail immediately took charge of the burial and ordered the same squad of soldiers who had unburied Hays to dig a new grave. To McPhaill's credit, he conducted the entire burial with enough decorum and ceremony to satisfy all of Hays' friends who were there to mourn him. Baldwin erected a cross of two whittled sticks and some rope and reverently placed it on Hays' grave.

During the burial ceremony Phelan tried his best to look sincerely sad, but because he felt no real sorrow in his heart he also felt very self-conscious standing next to so many teary-eyed mourners who seemed so genuinely sad about the death of the man in the grave. When the graveside prayers were finished, everyone slowly walked to the boat and boarded it like the orderly military party it was.

On the return voyage upriver, Phelan was greatly disturbed by what he overheard Baldwin say to Franklin Steele, immediately after an unintelligible conversation the Indian interpreter had with the lone Dakota on board the boat. Phelan had learned earlier (on the boat ride downriver) that the Dakota was the same man, Wabsheeda, who was with Baldwin's brothers-in-law when they had visited

Kaposia. Phelan now clearly heard Baldwin say something to Steele about Wabsheeda's claim that his son had actually first seen Hays' body further upriver. Phelan's heart raced and his stomach grew nauseous when he heard those words. The truth about Hays' body was coming out. But what could or should he do about it? Under the stressful circumstances, Phelan was too unsettled to think clearly; all he could do was sit quietly, pretend to be calm and wait to see what Baldwin and Steele would do with Wabsheeda's information.

Unfortunately for Phelan, the men decided it was important enough information to land the boat at the place Wabsheeda pointed to—a beach marked by a large, leaning cottonwood tree with its huge exposed roots rising dramatically out of the sand (the very same tree where Phelan had left his hat on the night he murdered Hays). Baldwin and Wabsheeda jumped off the boat and examined the shoreline. Phelan was pleased with how well he had concealed his tracks that morning—the beach showed no trace of footprints other than the new ones made by Baldwin and Wabsheeda—but he was still stunned that the two men were walking in the same general area where he had killed Hays, dragged his body into the river and then, weeks later, pushed him back into the river. Phelan grew more nervous when Baldwin and Wabsheeda followed the same path he had used the night he dragged Hays' body through the brush after he killed him. Phelan was a little relieved when Baldwin and Wabsheeda reappeared from the brush a few minutes later and calmly returned to the boat. But his tension turned to full relief when he heard Baldwin state matter-of-factly that all they could find was the apparent trail of some grey wolves who left their tracks and some of their hair on the brush and herbage they trampled through.

Phelan wanted to buy good old Bart a drink; for the second time now, Baldwin had saved him from an impending crisis. The fact was, wolf tracks or not, Phelan was the one who had made that trail through the herbage the night he dragged Hays' body to the river. He even suspected that some of those gray hairs may have actually been from Hays' battered head. Phelan was truly grateful to Baldwin but he never did reward him with a drink or invite him back to his home for a smoke.

Shortly afterward, when the boat reached his landing, Phelan said nothing to anyone, but simply jumped to shore and walked up the hill. He was still painfully aware that the men on the boat represented grave danger for him. Lieutenant McPhail in particular could cause him serious trouble when he made his report. Whatever he might report, one thing was certain: the investigation of Hays' murder was not over, it was just beginning.

As Phelan walked home from his landing, he contemplated what he should do if he was brought in for questioning. He thought back to his days in the slums of New York. There he had learned the standard rule for criminals who faced a police interrogation: "Don't incriminate yourself by talking too much." Phelan decided that if anyone questioned him about Hays he would do what he did back in New York when the police interrogated him; he would keep his answers short and provide as few details as possible. He would just stick to his well-rehearsed story and the minimum details that made it credible. He would not make the investigator's job easy. He would act cooperatively but be uncooperative.

The next day Phelan's strategy for handling questions was put to the test. Just before noon on Tuesday, October 1, the king of the fur traders, Henry Sibley—the region's first justice of the peace and "Law West of the Mississippi"—came to interview Phelan, accompanied by two burly voyageurs. The investigation into the murder of John Hays had come to the door of the murderer.

## Postscript

This fictional account does not include Alphonse Gervais' story about the bloody clothes found under Phelan's cabin. However, the account did set up the scene and situation whereby a number of different scenarios involving the bloody clothes could have played out. For instance, one could easily imagine that sometime shortly after Sibley and Brown's investigations, when Phelan was sitting in the

Fort Snelling guardhouse waiting for the steamboat to Prairie du Chien, another investigator (the county marshal or one of Hays' Fort Snelling friends) went to Phelan's home and conducted a more thorough search of his cabin. Such a search could have uncovered those bloody clothes under the floor boards. It would also have been possible that new investigators would enlist the help of Alphonse Gervais (and his blood-scenting dog), who lived near Phelan and was familiar with where he lived.

Scenarios of how the bloody clothes were eventually lost could also be easily imagined. Perhaps the Prairie du Chien court took issue with the legal chain of custody of the new evidence. In other words, if the discovery of the bloody clothes was not documented by some recognized legal authority who could verify that the evidence did come from Phelan's cabin, then that evidence may not have been admissible by the court. In that case, a jury would never hear about bloody clothes found at Phelan's cabin.

# CHAPTER TEN

## Phelan Gains His Freedom
## and Some Distinction

### (But Loses Valuable Land, All His Former
### Neighbors and Ultimately His Life)

*They are at rest now. It matters not what the present generation has
to say about the fellows. They had their faults, but are we perfect today, that we can go back and criticize with impunity the lives of these
old pioneers, who have been the forerunner's and helped us on the
way to the blessings we enjoy here? I say, no. Bury their imperfections
with them in their graves, keep their virtues in memory green like the
sward above them.*

—August Larpenteur, 1898

Sometime in the spring or summer of 1840, Edward Phelan was
released from his incarceration at Prairie du Chien and returned
home to his "hovel under the hill." A lot had changed in his frontier community since his forced departure in November 1839. Most
dramatic of all was an extraordinary development: all of the cabins
upriver had been razed. Yes, every cabin on the east bank from the
present-day Lake Street Bridge (Marshall Avenue in St. Paul) to the
west end of Phelan's land—including all of Rumtown and the Perry
and Gervais cabins around Fountain Cave—had been burned down
by orders of Pres. Martin Van Buren, Secretary of War Joel Poinsett,

and the commandant of Fort Snelling, Maj. Joseph Plympton. In response to the request of Commandant Plympton, the United States Government had expanded the Fort Snelling Military Reservation in October 1839 to cover a sizable portion of the east bank, including many homesteads claimed by settlers. The main reason for enlarging the military reservation was to do away with the sprawling Rumtown and Fountain Cave settlements, which Plympton deemed were too close to the fort and too permeated with liquor for the good of the soldiers, not to mention the local Indians who were becoming increasingly addicted to alcohol. After giving eviction notices to all the east bank settlers west of Phelan's Landing, on May 6, 1840, US Deputy Marshall Ira Brunson (the son of Methodist missionary Alfred Brunson) and a dispatchment of torch-bearing Fort Snelling soldiers burned down every building in Rumtown and every cabin downriver almost as far as Phelan's Landing. Both the Perrys and the Gervaises (as well as some Rumtowners) fought their evictions but the simple settlers were no match for the combined political power of the commandant of Fort Snelling, the Secretary of War, and the President of the United States.[1]

After the government-sanctioned destruction of their homes, most of the displaced settlers chose to resettle further downriver, east of the new reservation line, which was literally at the west end of Phelan's property. For Phelan the historic resettlement of 1840 meant that he no longer had any neighbors upriver; instead they were all downriver, confined between his land and William Evan's land. The new settlement was concentrated around the prominent exposed sandstone bluff that the Dakota called "Im-in-i-ja-ska," or "White Rock." Phelan's closest neighbor was no longer Pig's Eye Parrant, seven blocks downriver around the foot of present-day Robert Street, but a new homesteader just four blocks away, on top of the bluff, around the northwest end of the present-day Wabasha Street Bridge. In fact, Pig's Eye was no longer living at his old residence but had moved downriver a few more blocks to the foot of present-day Jackson Street, where once again he operated a crude saloon.[2] The saloon was the only business in the relocated settlement, and soon the two—saloon and settlement—became synonymous: people were calling the settlement "Pig's Eye" and as a result, Pig's Eye himself was becoming something of a local celebrity.

The new owner of Pig's Eye's former homestead was Phelan's old neighbor Ben Gervais who, in perhaps the bargain of the century, purchased Parrant's claim (roughly the area bounded by present-day Robert Street, Jackson Street, Fourth Street and Shepard Road) for a mere ten dollars.[3] But it was Gervais' neighbor, the homesteader who was now Phelan's nearest neighbor, who drew the big Irishman's attention and ire.

He was Vetal Guerin (1812-1870), the French Canadian and former voyager who had been employed by the American Fur Company and resided at Mendota, but even more recently had boarded with the Perrys. (He married Adele Perry on January 26, 1841.) Guerin, "a slender man, with sharp features and quiet in his manners," provoked Phelan's anger by having the audacity to build his home—a sixteen by twenty foot cabin "built of oak and elm, bark roof and floor of split hewed puncheons"—on the murdered man Sergeant Hays' claim.[4] Phelan believed he should have first dibs on Hays' land since he made the original claim and had been Hays' partner. Never mind that he had been gone six months because he had been arrested for Hays' murder.

Though he had just been released from jail, Phelan's aggressive, bullying manner had not been reformed. Learning that Guerin was a short and slender "quiet" French Canadian, Phelan relied on physical intimidation to persuade the claim jumper to leave the premises. Guerin's account of that encounter was recorded by J. Fletcher Williams, who interviewed Guerin about this episode twenty-six years later:

> *Phelan called at my cabin, accompanied by James R. Clewett as interpreter, as I could then talk no English. He demanded possession of the claim. I replied that I would not give it up, as I believed I was*

*rightfully entitled to it. Some more talk ensued, and, finding that I was not disposed to yield to him, Phelan told Jim to say that if I was not off by a certain day—say a week from then—he would put me off by force. As Phelan was a large, powerful man, and I was small and light, he could have easily picked me up and carried me outside the claim lines. After making this threat, Phelan went away.*

*As I knew I could not deal with Phelan single handed, I told some of my voyageur companions at Mendota how matters stood, and three or four of them, strong, "husky" fellows, came down to stay with me. A supply of liquor and some cards made time pass merrily. On the day Phelan had set to put me off the claim, sure enough, he made his appearance—axe in hand and sleeves rolled up—with Clewett as interpreter. Through the latter, Phelan inquired if I would leave. I replied, no. Phelan got very mad at this, and said, "Tell the d— little Frenchman I will take him under my arm and throw him off the claim."*

*I then said to my men, who were inside, that I thought it was time for them to interfere. They came out, and throwing off their coats, told Phelan that if he did not go away and leave me alone, they would pitch him over the bluff! And, moreover, if he ever molested me they would Lynch him. Phelan knew they were not fellows whom it would do to trifle with, and, as he had just got out of one bad scrape, didn't want to get into any further trouble, if he could avoid it. He finally left, saying he would take the law of me. He thereupon commenced an action before Joseph R. Brown, justice of the peace at Grey Cloud Island, to recover possession. Brown examined into the case, and found that Phelan was absent from his claim more than six months at one time. So he told Phelan that he had lost all title to it, and that I could not be ejected. I had no further trouble with him, and kept peaceable possession of the claim.*[5]

Guerin's reference to James Clewett as Phelan's interpreter is an interesting detail. Englishman Clewett (who was Rose Perry's husband, Vetal Guerin's future brother-in-law and Joseph R. Brown's

trading partner) was one of the men in the canoe who gave incriminating evidence against Phelan at the hearing conducted by Joseph
R. Brown. He was the same man who was later quoted by Williams
as saying that "he thought at the time the Indians had committed the
murder." Was the fact that Clewett (who now lived with his wife
and children and Mr. and Mrs. Perry in a large new cabin around
the present-day corner of Fourth Street and Lafayette Road) served
as Phelan's interpreter a sign that he believed Phelan was innocent
of murdering Hays and was rightfully entitled to his dead partner's
claim? If so, then Clewett was almost alone in his belief. According to
Williams, "of Phelan's guilt no one who was a resident in this vicinity had any doubt."[6] Perhaps Williams should have qualified his statement since apparently Clewett, James Thompson, and, a few years
later, August Larpenteur had doubts about Phelan's guilt. Nevertheless, there is no doubt that Phelan had few if any friends in the growing settlement. Naturally, the settlers would not have taken kindly to
someone whom they believed had gotten away with murder—especially when the victim was the "honest, good, courteous" gentleman,
"respected by everybody," Sergeant Hays.[7]

Phelan's lack of friends would certainly be a disadvantage if he
brought his land dispute before a judge and jury of his peers. But that
is exactly what he did on August 3, 1840. After issuing a formal complaint against Vetal Guerin on July 25, Phelan appeared at Justice of
the Peace Joseph R Brown's crude courthouse on Grey Cloud Island
nine days later to argue his right to Hays' claim. Though Guerin told
Williams that their land dispute was simply settled by a ruling from
Justice Brown, Brown's docket book shows that the case of "Edward
Phelan vs. Vetal Guerin" was a full-fledged jury trial. Brown even
recorded the names of the jurors, some of whom were well known
to Phelan: Pierre Gervais, William Evans, James Clewett, and Hazen
Mooers. (The others were Francis Chevallier, Jacques Des Cote,
Michael LeClaire, Joseph La Bissonierre, Henry Belland, Joseph
Haskell, and James Norris.)[8]

Brown didn't record any of the arguments; he only noted that one Joseph Rondeau (who we will say more about later) was sub-poenaed to appear for the plaintiff (Phelan) and Pierre Parrant was subpoenaed to appear for the defense (Guerin).[9] After the jury "had been out some time they returned and the foreman informed the court that no decision could be had."[10] Obviously, at least some jurors (perhaps Evans and Clewett) had voted for Phelan's side. Curi-ously, immediately after the announcement of a hung jury, "a second jury was summoned from the bystanders, consisting of H.C. Mencke, Antoine Roberts, Joseph Monjeau, Jos. Robinette, Baptiste Yea, J.B. Deniger, J.B. Tierrepain, J. Sanfacon Sr., Jos. Tierrepain Jr., J. Gregrich [and] J. Bruce."[11] The second jury, led by foreman Henry Mencke (another one of Brown's trading partners who had given incriminat-ing testimony against Phelan on November 1), also returned in an hour hopelessly deadlocked.[12]

After two deadlocked juries, both parties agreed to settle the mat-ter through arbitration. The dispute wasn't settled until June 1841 when Guerin amicably agreed to pay the court costs of the August 3 proceedings ($50.45) but he kept the claim.[13] The end result was that Guerin acquired property for $50 and change that only eight years later was valued at $150,000.[14] But Phelan's adversary was famously generous: he gave part of his claim to Pierre Gervais at no cost. (Might we assume that Pierre Gervais was one of the jurors that favored Guerin's claim argument?) Pierre and his wife and daughter then built their cabin near Guerin's claim, around the present-day intersection of Kellogg Boulevard and St. Peter Street. In October 1841, Guerin and Pierre's brother, Ben Gervais, donated parts of their land for the site of the settlement's first church, the historic chapel of St. Paul. The cha-pel was consecrated by Father Lucien Galtier, pastor of Minnesota's first Catholic parish, the Church of St. Peter at Mendota, on Novem-ber 1, 1841, coincidentally exactly two years after Phelan was charged with murder. It was on that historic consecration Sunday (All Saints Day) when the French-speaking Catholic congregation unanimously approved Father Galtier's suggestion to change the village's name from "Pig's Eye" to "St. Paul." Guerin, one of the principle founders, builders, and contributors of the village's namesake chapel, and the man who later also donated land for the town's first courthouse, eventually died penniless in 1870, due largely to his penchant for giving away property.[15] One can only wonder how differently the history of St. Paul might have unfolded had Phelan won the right to Hays' land. It is difficult to imagine the "unscrupulous" Phelan donating any of his land to any church, any person, or any public charity.

Around the same time that Phelan was engaged in his claim dispute with Vetal Guerin, one of the evicted settlers from Rumtown came to his door looking for land. He was Joseph Rondeau (1797-1885), another French Canadian who, like Ben Gervais, had immigrated from the Red River Colony after working for years in the far west as a voyageur for the Hudson Bay Fur Company. Rondeau (or Rondo), his wife Josephine, and their six children had been living comfortably in their home directly across the river from Fort Snelling until the soldiers burned down their cabin with the rest of Rumtown on May 6.[16] Thus, the Rondeaus were desperately looking for a new home. What drew the "stocky, sturdy Canadian" to Phelan's land was never recorded.[17] But a creek, a cleared canoe landing, and a standing cabin (with a root house) probably made the site an appealing one. The question was would Phelan be interested in selling his own undisputed claim, the land he had worked for over a year to turn it into a farm? No writer ever reported the discussions and negotiations that took place between the rough, tough French Canadian and the even rougher, tougher Irishman. But in the end they arrived at a mutually acceptable deal. Phelan agreed to sell his entire claim (cabin and root house included) for two hundred dollars.[18] The fact that Rondeau later stood as a witness for Phelan's side in the Irishman's land dispute hearing suggests that the deal was amicable and that Rondeau and Phelan were on good terms with each other.

Given the extremely high value of the property today (the Irvine Park/Excel Energy Center/Rice Park area is some of the most highly valued real estate in St. Paul), one might think that Phelan sold his claim too cheaply. However, $200 was serious money on the 1840 frontier. Indeed, $200 represented the entire life savings of Phelan's murdered partner, Sergeant Hays, and was $190 more than Parrant received for his equally valuable claim. Still, by any measure, Joseph Rondeau got a fabulous deal from Phelan. Just three years later (1843) he sold the same property— albeit with major improvements to the cabin but minus eighty acres of river bottom that he had already sold in 1842— to John Irvine for an impressive one hundred dollar profit. That profit did not include the unreported amount of money he received from Sgt. Richard Mortimer (1800-43), who purchased those eighty acres of bottomland, downriver from Phelan's Landing.

New York native John R. Irvine (1812-78)— the second American-born adult resident of St. Paul—was the ambitious, energetic, entrepreneur, who was mainly responsible for transforming the Rondeau's farm into the booming commercial-industrial-residential district of Uppertown— which included St. Paul's first two parks, Irvine Park and Rice Park, and the home of Minnesota's first Territorial Governor, Alexander Ramsey.[19] It was the forward-looking, enterprising Irvine who cleared the riverfront of its giant, old elm trees and ultimately transformed Phelan's crude canoe landing into an impressive, extensive steamboat dock (the Upper Landing)— which spurred continuous development in Uppertown, thus dramatically increasing the real estate value of the entire area.[20] In other words, the value of Phelan's land only increased after it was extensively (and expensively) developed— a project neither Phelan nor Rondeau, nor any other common backwoods farmer was realistically capable of doing.

Rondeau, for his part, was content to cash in on his land quickly and stake another claim further up the bluff, where he carved out a new farm and built his next home in the vicinity of present-day Rice Street and Interstate 94. (Old Rondo Street was named for him.)[21]

Like Rondeau, Phelan probably found it easier to cash in on his claim and relocate somewhere else. For Phelan that somewhere else was downriver by Evan's Landing. What drew Phelan farther eastward were several related factors. Undoubtedly, one underlying factor was that the presumed killer was not well liked or welcomed by the other settlers in the predominantly French-Catholic village. As tough as he was, even Phelan probably didn't care to live where he wasn't wanted. His oldest and perhaps truest friend, William Evans, lived away from the village, on the other side of the wide gorge, so it was natural for Phelan to look for his new home on the same east side of the gorge that Evans was on.

Phelan soon found good land north of Evan's home, along a creek—"a good trout stream"— that flowed into the river near Evan's Landing. That creek came to be known as "Phelan" or "Felyn's" or "Phalen" Creek, and later, when Phelan explored the stream north and found that its source was a "beautiful" 239-acre lake, that lake too would be named after Phelan.[22] Phelan chose to build his new cabin in a location that was, from the vantage point of the future, another prime piece of real estate. It was down in a lovely sandstone glen or hollow, near a cascade formed by "Felyn's Creek" which became known as "Felyn's Falls." (Years later Swedish immigrants would settle in that same hollow and dub it "Svenska Dalen," or Swedish glen. The place was later anglicized to "Swede Hollow," the name by which it is still known today.) St. Paul's first saw and flour mills were later built at Felyn's Falls, and most significantly, twenty-five years after Phelan claimed the site, one of Minnesota's greatest brewers, Theodore Hamm, built his historic landmark brewery, one of the most important big businesses in the history of St. Paul, on that site.[23]

But all that was in the future, back in 1840 Phelan was a true pioneer, blazing his own trail through the wilderness and building his cabin far away from any other settlers, with the single exception of William Evans, who lived about a mile away. For four years the lone wolf Phelan lived like a hermit down in the Phelan Creek hollow. Unfortunately, nothing was preserved in writing to detail Phelan's life in the hollow. The first detail of his stay there was recorded, ironically, when he was ready to leave the place. On September 22, 1844, Phelan made the second officially-recorded land transaction in the village of St. Paul when he sold "160 acres on Falyn's Creek and

Falls" to William Dugas for seventy dollars.[24] Dugas, another French Canadian but "a millwright by occupation," liked the water power potential of Felyn's Falls and with the help of yet another French Canadian, carpenter Charles Bazille (who later married the youngest of the Perry sisters, Annie Jane), built St. Paul's first saw mill there in less than a year. But the mill failed because it was too difficult and costly to get good timber, so on February 28, 1846, Dugas and his wife Susan sold their land and buildings for $835 to a Scotch Canadian fur trader named Alexander McLeod.[25]

Alexander R. McLeod (1817–64), the third owner of the Phelan Creek hollow, was surprisingly similar to Phelan in several interesting respects. For one, they were both legendary tough guys. In the words of Williams, "McLeod was a man of extraordinary powerful physique and great endurance."[26] And McLeod, like Phelan, would be arrested for killing a man and then acquitted of the crime. However, in McLeod's case, there was no mystery to the killing. Ten years after Phelan moved to the hollow, on February 27, 1850, a drunken man named Bill Gordon attacked McLeod with a whip, near Phelan's old cabin, which McLeod had remodeled into a trading post. McLeod, who was also drunk, responded by killing Gordon with his bare hands. The jury ruled that McLeod killed Gordon in self-defense. (McLeod's trial, presided over by the Territory of Minnesota's first Chief Justice, Judge Aaron Goodrich, was the first murder trial held in St. Paul.)[27]

Though McLeod left the hollow for good after his trial (and was ultimately killed fighting in the Civil War), he was Phelan's nearest neighbor for four years. After Phelan sold his creek land to Dugas in 1844, he moved above the hollow to "the ridge on the upper side of Phelan Creek," a place that became known as "Prospect Hill."[28] The exact location of Phelan's home on Prospect Hill is not known, but clearly it wasn't very far from McLeod's trading post down in the Phalen Creek hollow. (When McLeod lived there the stream was also known as "McLeod Creek.") Given the close proximity of the two English-speaking backwoodsmen, it is likely that Phelan and

McLeod had a number of interactions. Perhaps Phelan frequented McLeod's trading post for a drink of whiskey and a chat with the Scotsman and the people who lived with him, including his mixed-blood wife Nancy and his Irish American clerk William Quinn and his wife Angelique.[29]

What we do know for certain is that Phelan remained a farmer when he moved to the valley of Phalen Creek. The St. Croix County tax assessment records for 1848 (when Phelan was living at Prospect Hill) show that Phelan owned twelve head of cattle valued at $215, about $25 less than in 1847, and five hogs valued at $7.50, about $37 less than in 1847.[30] As speculated earlier, it's possible that some of those cattle once belonged to John Hays. Also noted earlier was the interesting fact that Phelan's ownership of a dozen cattle in 1847 made him one of the largest cattle owners in St. Paul in 1847. Interestingly, the tax rolls also reveal that in 1848 Phelan was listed as owning a dwelling valued at one hundred dollars. By 1848 standards that was an expensive cabin. William Evan's cabin had an estimated value of only twenty-five dollars. Indeed, among the thirty homeowners listed on the same tax assessment page with Phelan, twenty of them owned dwellings that were valued less than Phelan's and only seven of them owned dwellings that were valued more than his. The estimated values of those homes ranged from twenty-five dollars up to three hundred dollars. The high value of Phelan's cabin is even more striking considering that five of those seven higher-valued homes were owned by people known to have families residing with them (the other two owners were not found in census records). Phelan, however, was a bachelor farmer: he didn't run an inn or a trading post and he didn't need extra room for a large family.[31]

Add it all up: livestock, house, and land (which according to Williams included more than just his Prospect Hill claim) and clearly Phelan, the former shanty dweller, was one of the more affluent pioneers of the region. Perhaps that relative affluence helped him change his image as an undesirable ruffian, the rogue who got away with murder. But somehow or another Phelan succeeded in gaining some respect among his new neighbors east of the gorge—the great ravine that separated the central village from present-day Dayton's Bluff. Incredibly, in the summer of 1848, Phelan ended up being chosen as one of two representatives of the Prospect Hill area to attend the great Territorial Convention at Stillwater.

In Minnesota history the Stillwater Convention of 1848 is like a local version of what took place on the national arena in Philadelphia in 1776: the drafting of the Declaration of Independence that proclaimed the birth of a new nation. Likewise, on the smaller stage of Stillwater in August 1848, the birth of a new territory called Minnesota was proclaimed. Although the Territory of Minnesota was not officially born until President Polk signed the bill creating it on March 4, 1849, the Stillwater Convention was the great turning point that directly led to this new northern territory created by Congress less than seven months later. And just as the fifty-six members of the Continental Congress are considered the founding fathers of the United States, the sixty-two members of the Stillwater Convention can be considered the founding fathers of Minnesota. Significantly, those sixty-two delegates were the chosen representatives of virtually every settlement, however small, in the region that became the Territory of Minnesota.

To think that one of those founding father delegates was a man like Edward Phelan—the "immoral," "unscrupulous ruffian" who a preponderance of evidence points to as a brutal murderer—is to ponder one of the strange but true facts of Minnesota history. In most cases, those sixty-two founding fathers represented the best men of their communities, the most trusted men and the most able leaders. For the most part they were remembered as men of character and integrity.[32] Why would Edward Phelan's neighbors choose him, a man distinctly remembered for his lack of character and integrity, to represent them at such an important convention? Maybe the big, intimidating Irishman only represented a small number of people, and there wasn't much competition to be a delegate.

Phelan was not selected as a delegate representing St. Paul. The village of St. Paul sent ten representatives to Stillwater: August Larpenteur, David Lambert, J. W. Simpson, Henry Jackson, Louis Robert, Vetal Guerin, David Hebert, Oliver Rosseau, Ard Godfrey, and James Clewett.[33] Four of those men were important town builders who need to be introduced.

First was Henry Jackson (1811-57), a native of Virginia and a veteran of the Texas War for Independence, who in 1842 (two years after Phelan moved to Phelan Creek) became the first American-born adult to settle in St. Paul. A "self made man" with a sense of humor and a wide range of knowledge ("a walking encyclopedia"), Jackson bought three acres on top of the bluff from Ben Gervais, along the west side of what soon became known as "Jackson Street," and then built a "log pole" general store there that became a village landmark. Only a year after his arrival in 1843, Jackson became St. Paul's first resident justice of the peace and three years later he also became the village's first postmaster. That the "shrewd, active, jolly" Jackson— "a man to whom others looked to for general information" and who was "ever equal to any emergency"—was selected one of St. Paul's convention delegates is hardly surprising: he was clearly one of the emerging leaders of the growing town.[34]

Second was Missouri native Louis Robert (1811-74), another American-born new arrival to St. Paul, whose French Canadian ancestry and background in the fur trade made him naturally comfortable in the French-speaking voyageur village when he first settled there in 1844. "A tall, muscular man, with strong features, decided convictions and great energy," Robert (pronounced "Ro-bear") also bought land from Ben Gervais (which included Parrant's old log cabin) and quickly transformed it into valuable property. Significantly, in 1847 the namesake of Robert Street became "one of the original proprietors" of the "Town of Saint Paul" when it was surveyed and "laid out." Like Jackson, Robert was "a born leader of men" who "never followed, he always led." Like Vetal Guerin, he also donated generously to churches and charities. In the words of Williams, "his foresight and energy [were] a great value to the infant town."[35]

Third was David Lambert (1819-49), a native of Connecticut and a graduate of Trinity College in Hartford. Prior to settling in St. Paul, Lambert was editor of a Madison, Wisconsin newspaper; when he moved to St. Paul in 1848 he became St. Paul's first practicing attorney. "A man of considerable ability," a talented writer and orator and "an accomplished young lawyer," the newcomer Lambert was destined to play a major role at the convention.[36]

The fourth was James W. Simpson (1818-70), a Virginian like Jackson, who worked as a lay Methodist missionary to the Ojibwe at Sandy Lake before moving to the land of the Dakota and the village of St. Paul in October 1843, a year after Jackson arrived and the same year John Irvine bought the future Upper Landing property. "A small, thin, [frail] man," who was famously known for being "scrupulously just and honest," Simpson built a landmark stone warehouse ("the first stone building in St. Paul") at the foot of present-day Sibley Street near the "Lower Landing," before Irvine had even finished clearing all the elms from his Upper Landing. Like Jackson, Robert and others, Simpson also bought a parcel of bluff-top property from Ben Gervais and there, on Fourth Street, near present-day Mears Park, he built his home.[37]

One might wonder why Phelan's former neighbor Ben Gervais, who sold so much prime property to town builders like Jackson, Robert and Simpson, was not selected to be a delegate to the Stillwater Convention. The answer is simple: Ben Gervais was no longer a resident of St. Paul in 1848. Gervais left St. Paul in 1844 to found another settlement, and his son, Basil Gervais, later told the story of his father's move to the place he called Little Canada.

*Not long after we settled at the foot of Robert Street, the Indians began telling my father what a fine location for a farm the land was at their [summer] camping ground. My father and the Indians always got on pretty well together and they seemed to want to do him a favor. So he went out and examined the country and liked it so well that he determined to settle there.[38]*

There in Little Canada, along "Gervais Creek" and "Gervais Lake," seven miles north of St. Paul, Ben Gervais not only carved out another farm, he founded a village and also erected "the second grist mill built in Minnesota" with the help of his friend Charles Bazille, the same man who built the saw mill at Phelan Creek. A few years later Gervais played a major role in building another log chapel: The Church of St. John the Evangelist, the fourth Catholic parish in Minnesota. Pierre Gervais, who joined his brother in Little Canada in 1846, was selected as one of Little Canada's (also known as Gervais Mill) two delegates to the Stillwater Convention.[39]

Three of St. Paul's delegates to the Stillwater Convention were men with connections to Phelan: Vetal Guerin, August Larpenteur, and James Clewett. Interestingly, two of the three, Larpenteur and Clewett, were among a small number of people who in words or actions demonstrated support for the unpopular accused murderer. Larpenteur in particular was one of Phelan's strongest defenders, as reflected in the speech he gave to the Minnesota Historical Society decades later:

> *Edward Phelan ...never killed Hays; the Indians have told me since that Hays was not killed by Phelan.... Old Phelan was human. He took his toddy too, but would not injure a hair of your head while I knew him.*[40]

Though Clewett was not as direct in his defense of Phelan as Larpenteur was, it is clear that he was not convinced of Phelan's guilt and may have been on friendly terms with him (even though his testimony in Brown's hearing was not helpful to Phelan); he later served Phelan as an interpreter in his legal dispute with Vetal Guerin over land, and many years later he related the story to Williams that a son of Little Crow confessed to Hays' murder. Clewett, a native of England who had been a Canadian voyageur before becoming one of Joseph R. Brown's fur trading partners, was Phelan's neighbor when he boarded at the Perry home during most of 1839, and it is quite possible that during that time a friendly rapport developed between the two English-speaking neighbors who found themselves surrounded by French speakers.[41] Never mind that in the fictional account of Hays' murder the Northern Irishman Phelan was portrayed as disliking Clewett just because he was English and also because of jealousy over the fact that Clewett had married Rose Perry.

But any speculation that Clewett was friendly with Phelan has to be tempered with the fact that the Englishman's new brother-in-law and fellow delegate, Vetal Guerin (who married Clewett's wife's sister), was one of Phelan's known adversaries. Given the nature and duration of their land dispute and the low opinion most settlers had of Phelan, there is good reason to believe that Guerin would have held the big, bullying Irishman in contempt and would not have wanted anything more to do with him. Even if Clewett was on good terms with him, Guerin probably would have avoided the man who once threatened him. To repeat once again the plain words of Williams: "Phelan was regarded by the other settlers as a bad, unscrupulous, wicked man"—who "most civil and well disposed persons avoided as a dangerous person."[42]

But the "civil," honorable, and good Guerin would not be able to avoid the big, "bad" backwoodsman Phelan when he and the other civil and honorable delegates from St. Paul attended the Stillwater Convention, because Phelan was bound for Stillwater too. Again, how Phelan got to be a delegate to the convention is a mystery. But the fact that he represented Prospect Hill and not St. Paul is at least a clue. Prospect Hill was probably the name given to the small scattering of settlers who lived in the backwoods of the Phalen Creek valley extending north to Phalen Lake and maybe even beyond. (Later developers would name a part of that land "Arlington Hills.") Exactly how many people lived there in 1848 is unknown but the surviving evidence indicates that it would have been a very small number.

Thanks to Williams, we know there were at least two settlers living a mile or more south of Felyn's Falls in the present-day Dayton's Bluff/Mounds Park area. One was Phelan's old friend, William Evans, the first settler east of the ravine, who lived around the vicinity of what is now Mounds Boulevard and Conway Street, on the bluff overlooking the south end of Phalen Creek. Evans' life had radically changed since Phelan settled near Phalen Creek. Sometime around 1843 Evans married Elizabeth (Maxwell) Mortimer (1812–73), the Nova Scotia-born widow of Sgt. Richard Mortimer and mother of five children. Sergeant Mortimer, the Englishman who bought a parcel of Phelan's former bottom land from Rondeau in 1842, died on January 8, 1843. Thus the old bachelor Evans became both a husband and stepfather. His new family-man status and responsibilities that it incurred may explain why Evans—who had served in leadership roles as an election judge and road commissioner for the county before his marriage— was not a delegate to the Stillwater Convention.[43] The other settler south of the falls was newcomer Eben Weld, who lived down river from Evans, somewhere around present-day Mounds Park. Weld, another backwoods bachelor, purchased his land in 1848 from French Canadian Charles Mousseau (1806-82), a former American Fur Company voyageur who settled there in 1839, three years after marrying Fanny Perry, the second oldest of the Perry sisters.[44]

Aside from Evans and Weld, who we might assume were included in the Prospect Hill district because they lived east of the great ravine, there were only ten known adults residing in Phelan's valley in 1848. The original ninety- acre town site of St. Paul, surveyed and platted in 1847, only extended as far east as present-day Wacouta Street.

Six adults lived in the Phalen Creek hollow area: fur trader Alexander McLeod and his wife Nancy, McLeod's clerk William Quinn and his wife Angelique, and Mr. and Mrs. Louis Desnoyer, French Canadians from St. Louis, who built a cabin near the creek in 1846. The Desnoyers had close ties to both Louis Robert and James Simpson. (Mrs. Desnoyer was the sister of Louis Robert's wife, Mary (Turpin) Robert; the Desnoyer's daughter Mary was married to James Simpson on December 31, 1846.) Louis Desnoyer may have been the brother or cousin of Stephen Desnoyer (1805-77), another Stillwater delegate, who bought St. Paul's present-day "Desnoyer Park" neighborhood for "a barrel of whiskey and two Indian guns" in 1843 and five years later was selected as one of the delegates to represent the St. Anthony Falls area, which included what is now the northwestern area of St. Paul.[45]

Two more adults of the ten in Phelan's valley lived at the "foot of Phelan Lake": Louis Larrivier (1794-1874), an obscure French Canadian and his mixed-blood wife Charlotte (born in what is now Minnesota in 1798). They owned four head of cattle and four hogs, and had moved there around 1843 following a short stay in St. Paul.[46]

Finally, on the high ground above the hollow "near the bend of Phelan's Creek," was Prospect Hill's second delegate to the Stillwater Convention, William "Gip" Carter (1822-52), Henry Jackson's cousin from Virginia. In 1845 Carter, along with his Virginia-born wife Elizabeth and their young son George, settled on a parcel of Prospect Hill that was owned by Jackson, St. Paul's first justice of the peace.[47] Jackson originally purchased the parcel from Phelan, evidence that Phelan had connections to one of St. Paul's leading delegates to the Stillwater Convention. Of course, delegate Carter's connection to Jackson was even closer; they were blood relatives from old Virginia. Little is known of Carter, but if he had any of the same leadership qualities that his cousin Henry Jackson did, his selection as a convention delegate should not be surprising.

One additional settler, Stanislaus Bilansky (1805-59), may have been included in the Prospect Hill district. Although he lived on the west side of the ravine, he was still far northeast of the cluster of cabins on the river bluff called St. Paul. "A Polander by birth," Bilansky settled only about a mile west of the Phalen Creek valley in 1843 at a place called "Oak Point," around the vicinity of what is now University Avenue East and John Street. Years later Bilansky, "a heavy drinker and a man of violent temper," became sensationally famous when his fourth wife, Ann, was accused of poisoning him to death. Ann Bilansky was tried, convicted and then hanged for the crime on March 23,

1860, maintaining her innocence to the end. The "first white person executed in Minnesota," Ann Bilansky is also remembered as the only woman ever legally put to death in Minnesota.[48]

Phelan's selection as a delegate may seem strange but given the context of his time and place, maybe it shouldn't be. Considering how few settlers resided in Prospect Hill and the likelihood that all of them, except Carter, lacked formal education, (and some were illiterate), and further that most of them weren't likely interested in making the twenty-mile trip to Stillwater, then maybe Phelan got the job simply by default. In other words, aside from Gip Carter, maybe none of those dozen or so adults wanted to be a delegate. Even if Phelan was truly the popular choice of the Prospect Hill residents, he probably represented fewer people than most of the other delegates.

The details of Phelan's journey to Stillwater and his stay there are not known. He may have traveled to the St. Croix River town in his log canoe, or borrowed a horse and ridden the rough but passable trail through the wilderness called the "Stillwater Road," which started at "Evan's Farm".[49] We can only assume that Phelan reached the booming five-year-old lumber town on time and was able to find his way to the second floor of John McKusick's store, on Main and Myrtle Streets, before Joseph R. Brown called the convention to order on Saturday, August 26, at ten o'clock in the morning.[50]

Though most of the delegates were likely strangers to Phelan, there was one delegate from a far distant settlement who Phelan may have been pleasantly surprised to see. He was none other than the former St. Paul pioneer, Joseph Rondeau, the man Phelan sold his original claim to and his lone supporting witness during his land dispute trial. Now Rondeau was representing a place called "Sauk Rapids," seventy-eight miles upriver from St. Paul. His residency there had been brief and would prove to be short term. Around 1844, while still a property holder in St. Paul, Rondeau had staked a claim "north of the Falls of St. Anthony, on the East Side of the Mississippi," at Sauk Rapids. Rondeau was selected as one of the three delegates to represent that part of the Upper Mississippi frontier at the Stillwater Convention.*[51]

Aside from Rondeau and Phelan's Prospect Hill neighbor Gip Carter, there were at least eight other delegates at the convention that Phelan was well acquainted with: Pierre Gervais from Little Canada (also known as Gervais Mill); August Larpenteur, James Clewett, Vetal Guerin, and Henry Jackson from St. Paul; Franklin Steele from St. Anthony Falls (who was with Phelan and the "dispatchment of soldiers" at the official examination of Hays' body); Henry Sibley from Mendota ,who coincidentally was Steele's brother-in-law, (Sibley had married Steele's sister Sarah in 1843); and Joseph R. Brown, who was listed as a delegate from "Crow Wing" (a fur trading post at the confluence of the Crow Wing and Mississippi Rivers, near present-day Fort Ripley) but had older and stronger ties to both Stillwater and St. Paul. Brown owned property in both towns and lived periodically in both places, albeit his old, log home on the St. Croix, which was designated in 1839 to serve as a courthouse when needed, was technically outside of Stillwater's town limits just to the north.[52]

How much Phelan would have interacted with these and other delegates can only be imagined, but no doubt his encounters with some of those who knew him well would have been awkward. The ultimate awkward and ironic encounter would have occurred with convention leaders Joseph R. Brown and Henry Sibley, the two justices of the peace who had interrogated Phelan in 1839 and were convinced he was guilty of murder. Brown also had an earlier encounter with Phelan in August 1840 when he presided over the Phelan versus Guerin claim dispute as justice of the peace. But the convention setting in Stillwater eight years later was dramatically different. One can easily imagine Brown's astonishment when he saw the man he believed was a lying murderer among all the distinguished delegates at the convention. The same could be said for Henry Sibley, Phel-

---

* Today Sauk Rapids is a city in Benton County of 13,000 people.

*Phelan's bold signature from the Stillwater convention. Curiously, he used the modern spelling of "Phalen." Courtesy of the Minnesota Historical Society.*

an's original interrogator, who plainly told Williams that he had "no doubt of his guilt."[53]

How much Phelan contributed to the convention (or whether he even spoke at all) is not known. The conventions' elected secretary, David Lambert,* recorded only the essentials of the proceedings, and Phelan's name appears nowhere, except for his signature on the historic memorial petition to President Polk signed by sixty-one delegates. (Inexplicably, noted delegate Franklin Steele's name was not on the petition.) The two dominant figures at the assembly were, of course, Brown and Sibley. Sibley— "the most eminent and influential person in the region"—was unanimously elected to be the delegate to Washington to petition Congress for the quick passage of legislation creating the new Territory of Minnesota and placing its capital at St. Paul.[54] Sibley's unanimous election must mean, oddly enough, that Phelan also voted for him, the man who once arrested him and whom he may well have wished could be hanged.

We might also presume that Phelan was one of the delegates who voted for St. Paul as the territorial capital; it would have been in his own self-interest to do so. After all, Phelan owned a large tract of real estate just outside the town limits of St. Paul. Even an uneducated backwoodsman like Phelan would have realized that once the territory was formed and St. Paul became the capital, the town would boom and the value of local real estate would appreciate dramatically.

---

* Tragically, fourteen months later, on November 2, 1849, an intoxicated Lambert "leaped from the roof" of a St. Paul-bound steamboat "and was drowned." (Williams gives the account on p. 197 of *A History of the City of St. Paul*.)

CHAPTER TEN

Indecd, by 1849 St. Paul's population exploded to 840 and the next year it boasted 1,294 residents (including 257 families).[55]

But Phelan didn't remain in the St. Paul area long enough to benefit from the increasing value of his land. In the spring of 1850, two years after the Stillwater Convention and only a year after the territory of Minnesota was formed, Phelan abruptly slipped out of town. The details are sketchy and we only have J. Fletcher Williams to tell the story.

> *In the spring of 1850, Phelan was indicted by the first Grand Jury that ever sat in Ramsey County, for perjury. Phelan had fled his bailiwick, and in company with Eb Weld, started for California.*[56]

Exactly what Phelan perjured about was never reported but it certainly would not have been the first time he committed perjury, since the core of his testimony to both Sibley and Brown in 1839 was demonstratively false. And the fact that he skipped town with his neighbor Eben Weld is evidence that Phelan had at least one more friend. Phelan and Weld's flight to California, of course, corresponds perfectly with the great California gold rush at that time.

However, as Williams reported, Phelan never made it to California. After joining a wagon train west, Phelan's bad behavior finally caught up with him.

> *It was shortly afterwards reported here that Phelan had come to a violent end, while crossing the plains. The account states that he acted so brutally and overbearingly toward the other men in the same caravan, they were compelled to kill him in self defense. The murdered Hays was avenged!*[57]

And so on some forgotten part of the Great Plains, on some forgotten date, the overbearing, "bad," "brutal," "ruffian," who was prone to violence, Edward Phelan, died violently, at age thirty-nine or forty, leaving behind no known family and probably no real friends.

286

Yet his name lives on abundantly in St. Paul, Minnesota, the town he helped to pioneer and the place he gained some infamy. It may be odd and ironic that at least thirty public and private places in Minnesota's capital city now bear the name of the presumed murderer, "Phalen." And yet no places in St. Paul carry the names of such worthy pioneers as Hays, Guerin, Perry, Gervais, Clewett, Evans, Bazille, and even Parrant— who was, after all, never arrested for any crime and never known to do violence on any settler and was in fact long known as "the founder of St. Paul." ("Pig's Eye Lake," "Pig's Eye Lake Road," and "Pig's Eye Island," at the remote southern edge of St. Paul, were named for Parrant but no buildings or place names anywhere else in the city are named for him.)

J. Fletcher Williams, who lived in St. Paul when only the creek and the lake were named for Phelan, was outraged that anything was named for him. St. Paul's first historian reported that around the time he published his book in 1876 there was an attempt to change the name of the lake.

*It is a disgrace that the name of this brutal murderer has been affixed to one of our most beautiful lakes—one that supplies our households with water. Last winter, Senator W.P. Murray, made an effort to have the name changed to "Goodhue Lake" but it did not succeed as it should have done.* [58]

The senator who "made the effort" to change the name of Lake Phalen was state senator William Pitt Murray (1825-1910), an Irish American lawyer-politician from Ohio, who served in the Minnesota legislature and on the St. Paul City Council and had a county named for him. But Murray— "a good lawyer, a good talker, a good speaker, a good citizen"—was not persuasive enough to convince the city council to change the name of the lake from "Phalen" to "Goodhue." [59] Interestingly, Murray, who was president of the city council, wanted to replace the name of an unsavory alleged murderer with the name of early St. Paul's most honored murder victim (although it took him more than seventeen months to die), James Goodhue (1810–52).

The founder and editor of the *Minnesota Pioneer,* the first newspaper in Minnesota, James Madison Goodhue, was the single greatest promoter of Minnesota during the first three years it was a territory. But the pioneer newspaperman made the fatal mistake of publicly insulting one of Minnesota's first territorial judges, David Cooper. Goodhue ridiculed Judge Cooper unmercifully in print, calling him among other things "a miserable drunkard," who "off the Bench is a beast and on the Bench is an ass, stuffed with arrogance, self conceit and ridiculous affectation of dignity."[60]

Judge Cooper's brother, Joseph Cooper, was so outraged by those comments that the day after they were printed, on January 16, 1851, he angrily accosted Goodhue on a street in St. Paul and literally initiated a gun duel with the editor. The gun duel quickly turned into a mad brawl that ended with Cooper stabbing Goodhue twice with a knife, and Goodhue, in turn, wounding Cooper with a gunshot. Both men survived the fight but Goodhue's serious wounds no doubt contributed to his death on August 27, 1852.[61] Goodhue's passing was mourned near and far, and soon after his death a county, a township and a street (in St. Paul) were all named in his memory.

Perhaps the fact that Goodhue had already been duly honored compelled the city council to reject Murray's proposed name change for a lake to which Goodhue plainly had no connection. In addition, the fact that none of the councilmen of 1875–76 had known Phelan or lived in the St. Paul area when he did may account for their reluctance to change the name of a landmark lake that had already been known by the name of Phelan for over thirty years.*

Today that landmark lake has carried the name Phelan for over 170 years and has inspired the name of Phelan for many other place names in St. Paul. Generations of St. Paulites have grown quite accus-

---

* Williams' rosters of pioneers and councilmen in 1875–76, and their respective arrival dates in St. Paul, indicate that none of them would have overlapped with Phelan's dates in the St. Paul area.

tomed to the name "Phalen" and no doubt associate it not with a murderer from the city's remote past, but rather a lovely lake and creek, the large recreational park that developed around the lake beginning in 1894, the beach house on the lake that opened in 1903, the memorable grammar school that opened in 1902, ten blocks southwest of the park at 650 East Rose Street, and the popular golf course near the lake that opened around 1925.[62] All these old public places named "Phalen" are and were part of the lifelong memories of a great multitude of people living and dead.

Given the passage of time and the sheer number of places that carry the name of Phalen, any proposal now to expunge the name from St. Paul public places (never mind the private ones) would be impractical, unfeasible, and unsettling to many people who hold dear the memories of old places named Phalen. But after learning the full record of Edward Phelan's unusually flawed life, readers may be struck by the absurd irony that so many places were named for him. Like J. Fletcher Williams, they will be embarrassed that a lying, pig stealing, big bad bully—whom a preponderance of the evidence points to as St. Paul's first murderer—has his name affixed to so many places in the city that was named for a saint and mostly founded by generally good people who followed the teachings of that great saint.

# ACKNOWLEDGMENTS

A special thanks to my mother, retired secretary Marianne Brueggemann—the fastest eighty-nine year-old typist in Minnesota (now she's over 90)—who amazingly typed most of the original manuscript. I also want to thank my saintly wife, Jacqueline, for all the work, support, and encouragement she gave to this long-term project. I was most fortunate to have found the perfect editor for this book, right in my own neighborhood and in my own church, Ann Schroeder. Ann, you know how much I appreciate your editing talents. Finally, I would like to acknowledge my goddaughter, Mary Brueggemann, who on short notice created a colorful, custom-made map of frontier St. Paul; and my old friend Jim ("J. D.") Kerrigan, who was the first person to read the full manuscript and became one of my most trusted advisors and supporters.

# ABOUT THE AUTHOR

**Gary Brueggemann** teaches history at Century and Inver Hills Community Colleges. A lifelong resident of St. Paul, he has spent the last 35 years researching, writing and teaching Minnesota History. He is the author of numerous works on St. Paul History, including at least 40 newspaper and magazine articles.

# ENDNOTES

## Notes to Introduction

1. J. Fletcher Williams, *A History of the City of Saint Paul, and of the County of Ramsey, Minnesota* (St. Paul: Minnesota Historical Society, 1876; reprint edition, 1983), 71, 90.
2. Rev. Edward D. Neill, *History of Ramsey County and the City of St. Paul* (Minneapolis: North Star Publishing Company, 1881), 182, 302.
3. Frank C. Bliss, *St. Paul: Past and Present* (St. Paul: F.C. Bliss Publishing Company, 1888), 37.
4. Alix J. Muller, *History of the Police and Fire Departments of the Twin Cities* (St. Paul: American Land & Title Register Association Publishers, 1899), 22.
5. W.B. Hennessy, *Past and Present of St. Paul, Minnesota* (Chicago: S.J. Clarke Publishing Company, 1906), 47.
6. Nancy Goodman, ed. *Minnesota Beginnings: Records of St. Croix County, Wisconsin Territory, 1840-1849* (Stillwater, Minn.: History Network of Washington County, 1999). This volume includes a complete transcription of Joseph R. Brown's casebook and includes the Hays murder testimony. All subsequent citations to the casebook refer to this edition and are abbreviated as "*Brown's Casebook.*" Brown's original casebook is in the Joseph R. Brown Papers at the Minnesota Historical Society archives in St. Paul. Subsequent citations to material from this volume other than the casebook material are referenced as "*Records of St. Croix County.*"
7. *Ibid*
8. Wisconsin Territorial Papers, *St. Croix County Proceeding of Board of Supervisors, October 5, 1840–April 2, 1849* (Madison: Wisconsin Historical Society Records Survey, 1941).

## Notes to Chapter One

1. Williams, *A History of St. Paul*, 71.
2. "History of Derry," Original Official Site of Northern Ireland Tourist Board, accessed June 16, 2011, http://www.geographia.com/northern-ireland/ukideroohtm; "The Walled City of Derry," accessed June 16, 2011, http:// www.discovernorthernireland.com/walledcity.
3. "Last name: Phelan," The Internet Surname Database, accessed June 7, 2007, www.surnamedb .com/surname/Phelan; Londonderry Ireland Genealogy Forum, accessed July 14, 2009, www .genforymgenealogy.com/Ireland/Londonderry.
4. *St Peter and St. Paul Register*, Vol. *1, 1841-47*, Minnesota Historical Society archives.
5. "Passenger Lists," accessed June 3, 2008, www.ancestry.com, http://search.ancestry.com/ search/default.aspx?cat=112&0.xid=21837&0_Sch=search;
6. Williams, *A History of St. Paul*, 70-71.

7.  Ibid, 70-71
8.  August L. Larpenteur, "Recollections of the City and People of St. Paul 1843-1898," *Collections of the Minnesota Historical Society* 9 (1898-1900): 391.
9.  Williams, *A History of St. Paul*, 40, 71; Marilyn Ziebarth and Alan Ominsky, *Fort Snelling: Anchor Post of the Northwest* (St. Paul: Minnesota Historical Society, 1970), 1; Helen White and Bruce White, *Fort Snelling in 1838: An Ethnographic and Historical Study* (St. Paul: Turstone Historical Research, 1998), 11.
10. Marcus L. Hansen, *Old Fort Snelling* (Mpls: Ross & Haines Inc., 1958), 84-102; Ziebarth and Ominsky, *Fort Snelling: Anchor Post of the Northwest*, 11-17; Barbara K. Luecke and John C. Luecke, *Snelling: Minnesota's First Family* (Cannon Falls, Minn.: Cannon Falls Beacon, 1893), 154.
11. Helen and Bruce White, *Fort Snelling in 1838*, 65. The Whites' height table for soldiers at Fort Snelling in 1838 shows only one man (Phelan?) over 6'1" and he was 6'2½"; Williams, *A History of St. Paul*, 70.
12. Neill, *History of Ramsey County*, 182; Williams, *A History of St. Paul*, 212.
13. Gen. Richard W. Johnson, "Fort Snelling From Its Foundation to the Present Time," *Collections of the Minnesota Historical Society*, 8 (1895-98): 430; Edward D. Neill, "Early Days at Fort Snelling," *Collections of the Minnesota Historical Society*, 1 (1850-56): 355-59; Colonel John H. Bliss, "Reminiscences of Fort Snelling," *Collections of the Minnesota Historical Society*, 6 (1894): 342; Williams, *A History of St. Paul*, 212.
14. For a full biography of J. Fletcher Williams, see Lucile M. Kane's introduction to the 1983 edition of Williams, *A History of the City of Saint Paul;* Williams, *A History of St. Paul*, 205.
15. John Fletcher Williams Papers, Minnesota Historical Society collections; Williams, *A History of St. Paul*, 71.
16. Williams, *A History of St. Paul*, 146.
17. Williams, *A History of St. Paul*, 71.
18. Herbert Asbury, *The Gangs of New York* (New York: Old Town Books, 1927), 9-12.
19. Gregory Cristiano, "Where the Gangs Lived: New York's Five Points District," Urbanography, http://www.urbanography.com/5-points/, accessed June 10, 2007; Ted Chamberlain, "Gangs of New York: Fact vs. Fiction," *National Geographic News*, updated March 24, 2003, http://news.nationalgeographic.com/news/2003/03/0330-030320_0SC05_gangs.html.
20. Asbury, *The Gangs of New York*, 9.
21. Ibid., 1.
22. Barbara and John Luecke, *Snelling*, 63.
23. Asbury, *The Gangs of New York*, 22.

## Notes to Chapter Two

1.  Williams, *A History of St. Paul*, 57-58, 71.
2.  Ibid., 64-68; Gary Brueggemann, "The Perret Family's Forgotten Farm at Buttermilk Falls," *Community Reporter: Serving Fort Road Neighborhoods, Downtown St. Paul to Fort Snelling*, Feb. 2000, special edition.
3.  Williams, *A History of St. Paul*, 72.
4.  Ibid.
5.  Ibid.
6.  Helen and Bruce White, *Fort Snelling in 1838*, 57; Barbara and John Luecke, *Snelling*, 253; A good detailed description of a frontier cabin is presented in Merrill E. Jarchow, *The Earth Brought Forth: A History of Minnesota Agriculture to 1885* (St. Paul: Minnesota Historical Society, 1949), 81.

7. Williams, *A History of St. Paul*, 72-73.

8. Ibid.

9. Gary Clayton Anderson, *Little Crow: Spokesman for the Sioux* (St. Paul: Minnesota Historical Society Press, 1986), 11-13, 196; Gary Brueggemann, "Rendezvous at the Riverbend: Pike's Seven Days in the Land of Little Crow, the Wilderness that Later Became St. Paul," *Ramsey County History* (Summer 2005), 5-9; *Records of St. Croix County*, 270.

10. Thomas M. Newson, *Pen Pictures of St. Paul, Minnesota and Biographical Sketches of Old Settlers* (St. Paul: T.M. Newson Publishing, 1886), 6; W.B. Hennessy, *Past and Present*, 20; Williams, *A History of St. Paul*, 65.

11. Williams, A History of St. Paul,, 64-65; Francis Paul Prucha, *American Indian Policy in the Formative Years* (Lincoln: University of Nebraska Press, 1962), 127.

12. Williams, *A History of St. Paul*, 72-73.

13. Ibid., 73.

14. Warren Upham, "Minnesota Biographies 1655-1912," *Collections of the Minnesota Historical Society*, 19 (1912): 546; Newson, *Pen Pictures*, 9-11.

15. T. Otto Nall, *Forever Beginning: A History of the United Methodist Church and Her Antecedents in Minnesota to 1969* (Nashville: Parthenon Press, 1973), 12-13, 101; William D. Green, *A Peculiar Imbalance: The Fall and Rise of Racial Equality in Early Minnesota* (St. Paul: Minnesota Historical Society Press, 2007), 17-36; Newson, *Pen Pictures*, 9-12; Alfred Brunson, *Western Pioneer*, 2 (Cincinnati. Walden and Stowe, 1880), 32; Rev. S.R. Riggs, "Protestant Missions in the Northwest," *Collections of the Minnesota Historical Society*, 6 (1894): 136-40.

16. Green, *A Peculiar Imbalance*, 19-27; Evan Jones, *Citadel in the Wilderness: The Story of Fort Snelling and the Northwest Frontier* (New York: Coward-McCann, Inc., 1966), 164.

17. Newson, *Pen Pictures*, 11.

18. Ibid., 10.

19. Ibid.

20. Williams, *A History of St. Paul*, 72-73

21. *Brown's Casebook*, 252.

22. Gary J Brueggemann, *Seven Generations: A People's History, Calendar of Little Canada, Minnesota* (St. Paul: Little Canada Historical Society, 1984). See opening article: "The Adventures of Ben Gervais, the Founder of Little Canada"; Gary J. Brueggemann, "From Gervais Glen to the West End Flats to Junkyard Hollow: The South End of Randolph Avenue Has a Remarkable History," *Community Reporter*, October 2004; Joan Stoltzman Jansen, "The Benjamin Gervais Family: First Settlers and Founders of Little Canada," (unpublished manuscript, April 1989); Williams, *A History of St. Paul*, 69-70. Williams was mistaken on the birth year of Ben Gervais.

23. Gary J. Brueggemann, "Backwoodsmen, Farmers and Bootleggers: Saint Paul Pioneers of the Far West End" (Master's thesis, University of Wisconsin, River Falls, 1981), 97-98; Helen and Bruce White, *Fort Snelling in 1838*, 133-39

24. Edward K. Smith, "Map of Fort Snelling and Vicinity," 1837, Minnesota Historical Society collections; James L. Thompson, "Map of Military Reserve Embracing Fort Snelling," October 1839, Minnesota Historical Society collections; Williams, *A History of St. Paul*, 66-67; Vera Kelsey, *Red River Runs North* (New York: Harpers Brothers, 1951), 70-140; William Watts Folwell, *A History of Minnesota* (St. Paul: Minnesota Historical Society, 1921) 1:217.

25. *St. Paul Pioneer Press*, August 8, 1920, 3; Thompsons Map of Military Reserve, 1839; Neill, *History of Ramsey County*, 279; Edward Neill, *History of Minnesota* (Minneapolis: Minnesota Historical Company, Fourth Edition, Revised and Enlarged, 1882), 911-912; Williams, 101.

26. "First By Birth", *St. Paul Pioneer Press*, May 6, 1894, 11.

## Notes to Chapter Three

1. "First By Birth", *St. Paul Pioneer Press*, May 6, 1894,11; *Records of St. Croix County*, 343.
2. Williams, *A History of St. Paul*, 72; Neill, *History of Ramsey County*, 302.
3. *Brown's Casebook*, 250.
4. Ibid.
5. Ibid., 248.
6. Ibid., 252
7. Ibid., 248.
8. Ibid., 250; John H. Case, "Historical Notes of Grey Cloud Island and its Vicinity," *Collections of the Minnesota Historical Society*, 15 (1909-1914): 371-378.
9. *Brown's Casebook,* 252.
10. Williams, *A History of St. Paul,* 101, 105; *Minnesota Territorial Census, 1850*, Patricia C. Harpole and Mary D. Nagle, eds. (St. Paul: Minnesota Historical Society, 1972), 40, 52.
11. *Brown's Casebook*, 250.
12. Ibid.
13. Muller, *History of Police and Fire,* 22; Brueggemann, *People's History Calendar of Little Canada*, 1-2.
14. *Brown's Casebook*, 250-53.
15. A good map of the old St. Paul riverfront appears in G.M. Hopkins, *Atlas of the Environs of St. Paul* (Philadelphia: G.M. Hopkins Co., 1886), plate 23; *Brown's Casebook*, 252.
16. Jansen, "The Ben Gervais Family."
17. *Wiskonsan Enquirer*, April 13, 1839, as quoted in Nancy and Robert Goodman, *Joseph R. Brown: Adventurer On the Minnesota Frontier 1820-1849* (Rochester, Minnesota: Lone Oak Press, 1996), 162.
18. Brueggemann, "Rendezvous at the Riverbend," 8; Nall, *Forever Beginning,* 13-14; Green, *A Peculiar Imbalance,* 20; *Brown's Casebook*, 252.
19. *Brown's Casebook*,252
20. Ibid., 248, 252.
21. A mini-biography of Baldwin appears in the appendix of *Minnesota Beginnings: Records of St. Croix County*, 291.
22. *Brown's Casebook*, 249.
23. Ibid., 248.
24. Ibid.
25. Ibid., 252.
26. Ibid., 248.
27. Ibid.
28. Ibid.
29. Williams, *A History of St. Paul*, 68.
30. *Lawrence Taliaferro Journal* 1820-39 (Aug. 27, 1834), Lawrence Taliaferro Papers, Minnesota Historical Society collections.
31. W.B. Hennessy, *History of the St. Paul Fire Department* (St. Paul: St. Paul Fire Department Relief Fund Assn., 1909), 6-7.
32. Williams, *A History of St. Paul*, 105-6.
33. Ibid., 106.
34. "Vetal Guerin Statement," John Fletcher Williams Papers, Minnesota Historical Society collections.
35. *Brown's Casebook*, 249-50.
36. Williams, *A History of St. Paul*, 91.

37. Samuel W. Pond, *The Dakota or Sioux in Minnesota As They Were in 1834* (St. Paul: Minnesota Historical Society Press, 1986, first published in 1908 in *Minnesota Historical Collections*, Vol. 12, 1908), 9.

38. Ibid., 9.

39. Ibid., 8-9; "Autobiography of Maj. Lawrence, written in 1864," *Collections of the Minnesota Historical Society*, 6 (1894): 189, 200-238; Folwell, *A History of Minnesota* 1: 140-142.

40. *Brown's Casebook*, 249.

## Notes to Chapter Four

1. Williams, *A History of St. Paul*, 91.

2. Ibid.

3. *Brown's Casebook*, 248; Williams, *A History of St. Paul*, 86-88, 108-9; Jonathan Carver, *Three Years' Travels Through the Interior Parts of North America* (Walpole, N. H.: Isaiah Thomas & Co., 1813), 48-49; Brueggemann, "Rendezvous at the Riverbend," 6, 9, 15.

4. *Brown's Casebook*, 248.

5. Ibid.

6. Ibid., 249.

7. Ibid.

8. See Don E. Fehrenbacker, *The Dred Scott Case* (New York: Oxford University Press, 1978); Return I. Holcombe, *Minnesota in Three Centuries* (Mankato: The Publishing Society of Minnesota, 1908), 2:95-97.

9. *Brown's Casebook*, 249.

10. Ibid.

11. Ibid.

12. Ibid., 251.

13. Ibid., 247.

## Notes to Chapter Five

1. Nathaniel West, *The Ancestry, Life and Times of Hon. Henry Hastings Sibley* (St. Paul: Pioneer Press-Company, 1889), 57, 80; Folwell, 1:161; Rhoda R. Gilman, *Henry Hastings Sibley—Divided Heart* (St. Paul: Minnesota Historical Society Press, 2004), 4-78.

2. Newson, *Pen Pictures*, 432.

3. Williams, *A History of St. Paul*, 91.

4. *Brown's Casebook*, 247.

5. Ibid., 248.

6. Ibid.

7. Williams, *A History of St. Paul*, 92.

8. *Brown's Casebook*, 248.

9. Ibid., 250.

10. Ibid., 248.

11. Williams, *A History of St. Paul*, 92.

12. John Porter Bloom, ed., *The Territorial Papers of the United States, Volume 27: The Territory of Wisconsin Executive Journal, 1836-1848 and Papers, 1836-1839* (Washington D.C. The National Archives Records Service, 1969), 185; *Records of St. Croix County*, introduction.

13. Newson, *Pen Pictures*, 201-9; W.H.C. Folsom, *Fifty Years in the Northwest* (St. Paul: Pioneer Press Company, 1888), 52-53.

14. Augustus B. Eaton, *History of the Saint Croix Valley*, 1 (Chicago: H.C. Cooper Jr. & Company,

1909), 7-11; Folwell, *A History of Minnesota*, 1: 231-38; Williams, *A History of St. Paul*, 41-42; Holcomb, *Minnesota in Three Centuries*, 2: 91-93; The best and only book-length biography of Brown is Nancy and Robert Goodman, *Joseph R. Brown: Adventurer on the Minnesota Frontier*.

15. Nancy and Robert Goodman, *Joseph R. Brown*, 161-65.
16. Ibid., 161-165; "Autobiography of Major Lawrence Taliaferro," 226-27.
17. Nancy and Robert Goodman, *Joseph R. Brown*, 161-65.
18. "Henry Sibley, Reminiscences Historical and Personal," *Collections of the Minnesota Historical Society*, 1 (1850-56), 383-384; Nancy and Robert Goodman, *Joseph R. Brown*, 115, 147-48; Pond, *The Dakota in 1834*, 18-19.
19. Folsom, *Fifty Years in the Northwest*, 53.
20. William J. Petersen, *Steamboating on the Upper Mississippi* (Iowa City: State Historical Society of Iowa, 1968), 153-54.
21. *Brown's Casebook*, 246-47.
22. Ibid., 248.
23. Ibid., 249-50.
24. Pond, *The Dakota in 1834*, 137-39.
25. *Brown's Casebook*, 249-50.
26. Ibid.
27. Carver, *Three Years' Travels*, 48.
28. *Records of St. Croix County*, 316, 350.
29. *Brown's Casebook*, 250-51.
30. Ibid.
31. Ibid.
32. Ibid.
33. Ibid.
34. Ibid.
35. Ibid.
36. Ibid., 247-48.
37. Ibid., 251.
38. Ibid., 249.
39. Ibid., 248.
40. Ibid., 249.
41. Williams, *A History of St. Paul*, 88-89.
42. *Brown's Casebook*, 251-52.
43. Neill, *History of Minnesota*, 916; Nancy and Robert Goodman, *Joseph R. Brown*, 157-65; *Taliaferro Journal*, Sept. 8, 21, Oct. 5, 1839; *Autobiography of Maj. Lawrence Taliaferro*, 226-27.
44. *Brown's Casebook*, 252.
45. Ibid., 251.
46. Ibid., 250-51.
47. Ibid.
48. Ibid., 252.
49. Ibid.
50. Ibid.
51. Ibid.
52. Ibid.
53. Williams, *A History of St. Paul*, 92.
54. Williams, *A History of St. Paul* (1983 ed.), introduction and preface.
55. Brueggemann, *History Calendar of Little Canada*.

56. *St. Paul Pioneer Press*, May 6, 1894, 11.
57. Ibid.
58. Brown's Casebook, 250
59. Ibid., 249.
60. Ibid.
61. Williams, *A History of St. Paul*, 91.

## Notes to Chapter Six

1. *Brown's Casebook*, 252.
2. Ibid., 250.
3. Ibid.
4. Ibid., 251.
5. Ibid., 250-51.
6. Ibid., 253,
7. Williams, *A History of St. Paul*, 92.
8. St. Gabriel Catholic Church, Prairie du Chien, baptismal records, May 10, 1840; Williams, *A History of St. Paul*, 90.
9. Telephone interviews by author with file clerks of Crawford County Courthouse, June 11, 2007.
10. Ibid.
11. Williams, *A History of St. Paul*, 92; Neill, *History of Ramsey County*, 182; Larpenteur, "Recollections," 391; *Brown's Casebook*, 247, 252-253.
12. *The Territory of Wisconsin Executive Journal and Papers*, 185; *Brown's Casebook*, 246.
13. Williams, *A History of St. Paul*, 59, 77-79.
14. *Brown's Casebook*, 251.
15. Ibid., 252.
16. Williams, *A History of St. Paul*, 91.
17. *Records of St. Croix County*, 84-85.
18. Death Penalty in Wisconsin, Dictionary of Wisconsin History, Wisconsin Historical Society, accessed June 11, 2010, http://www.wisconsinhistory.org/dictionary/index .asp?action=id=11148&research_term=death.
19. *Brown's Casebook*, 247.
20. Ibid., 249.
21. Williams, *A History of St. Paul*, 72.
22. Ibid.
23. Ibid., 92.
24. Newson, *Pen Pictures*, 11.
25. Ibid., 30-31; Williams, *A History of St. Paul*, 122-25; Larpenteur, "Recollections," 373-75; Folwell, *A History of Minnesota* 1: 179-80; Donald Dean Parker, ed., *The Recollections of Philander Prescott Frontiersman of the Old Northwest 1819-1862* (Lincoln: University of Nebraska Press, 1966), 175-76; Neill, *History of Minnesota*, 469-70. Neill reported that Dancer was "skinned" by the Ojibwe.
26. Newson, *Pen Pictures*, 11-12, 51-52; Green, *A Peculiar Imbalance*, 18, 26-27, 29, 34.
27. *Minnesota Territorial Census, 1850*, 44, Williams, *A History of St. Paul*, 123; Newson, *Pen Pictures*, 12.
28. Williams, *A History of St. Paul*, 123.
29. Ibid., 158; Newson, *Pen Pictures*, 51.
30. Williams, *A History of St. Paul*, 123.
31. Ibid., 125.

32. Newson, *Pen Pictures*, 11.
33. Ibid.
34. Larpenteur, "Recollections," 391.
35. Ibid., 367-70, 379-83.
36. Ibid.
37. Ibid., 263-66; Williams, *A History of St. Paul*, 279; J.W. Bond, *Minnesota and Its Resources* (New York: Redfield, 1853), 112-113; E.S. Seymour, *Sketches of Minnesota, the New England of the West* (New York: Harper and Brothers Publishers, 1850), 95.
38. Larpenteur, "Recollections," 371; Williams, *A History of St. Paul*, 293-94.
39. Larpenteur, "Recollections," 373.
40. Ibid.
41. Williams, *A History of St. Paul*, 92.
42. Anderson, *Little Crow*, 9, 184-85.
43. Ibid., 33.
44. Holcombe, *Minnesota in Three Centuries*, Vol. 2: 170, 169-175; Edward D. Neill, "Battle of Lake Pokegema," *Collections of Minnesota Historical Society*, 1 (1850-1856), 146-56.
45. *Brown's Casebook*, 248.
46. Williams, *A History of St. Paul*, 92.
47. Gilman, *Henry Hastings Sibley*, 75-76.
48. Lucy Leavenworth Wilder Morris, ed., *Old Rail Fence Corners* (Austin, Minn., F.H. McCulloch Printing, 1914), 43-46; Big Thunder's death is also covered in Holcombe, *Minnesota in Three Centuries*, 2: 180.
49. Gilman, *Henry Hastings Sibley*, 76.
50. "Henry Sibley, Reminiscences, Historical and Personal," 389.
51. Pond, *The Dakota in Minnesota in 1834*, 124, 128, 129.
52. Ibid., 131.
53. Helen and Bruce White, *Fort Snelling in 1838*, 11.
54. Williams, *A History of St. Paul*, 64-65.
55. Newson, *Pen Pictures*, 15-16.
56. Neill, *History of Ramsey County*, 113.
57. Colonel John Hankins, *Dakota Land or the Beauty of St. Paul* (New York: Hankins & Sons Publishers, 1869), 30.
58. Christopher C. Andrews, *History of St. Paul, Minn.* (Syracuse, N.Y.: D. Mason & Co. Publisher, 1890), 52.
59. Williams, *A History of St. Paul*, 84-85.
60. Larpenteur, "Recollections," 391.
61. Williams, *A History of St. Paul*, 65-66, 71.
62. Ibid., 65.
63. *Brown's Casebook*, 247, 253; Williams presents the popular legend of the dispute: Williams, *A History of St. Paul*, 146-48.
64. Williams, *A History of St. Paul*, 92.
65. *Brown's Casebook*, 248.

## Notes to Chapter Seven

1. Williams, *A History of St. Paul*, 71.
2. Newson, *Pen Pictures*, 3, 4; Upham, *Minnesota Biographies*, 169; Jim Sazevich, St. Paul's "house detective" and leading expert on the city's old homes, including the Dayton Mansion, telephone interview by author, July, 2009.

3. *Brown's Casebook*, 250-52—.

4. Josiah B. Chaney, "Early Bridges and Changes of the Land and Water Surface in the City of St. Paul," *Collections of the Minnesota Historical Society*, 12 (1908): 139; Minnesota Historical Society Photograph Collection: see "St. Paul panoramic views" and "views from Dayton's Bluff."

5. A.T. Andreas, *Illustrated Historical Atlas of the State of Minnesota* (Chicago: A.T. Andreas, 1874), 15-16.

6. *Brown's Casebook*, 250.

7. Ibid., 252.

8. Ibid., 251.

9. Ibid.

10. Ibid., 252.

11. Ibid.

12. Ibid., 251.

13. Ibid., 250.

14 Ibid., 250-51.

15. Ibid., 251.

16. Ibid., 251-52.

17. Ibid., 252.

18. Ibid., 250-51.

19. Ibid., 249.

20. Ibid., 250.

21. Ibid.

22. Ibid.

23. Ibid.

24. Williams, *A History of St. Paul*, 90, 101; *Minnesota Territorial Census, 1850*, 40.

25. *Brown's Casebook*, 250.

26. Ibid., 248.

27. Ibid.

28. Ibid.

29. Ibid., 249.

30. The author has close relatives on both sides of his family that are or were farmers and has had numerous occasions to eat breakfast with them; Margaret Visser, *The Rituals of Dinner* (New York: Penguin, 1991), 159-60, 205; Andrew F. Smith, ed., *Oxford Encyclopedia of Food and Drink in America* (New York: Oxford University Press, 2004) 1: 127-37; Vol. 2: 65-67; "Breakfast: America," The Food Timeline, accessed July 20, 2011,

31. Williams, *A History of St. Paul*, 72.

32. *Webster's Ninth New Collegiate Dictionary* (Springfield, Mass.: Merriam-Webster Inc., 1986), 730.

33. *Brown's Casebook*, 251.

34. Ibid., 248.

35. Ibid., 251.

36. Ibid., 252.

37. Ibid., 250.

38. Ibid., 251.

39. G. M. Hopkins Atlas of St. Paul, 1886, Plate 23.

40. *Brown's Casebook*, 250.

41. Ibid., 251.

42. Ibid., 247-48.

43. Ibid., 250.

44. Ibid., 251.
45. Ibid., 249-50.
46. Charlotte Ouisconsin Van Cleave, *Three Score Years and Ten Life-Long Memories of Fort Snelling Minnesota* (Mpls: Harrison and Smith, 1888), 62-67; Williams, *A History of St. Paul*, 82.
47. *Brown's Casebook*, 250.
48. Ibid.
49. Ibid.
50. Williams, *A History of St. Paul*, 90.
51. *Brown's Casebook*, 251.
52. Ibid., 252.
53. Ibid.
54. Ibid.
55. Williams, *A History of St. Paul*, 84-85.
56. *Brown's Casebook*, 250.
57. Ibid., 252.
58. Williams, *A History of St. Paul*, 92.
59. *Brown's Casebook*, 250-51.
60. Ibid., 251.
61. Ibid., 248.
62. Ibid., 252.
63. Pond, *The Dakota in Minnesota in 1834*, 26-31, 65-66; Theodore Blegen, ed., "The Narrative of Samuel W. Pond," *Minnesota History*, 21 (1940), 23-24, 171; Stephen R. Riggs, *Mary and I: Forty Years with the Sioux* (Minneapolis: Ross and Haines Inc., 1880, reprint 1969), 78, 110, 127, 388, 425.

## Notes to Chapter Eight

1. *Brown's Casebook*, 249-50.
2. Ibid.
3. Ibid., 249.
4. Ibid.
5. Ibid., 248-49, 252.
6. Dennis Claugherty, retired Senior Investigator with the Ramsey County Medical Examiner's office, interviewed by author, Dec. 2007, Dec. 2008.
7. *Alexis Bailly Ledger Book*, March 14, 1826, *Alexis Bailly Papers*, 1821-1898, Vol. 7, Box 3, Minnesota Historical Society collections.
8. Nancy and Robert Goodman, *Joseph R. Brown*, 307.
9. Carolyn Gilman, *Where Two Worlds Meet: The Great Lakes Fur Trade* (St. Paul: Minnesota Historical Society, 1982), 96.
10. Pond, *The Dakota in Minnesota in 1834*, 32-33.
11. Williams, *A History of St. Paul*, 92.
12. Interviews with Dennis Claugherty, 2007-2008.
13. Ibid.
14. *Brown's Casebook*, 247-49.

## Notes to Chapter Nine

1. Williams, *A History of St. Paul*, 91.
2. Ibid., 72.

3. Ibid., 71; Muller, *History of Police and Fire*, 22.
4. *Brown's Casebook*, 249; *Records of St. Croix County*, 84, 104.
5. Neill, *History of Minnesota*, 911–912.
6. Jansen, "The Ben Gervais Family"; *Minnesota Territorial Census, 1850*, 38, 39.
7. *Minnesota Territorial Census, 1850*, 59; *Records of St. Croix County*, 322.
8. *Brown's Casebook*, 248.
9. Ibid., 252.
10. Ibid., 248.
11. Ibid.
12. Ibid.
13. Ibid., 249.
14. Ibid., 247.
15. Ibid.

## Notes to Chapter Ten

1. Williams, *A History of St. Paul*, 69–70, 77–82, 99–100, 16; Neill, *History of Minnesota*, 459.
2. Williams, *A History of St. Paul*, 84–85, 98.
3. Ibid., 101.
4. Ibid., 98.
5. Ibid., 102, 103.
6. Ibid., 92
7. Ibid., 72; Neill, *History of Ramsey County*, 302.
8. *Brown's Casebook*, 258–59.
9. Ibid.
10. Ibid.
11. Ibid.
12. Ibid.
13. Ibid.
14. Ibid.
15. Newson, *Pen Pictures*, 17.
16. Ibid., 19; Williams, *A History of St. Paul*, 103, 111.
17. "The Unpublished Memoirs of the Very Reverend Alexius Hoffman," in the possession of the *Grand Gazette*, 867 Grand Avenue, St. Paul, Minn. Quoted from *Grand Gazette*, October 1979. see CMS 14.225 re indication of format, also not sure what last phrase refers to "Quoted from…."
18. Williams, *A History of St. Paul*, 104.
19. Ibid., 126–29; Gary Brueggemann, "The Historic Upper Landing: The Lost Legacy of the Chestnut Street Levee," *Community Reporter*, January 1985, 1, 5.
20. Williams, *A History of St. Paul*, 128.
21. Joseph Corrigan, *The History of St. Mark's and the Midway District* (St. Paul: publisher unknown, 1939), 17-18, 21; unpublished "Report on Joseph Rondeau" by Virginia Kunz, submitted to Felix Rondeau, July 14, 1979. see CMS 14.225 re indication of format for citation to unpublished works
22. Williams, *A History of St. Paul*, 104, 146; Brueggemann, *A People's History Calendar of East St. Paul* (St. Paul: St. Paul Community Education, 1985), 2, 15; Seymour, *Sketches of Minnesota*, 178.
23. Williams, *A History of St. Paul*, 104, 144; Brueggemann, *History Calendar of East St. Paul*, 3.
24. Williams, *A History of St. Paul*, 144.

25. Ibid.
26. Ibid., 136.
27. Ibid., 135-36, 258.
28. Ibid., 145.
29. Ibid., 136; *Minnesota Territorial Census, 1850*, 55.
30. *Records of St. Croix County*, 84, 104.
31. Ibid.
32. Holcombe, *Minnesota in Three Centuries*, 361-69; Henry Moss, "Last Days of Wisconsin Territory and Early Days of Minnesota," *Collections of the Minnesota Historical Society*, 8 (1895-1898)· 66-88; Neill, *History of Minnesota*, 491.
33. Holcombe, *Minnesota in Three Centuries*, 368-69.
34. Williams, *A History of St. Paul*, 117-18; Henry Moss, "Biographical Notes on Old Settlers," *Collections of the Minnesota Historical Society*, 9 (1898-1900): 144-45; Newson, *Pen Pictures*, 27-29.
35. Newson, PenPictures, 43; Williams, *A History of St. Paul*, 141-42.
36. Williams, *A History of St. Paul*, 197, Newson, *Pen Pictures*, 87.
37. Ibid., 130-31; Ibid., 35-36; *Minnesota Pioneer*, June 1, 1870, obit.
38. *Minnesota Pioneer*, May 6, 1894, 11.
39. Brueggemann, *History Calendar of Little Canada, 1-2.*
40. Larpenteur, "Recollections," 391.
41. Williams, *A History of St. Paul*, 88-89.
42. Ibid., 71.
43. Larpenteur, "Recollections," 371-72; Williams, *A History of St. Paul*, 118-20, *Minnesota Territorial Census, 1850*, 41.
44. Williams, *A History of St. Paul*, 88.
45. Ibid., 63, 159,; *Records of St. Croix County*, 78.
46. Williams, *A History of St. Paul*, 138; *Records of St. Croix County*, 84; *Minnesota Territorial Census, 1850*, 60.
47. Williams, *A History of St. Paul*, 145, 150, 177; *Minnesota Territorial Census, 1850*, 37.
48. Williams, *A History of St. Paul*, 121, 388-89, 392-93; Walter Trenerry, *Murder in Minnesota* (St. Paul: Minnesota Historical Society, 1962), 26.
49. *Records of St. Croix County*, 21.
50. Holcombe, *Minnesota in Three Centuries*, 363.
51. Ibid., 369; Kunz, "Report on Rondeau,"
52. Holcombe, *Minnesota in Three Centuries*, 368-69, 93.
53. Williams, *A History of St. Paul*, 92.
54. "Organization of Minnesota Territory," *Collections of the Minnesota Historical Society*, 1 (1850-53): 53-68.
55. Williams, *A History of St. Paul*, 224, 228, 266.
56. Ibid., 146.
57. Ibid.
58. Ibid.
59. Newson, *Pen Pictures*, 149-50.
60. Mary Wheelhouse Berthel, *Horns of Thunder: The Life and Times of James Goodhue* (St. Paul: Minnesota Historical Society, 1948), 65.
61. Berthel, *James Goodhue*, 260; Donald Empson, *The Street Where You Live* (Minneapolis: University of Minnesota, 2006), 107.
62. Brueggemann, *History Calendar of East St. Paul,* .